Melancholy and the Secular Mind
in Spanish Golden Age Literature

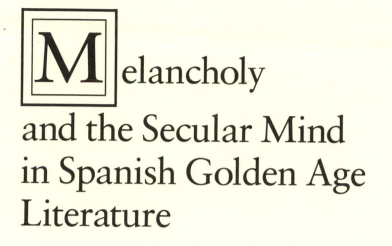

Melancholy
and the Secular Mind
in Spanish Golden Age
Literature

Teresa Scott Soufas

University of Missouri Press
Columbia and London

PQ
6066
S68
1990

Library of Congress Cataloging-in-Publication Data

Soufas, Teresa Scott.
    Melancholy and the Secular Mind in Spanish Golden Age Literature /
Teresa Scott Soufas.
        p. cm.
    Bibliography: p.
    Includes index
    ISBN 0-8262-0714-6 (alk. paper)
    1. Spanish literature—Classical period, 1500-1700—History and criticism.
2. Melancholy in Literature. I. Title.
PQ6066.S68   1989
860.9′003—dc20   89-4852
                                                                    CIP

This book was brought to publication with the generous assistance of the
Program for Cultural Cooperation Between Spain's Ministry of Culture
and United States' Universities

Designer: Barbara J. King
Typesetter: Connell-Zeko Type & Graphics
Printer: Thomson-Shore, Inc.
Binder: Thomson-Shore, Inc.
Type face: Sabon

5 4 3 2 1   94 93 92 91 90

for
Chris

Contents

Preface

The Spanish Renaissance and Baroque literary articulation of Europe's discursive transition from pre-Cartesian thinking to the more modern understanding of the nature of thought encompasses varied representations and examinations of humoral melancholy in numerous canonical Golden Age works. This study considers the dialectical manner in which the Golden Age prose writers, dramatists, and poets respond to new evaluations of human thought by means of their depiction of melancholy figures, a character type integrally linked during the Renaissance to intellectual endeavors and a European literary phenomenon easily identified in Spanish works in all major genres. The approach I suggest maintains its own dialectical relationship to the theocentric critical bias that has long dominated Golden Age studies. Although I consider how the conservative and mainstream Spanish authors and scholars of that period endeavor to reaffirm the more medieval, God-centered universe, my examination reveals their simultaneous uneasy acknowledgment of a new epistemological order that values highly the autonomous, secular mind and anticipates the emergence of the modern bourgeois individual, a "thinking subject" independent of the traditional hierarchies. The new order becomes dominant sooner in the scientific and intellectual activity of other European nations as the Baroque era progresses, but the late sixteenth and early seventeenth centuries represent a period when writers in other countries also register their mistrust of the highly active melancholy mind that their Spanish contemporaries communicate in numerous literary works.

Eschewing, therefore, the persistent image of Golden Age Spain's radical difference from the rest of Europe in the hope of further dispelling the heavy critical emphasis upon Spanish "uniqueness," my arguments address the need to understand how the inarguably Catholic authors of post-Tridentine Spain use melancholy in order to engage in a dialectical transvaluation of values, that is, a reexamining and redefining of society and traditional norms that nevertheless does not seek to invalidate those norms or their inversion. This transvaluational process is evident throughout Europe in the sixteenth and seventeenth centuries in the aftermath of Erasmus's seminal *Praise of Folly*.[1] As other scholars have argued, furthermore, the scientific discoveries of the sixteenth century do not easily penetrate the European literary discourse of seventeenth-century literature in a consistent way.[2] The strength of the accepted belief in the medieval

---

1. For a thorough discussion, see Walter Kaiser, *Praisers of Folly*, 19–100.
2. See Jean Starobinsky, *History of the Treatment of Melancholy from the Earliest Times to 1900*, 42–44; Bridget Gellert Lyons, *Voices of Melancholy*, 1; Louise Fothergill-Payne, "The

Christianized version of ancient cosmology and the system of correspondences between humans and the objects and forces of the universe are under scrutiny and are attacked by various scientists and philosophers whose mathematical calculations and new instruments of direct observation lead them to discoveries that undermine or destroy the conceptual premises of analogical patterns and the geocentric universe. The older system, however, lends itself quite readily to literary images and representation, and this in part helps to explain the continued literary recourse to the medieval theories of humoral medicine, concentric globes, and the delicate balance of the fabric and construction of the universe.[3] Important to consider with Spanish Golden Age authors, therefore, are the positions they articulate, by means of their varied portrayals of melancholia, on the reorganization of the structure of thought undertaken in the sixteenth and seventeenth centuries in Europe, a reorganization that provides the framework into which the varied fields of knowledge—science and literary representation among them—find their place in an emerging order.

As Michel Foucault and, after him, Timothy J. Reiss have explained, the system of analogical thinking operative from ancient times until approximately the end of the sixteenth century is replaced by a system based on logical identity. Reiss defines this as a passage from a discourse of patterning to a serial one of analytico-referentiality, or what he calls a passage from an orientation toward a "discursive exchange within the world to the expression of knowledge as a reasoning practice upon the world."[4] Reiss describes an evolution from an earlier mode of thought in which the human mind is intimately involved with a context, a social, historical, and religious milieu, to one in which the mind understands from a vantage point of autonomy, epitomized in the Cartesian dictum *cogito ergo sum*. Reiss's notions on the structure of intellectual discourse rely heavily upon the arguments Foucault offers in *The Order of Things* about a rupture in the traditions of Western thought in the sixteenth and seventeenth centuries, during which resemblance ceases to play a "constructive role in the knowledge of Western culture" and an emerging system of thought based on a paradigm of identity and difference becomes important.[5] Within the pre-Cartesian system of conceptualization, the primary emphasis is upon likenesses, a configuration

World Picture in Calderón's *Autos Sacramentales*," in *Calderón and the Baroque Tradition*, ed. Kurt Levy, Jesús Ara, and Gethin Hughes, 33; Marjorie Hope Nicolson, *The Breaking of the Circle: Studies in the Effect of the "New Science" upon Seventeenth Century Poetry*, 122; Daniel Heiple, *Mechanical Imagery in Spanish Golden Age Poetry*, 1–14, 179–81.

3. See Lyons, *Voices of Melancholy*, 13–14; Fothergill-Payne, "The World Picture in Calderón's *Autos Sacramentales*," 34. Lawrence Babb, *The Elizabethan Malady: A Study of Melancholia in English Literature from 1580 to 1642*, 1–20.

4. Timothy J. Reiss, *The Discourse of Modernism*, 30, also 46.

5. *The Order of Things*, 17.

that Foucault considers "[p]lethoric because it is limitless. . . . Each resemblance . . . has value only from the accumulation of all the others, and the whole world must be explained if even the slightest of analogies is to be justified and finally take on the appearance of certainty." Further characterizing this older epistemological order, Foucault explains:

> As a "category of thought," it applies the interplay of duplicated resemblances to all the realms of nature; it provides all investigation with an assurance that everything will find its mirror and its macrocosmic justification on another and larger scale; it affirms, inversely, that the visible order of the highest spheres will be found reflected in the darkest depths of the earth. But, understood as a 'general configuration' of nature, it poses real and, as it were, tangible limits to the indefatigable to-and-fro of similitudes relieving one another. It indicates that there exists a greater world, and that its perimeter defines the limit of all created things.[6]

Inquiry of whatever kind, then, provides an opportunity to reaffirm the essential sameness of the world and each person's place within a "great chain of being." Humoral medicine is one example of such intellectual effort, for within that context, health and illness are explained in terms of an equilibrium or an imbalance in the four bodily substances—blood, choler, melancholy, and phlegm—all of which fit into the scheme of the human being as a little universe reflecting the ordered tension of the elements, the seasons, and the heavenly bodies. Indeed, such articulation and representation of relationships and connections are evidence of the thought process which necessitates that "the relation of microcosm to macrocosm should be conceived as both the guarantee of . . . knowledge and the limit of its expansion."[7]

The chapters in this book contain examinations of specific melancholy disorders that are documented in the medical texts chosen for consideration as well as depicted in important works of artistic literature in Spain and other European nations. Though my approach is not comparative in nature, some points of reference to other national literatures are supplied as necessary explanations of the broader context of the Spanish portrayal of melancholy and its implications for

6. Ibid., 30, 31.
7. Ibid., 32. Starobinski also asserts that "the doctrines of antiquity are, for the Middle Ages, the basis of all medical teaching: but they are subject to variants, commentaries and speculations which aim at reinforcing the coherence and symmetry of a universe which they insist must be flawless. Assertions as attractive as they are unverifiable are given out as tangible truths, simply in order to strengthen the analogies which unite the microcosm with the macrocosm. This extraordinary edifice of ideas was not completed until the Renaissance, by which time its structure had become so intricate that every phenomenon in the natural world was dependent on, and explained by, every other, in a network of imaginary interrelationships" (*History and Treatment of Melancholy*, 35).

the highly active secular mind. This is, moreover, a study meant to be, rather than definitive and exhaustive, provocative and suggestive through a demonstration of the artistic and intellectual importance of melancholy in selected canonical Golden Age works that clearly portray the principal categories of melancholia. I have chosen well-known works for close scrutiny because, for the most part, Hispanic criticism has neglected (or misinterpreted) the depictions of melancholy in them, and my analyses are offered as a methodology that complements, as well as challenges, established practices in Golden Age scholarship. I hope to stimulate further consideration of the issues raised and suggest new areas for investigation concerning melancholy in Spanish literature.

The scope of my study reexamines and reassesses the intellectual conservatism and the mistrust of the secular mind's independence and creative strength that Spanish Golden Age authors generally express. I begin with a discussion of melancholy in its medical context and argue for an understanding of Don Quijote as the paradigmatic transvalued melancholic and the literary figure whose passage from sanity to insanity and back again best represents the dialectical quality of both the Spanish and the general European evaluations of the melancholic mind in the early seventeenth century. Chapter 2 comprises an examination of Tirso de Molina's depiction of *acedia* in *El condenado por desconfiado* (Damned for disbelief), in which the mythological connection between melancholy and Saturn is also an important component. *Acedia* is one of the forms of melancholia with the longest medical and philosophical background. As such it serves as an appropriate topic with which to begin the series of chapters that follow the historical discussion of the theories about melancholic disorders. Indeed, I have chosen to organize my discussion around relevant areas within the discourse on melancholy rather than to observe a strict chronology of composition and publication of the literary works to be considered. In chapter 3, I examine Lope de Vega's dramatic treatment of melancholy lovesickness, a disorder also known as heroical love, which enjoys a lengthy history of medical interest and literary portrayal. Through a presentation of love melancholy's dual context of comicity and tragedy in *El caballero de Olmedo* (The knight from Olmedo), Lope depicts his protagonist Alonso as an initially silly, conventional, and affected stage lover who meets a sad end as a result of the more serious and pathological love melancholia of his rival, which has much in common with the melancholia that deranges Calderón's wife-murderers. The sixteenth- and seventeenth-century melancholy malcontentedness is a social and literary phenomenon in Elizabethan England, and the Spanish *pícaro* (rogue) is, as I argue in chapter 4, a particularly well-developed and fully human characterization of this often highly conventionalized melancholy type who embodies the irony of the corrupted moralist and the digressive discourse of the self-contemplative melancholic. Finally, in chapter 5, the polemical tension generated between Góngora and his detractors (or between the literary factions today known as *culteranos* and *conceptistas*) can be understood as an ideological dispute over Góngora's recognition of the value of the melancholy mind and its power to undermine the analogical thought that informs the traditional poetics that his *poesía culta* (precious poetry) challenges. The focus of these chapters, therefore, reveals the dialectical efforts of the majority of Spain's publishing intellectuals who, in the face of a growing body of opinion that affirms the superiority of the autonomously functioning mind, endeavor to reaffirm the traditionally appropriate application of human thought in a God-centered universe through the medium of superiority and distemper known as melancholy.

Acknowledgments

I wish to express my appreciation to the National Endowment for the Humanities for a Summer Stipend and to Ursinus College for summer research support during the investigation phase of my work, both of which helped to hasten the completion of this project. I should also like to thank the Program for Cultural Cooperation Between Spain's Ministry of Culture and United States' Universities for a grant awarded to the University of Missouri Press to help defray publication costs. Parts of chapters 2 and 3 are based on arguments put forward in the previously published articles "Religious Melancholy and Tirso's Despairing Monk in *El condenado por desconfiado*," *Romance Quarterly* 34 (1987) and "Calderón's Melancholy Wife-Murderers," *Hispanic Review* 52 (1984).

The translations into English of the Spanish passages cited throughout the book are my own, prepared in consultation with Professor Vern G. Williamsen, whose assistance in this task is gratefully acknowledged. These translations are provided as informal aids to help nonreaders of Spanish follow the text. Regarding the quotations from sixteenth- and seventeenth-century Spanish theoretical works, I have chosen not to regularize the spelling and accentuation in order to remain faithful to the originals.

Melancholy and the Secular Mind
in Spanish Golden Age Literature

1

Melancholy and Its Scientific and
Literary Transvaluation (Cervantes)

thoughts beget melancholy, and that, thoughts alternatively
Dudley North

O ne result of the proliferation of secular philosophies during the Renaissance, of which Cartesianism is a late manifestation, was an undermining of the medieval foundation of knowledge. The sixteenth century was marked by an uneasiness over the evolution from the extant epistemological orientation of correspondences to the emerging, more modern one, a tradition within which the contemporary structure of thinking still largely participates. The resultant dialectical tension is evident among writers and thinkers who were recognizing the growing hegemony of a discourse that appreciates the individual, secular mind. Edgar Wind and others have discussed what he terms the "transvaluation of values" effected during the Renaissance, through which society's accepted notions were reexamined and redefined.[1] Such a phenomenon brings about a reconsideration of the society that upholds a system of values and traditions being actively questioned. While the transvaluational dialectic provides further evidence of a massive intellectual struggle to accommodate the new and freer system of thought, it nevertheless proceeds in such a way that does not entirely invalidate the older system. In a study of the self-conscious quality of the Renaissance's literary and extraliterary preoccupation with the framework for expressing human thought, Ronald Levao also ponders the survival of the traditional harmonies. He questions whether Renaissance texts "certify a continuity of attitude or reveal a willed conservatism, a strenuous and self-conscious effort to shore up a profoundly unsettled edifice," and he speculates on the possibility that "the most distinguished of such texts are merely reactionary."[2] Levao's considerations echo another question posed by Dominick La-

1. Edgar Wind, *Pagan Mysteries in the Renaissance*, 69-70. See also Walter Kaiser, *Praisers of Folly*, 51-83.
2. Ronald Levao, *Renaissance Minds and Their Fictions*, xviii.

1

Capra, who asks, "Do certain works themselves both try to confirm or establish something—a value, a pattern of coherence, a system, a genre—and call it into question?"[3] As it is in many texts written in the rest of Renaissance and Baroque Europe, this process is evident in the treatment of melancholy in Golden Age Spain.

Walter Kaiser has examined the process of transvaluation within the European tradition of the wise fool and Erasmus's paradigmatic representation of that figure in the *Praise of Folly*. Kaiser contends that "the ironic inversion of values which Stultitia performs . . . redefines the nature of sobriety and happiness and truth itself. Erasmus *pretends* to espouse the most Epicurean licenses in order to show the fallacies of their Stoic restraints. He does so not to advocate without qualifications the former, but rather to redefine the latter."[4] Humoral melancholy is one such transvalued concept within this dialectical process through which the Renaissance epistemology neither completely affirms nor denies the validity of either side of an issue, but embraces both in a process that accomplishes a reevaluation of the basic intellectual assumptions inherent in a given discourse. The notions that the Renaissance inherited from antiquity were handed down by way of medieval glossing and reinterpretation, and humoral melancholy is important among them. In his discussion of Marsilio Ficino's transmutation of the vices *acedia* and *ira,* Wind defines the transvaluation of *voluptas,* saying:

> It is with these Renaissance vindications of melancholy and rage as noble passions that the cult of noble *voluptas* should be compared. Like *acedia* and *ira,* the vice of *luxuria* continues to be classed as a deadly sin, and the vulgar *voluptas,* that is, incontinence, was pictured in her image. And yet, on the authority of Plotinus, sustained in this instance by Epicurus, a noble *voluptas* was introduced as the *summum bonum* of Neoplatonists.[5]

Appropriately included, therefore, among the many issues for examination under such a heading as Renaissance transvaluation of values is humoral melancholy, the condition of body and mind that intensifies the tendencies for isolation, self-conscious contemplation, and a hyperactive mind—considered historically, and depicted literarily, either as an attribute of brilliance or as a dangerous and marginalized aberrant pathology. The redefinition of melancholy that the Neoplatonists effect is itself a product of the early fifteenth-

3. Dominick LaCapra, *Rethinking Intellectual History,* 29.
4. *Praisers of Folly,* 53–55.
5. *Pagan Mysteries,* 69–70.

century reevaluation of melancholia as a special kind of grief commingled with thoughtfulness, withdrawal, unhappy love, and sickness, a definition that also demonstrates an affinity between melancholy and notions of death and self-awareness. By the end of the fifteenth century and well into the next "this consciousness became so much a part of self-awareness that there was scarcely a man of distinction who was not either genuinely melancholic or at least considered as such by himself and others."[6] Unlike the medieval thinker for whom the "vita contemplativa" was a means of drawing closer to God and not of affirming a world intellectually centered in the individual, the Renaissance mind celebrated the "vita speculativa" in which the humanistic view of meditation brought with it an enhancement of the polarity inherent in the danger and the freedom of mental sovereignty within the framework of Christian culture. Raymond Klibansky and his coauthors explain:

> The birth of this new humanist awareness took place, therefore, in an atmosphere of intellectual contradiction. As he took up his position, the self-sufficient "homo literatus" saw himself torn between the extremes of self-affirmation, sometimes rising to hubris, and self-doubt, sometimes sinking to despair; and the experience of this dualism roused him to discover the new intellectual pattern, which was a reflection of this tragic and heroic disunity . . . There was therefore a double renaissance: firstly, of the neoplatonic notion of Saturn, according to which the highest of the planets embodied, and also bestowed, the highest and noblest faculties of the soul, reason and speculation, and secondly, of the "Aristotelian" doctrine of melancholy, according to which all great men were melancholics.[7]

The acknowledgment of the concurrent negative and positive aspects of melancholy and its mythological and planetary mate Saturn thus resulted in a heightened perception of the melancholic mind as studious and thoughtful as well as diseased and even blasphemously hypertrophic and introspective.

The microcosmic-macrocosmic equivalents and the interconnections between science, ethics, philosophy, art, and religion that humoralism effects underscore the discourse of similitude that Renaissance conservatism struggles to keep viable in the face of an emerging paradigm of difference. Within this pseudo-scientific field, the melancholic becomes the focus of attention and offers the widest variety of interesting case studies (and therefore literary portrayals as well)—the villainous criminal, the seditious political conniver, the meditative scholar, the lovesick individual, the poet, and the discontented social misfit, among others. Through portrayal of these sorts of figures, melancholy is

6. Raymond Klibansky, Erwin Panofsky, and Fritz Saxl, *Saturn and Melancholy,* 231–32.
7. Ibid., 247.

linked with contemplation, rumination, and excessive mental activity, calling into question both the embrace and the rejection of the Cartesian *cogito* and serving as both a subject and a medium of Golden Age *desengaño* (clarity after deception). The artistic use of humoralism, and more specifically melancholy with all the struggles it connotes, moreover, implies a response to the admonition *nosce teipsum*, the underlying ethical principle of that age, and so the efforts that produce the more scientific expository works on melancholy complement the literary premise to instruct and to entertain within a discourse that becomes increasingly more self-conscious.

As many Hispanists have affirmed, Spain's Baroque was indeed a continuation of its Renaissance.[8] Referring to the intense intellectual and emotional tensions articulated in seventeenth-century Spanish literature over the heightened awareness of such dichotomies as *desengaño* and illusion, Wardropper says: "Como las apariencias nos engañan continuamente, el corolario del desengaño es la admisión de que el mundo del hombre está desquiciado . . . a que necesita que se inviertan sus valores . . . así como el tratamiento literario del tema de la soledad del hombre, comunión con la naturaleza y con Dios en el siglo XVI, [es] fuente de desengaño en el Barroco" (Since appearances deceive us continuously, the corollary of disillusion is the admission that man's world is unbalanced . . . that it needs to invert its values . . . so that the literary treatment of the theme of man's solitude, communion with nature and with God [is], in the sixteenth century, the source of the Baroque's disillusion).[9] These issues are fundamentally connected to the ideological and stylistic representation of the contemplative, isolated, and disapproving melancholic as well, and, indeed, Klibansky singles out Baroque Spain and England as the sites of the fullest and most profound articulation of the discourse of melancholy, an articulation that is also linked to the deeply felt religious tensions of the sixteenth and seventeenth centuries and the efforts of Catholics and Protestants to bring about a religious reform from within their ranks.[10]

In seventeenth-century Spain, the melancholic became a predominant literary vehicle for the conservative attempt to discourage the active use of the disassociated secular intellect, and in few instances does the melancholy figure receive unequivocally positive treatment by Siglo de Oro authors (an outstanding exception, discussed in chapter 5, is Góngora). The physical and spiritual

8. See Dámaso Alonso, ed., *Poesía de la Edad Media y poesía de tipo tradicional;* Theodore S. Beardsley, *Hispano-Classical Translations Printed Between 1482–1699;* María Rosa Lida de Malkiel, *La tradición clásica en España;* Bruce W. Wardropper, "Temas y problemas del barroco español," in *Historia y crítica de la literatura española (Siglos de Oro: Barroco),* vol. 3.
9. *Historia y crítica,* 9–10.
10. *Saturn and Melancholy,* 233.

aspects of melancholia are attractive subjects for literary representation in a conservative society, for the systemic imbalance of the overly thoughtful, solitary, and obsessive melancholic individual is a perfect medium for portraying the failure of the independent mind in a secular context.[11] The negative disillusionment that results from the melancholy heightened self-awareness produces dissatisfaction but, at the same time, also strengthens the intense appreciation of the *ingenio* (ingenuity) and *agudeza* (wit) that are considered the basis of the poetic *concepto* (poetic conceit). This poetic wit, however, is itself evidence of the conservative effort to reaffirm traditional modes of thinking, for it values the brilliant metaphor and thus a method of conceptualization that seeks to establish connections between all objects in the universe.[12]

Jean Starobinsky has declared that the Renaissance was the age of gold for melancholy,[13] and certainly textual evidence provides ample indications of the frequency with which Spain's Golden Age authors portray melancholy figures and imagery in their works. Throughout Europe during the epistemological transition of the sixteenth and seventeenth centuries, humoral melancholy received more scholarly and artistic literary attention than blood, choler, and phlegm. The roots of the humoral theory itself can be traced to Pythagorean philosophy and its insistence upon tetradic categories of time and natural elements, a system that eventually merged with other notions to accommodate the idea of four substances within the body, each with physical properties of heat, cold, dryness, and moisture that match it to one of the four elements, to a season, to a planetary or stellar body, and to one of the ages of man. Thus because melancholy or black bile was thought to be cold and dry, it became paired with the element earth, with winter, with the planet Saturn, and with old age. Through contributions from Hippocrates, Galen, Plato, Aristotle, St. Augustine, Avicenna, Averroes, St. Thomas Aquinas, and countless others, humoralism became from ancient through medieval times the basis for explaining health and illness.[14] An overabundance in the body of one of the humors was believed to be the cause of illness of one sort or another, and, as the notions evolved, the humors were believed responsible for dispositions or temperaments as well. Influences by the passions and external factors known as the non-

11. As I also argue in chapter 2, these implications likewise obtain in the religious context that many Hispanists consider the central focus of the later Golden Age; see, for example, Leo Spitzer, "El barroco español," and Wardropper, "Temas y problemas," 11-12.
12. See Michel Foucault, *The Order of Things*, 17-44; Timothy J. Reiss, *The Discourse of Modernism*, 21-54; and also Daniel L. Heiple, *Mechanical Imagery in Golden Age Poetry*, 1-14.
13. Jean Starobinsky, *History of the Treatment of Melancholy from the Earliest Times to 1900*, 40.
14. See summaries of these works in Lawrence Babb, *The Elizabethan Malady*, 1-72; Stanley W. Jackson, *Melancholia and Depression: From Hippocratic Times to Modern Times*, 3-77.

naturals could affect the physical and psychological characteristics and bring about an abundance of melancholy or one of the other humors and thus alter one's health and/or behavior.[15]

By the time the term "melancholy" and its connotations had passed through many centuries of popular tradition, medical practice, artistic depiction, and philosophical theorizing, it had become complex in meaning for the Renaissance. Alonso de Freylas's work of 1605 on the more clinical subject of the treatment of plague contains descriptions of the humoral types that synthesize contemporary notions about them. Like many other doctors and scientific philosophers of the sixteenth and seventeenth centuries, he is careful in his explanation of melancholy to make a distinction among its recognized types.[16] As explained by these myriad doctors, the word "melancholy" (*melancolía*) identifies the natural bodily humor; Andrés Velásquez, for example, explains that in this sense melancholy is "uno de los quatro humores, que naturalmente se engendran en el higado, para nuestra nutricion. Este de su temperamento es frio y seco" (one of the four humors, that are naturally produced in the liver for the purposes of digestion. By nature it is cold and dry).[17] Luis Lobrera de Avila records that when this natural humor is found in excess in the body, a person begins to experience "malos pensamientos y tristeza sin causa: y temor de cosas que no son de temer . . . [aparta]se mucho de la conversacion humana . . . y [tiene] los pensamientos mas danados" (bad thoughts and sadness without cause; and fear of things that do not frighten . . . he/she [withdraws] from human contact . . . and [has] rather harmful thoughts).[18]

The corrupted substance believed left behind in the system through a burning of any one of the humors by a strong emotion is also called melancholy, or may be known as adust melancholy or *atrabilis*. Velásquez describes "lo mismo que los medicos llaman atra bilis" (what doctors call atra bilis) in metaphorical terms: "Como lo vemos en la ceniza, que aunque fria y seca de su naturaleza,

---

15. See Jackson, *Melancholia and Depression*, 11–12.

16. *Conocimiento, curacion y preservacion de la peste y un tratado de arte de descontagiar las ropas de sedas y un discurso si los melancolicos pueden saber lo que esta por venir con la fuerza de la imaginacion*, fols. 226r–228r.

17. Andrés Velásquez, *Libro de la melancholia*, 48r.

18. Luis Lobrera de Avila, *Remedios de cuerpos humanos y silva de experiencias y otras cosas utilísimas*, fol. xxxvij r–v. Descriptions of the fear and sorrow without cause that melancholics typically suffer are traceable to the aphorisms of Hippocrates (*Works of Hippocrates*, trans. and ed. W. H. S. Jones and E. T. Withington [Cambridge: Harvard University Press, 1931], 4:185). Among the well-known literary passages that express the same ideas is Fénix's speech about her sorrow in Calderón's "El príncipe constante": "pero de la pena mía / no sé la naturaleza: / que entonces fuera tristeza / lo que hoy es melancolía" (but of my sorrow / I know not its nature: / because what was then sadness / today is melancholy); "El príncipe constante," in *Obras completas*, ed. A. Valbuena Briones, 1:250.

guarda en si aquella ignicion que dezimos" (Like we see in ash, which although cold and dry by nature, holds within itself that ignition of which we speak).[19] This substance is considered harmful and the cause of a variety of mental and physical problems. Like his colleagues throughout Europe, Velásquez describes this more extreme pathological condition as the result of excessive amounts of the natural humor or from the extended presence of adust melancholy in the body.[20] The varying symptoms that it produces such as insomnia, hallucinations, desire for darkness and solitude, discontentment, and villainous tendencies are also characteristics associated with insanity.

Whereas an individual with a system dominated by natural melancholy is clearly labeled melancholic and is usually described as fearful and/or sorrowful, the adust melancholic is thought to exhibit more aggressive behavior and more mental alertness. Velásquez notes: "este humor es, el que mas bravos y terribles accidentes haze en los cuerpos humanos . . . esta atrabilis diffiere de la natural melancholia en el sabor muy azedo, y accerbo" (this humor is that which causes more fierce and terrible accidents in the human body . . . this atrabilis differs from natural melancholy in having a bitter and acid taste).[21] Because of its heat, adust melancholy produces more violent or active behavior than the colder, natural melancholy, but it is often described as having variable stages: "A case of melancholy due to an adust humor, therefore, has two phases: a hot phase characterized by energetic extravagances and a cold phase with . . . dull and passive melancholic symptoms."[22] Lobrera de Avila records just such alternations in his description of "melancholia adusta" and notes specifically its association with mania;[23] and Velásquez writes in detail about "melancholia morbus," the pathological state without fever, whose name is interchangeable with "melancholia," "furor," "insania," and "mania."[24] He insists: "infinitos son en especie, los modos de locura: pero todos caen debaxo de un genero. Porque no hay mas en los furiosos, maniacos, insanientes, o melancholicos: que ser una enagenacion de razon o entendimiento, sin calentura" (the sorts of insanity are infinite in kind: but all fall under one classification. Because there is

19. *Libro de la melancholia,* 48r-v.

20. See, for example, Sir Thomas Elyot, *The Castel of Helth,* fol. 72v; Levinus Lemnius, *The Touchstone of Complexions,* trans. Thomas Newton, fols. 146–47; Luis Mercado, *Opera,* 1:218–20 and 2:88–89; Timothy Bright, *A Treatise of Melancholie. Containing the Causes Thereof, & Reasons of the Strange Effects It Worketh in Our Minds and Bodies: with the Physicke Cure, and Spitiruall Consolation for Such as Have Thereto Adioyned an Afflicted Conscience,* 32.

21. *Libro de la melancholía,* fols. 48–49r; see Babb, *Elizabethan Malady,* 212–23 and 33–37 for a further description of "adust melancholy."

22. Babb, *Elizabethan Malady,* 34.

23. *Remedios de cuerpos humanos,* fol. xl.

24. *Libro de la melancholia,* fol. 55v.

no other cause in the furious, maniacs, insane, or melancholics: than to be a mental derangement without fever).[25]

In Spanish medical treatises a further complication results from the interchangeability of the word *cólera* (choler) with terms that label melancholic conditions. The definition of *cólera* found in the *Diccionario de Autoridades* of 1732 evinces the confusion that can result if one does not recognize this overlap—a problem, as I will argue, that concerns readings of *Don Quijote*. The *Diccionario*'s definition is:

> Humor cálido, seco y amargo, que imita el colór amarillo. Es uno de los quatro que residen en el cuerpo humano. Se halla en el estómago, passa a las venas y al intestino: y segun la parte en que predomina, o se destempla, causa diferentes enfermedades, como vómitos y otras. Son varias sus diferéncias, porque tambien le hai frio y seco, que imita al colór negro u de centella muerta, otro que se compone de los dos referidos por lo que se llama Atrabilis: y assi otros muchos que conocen y distinguen mui bien los Physicos.

> (Hot, dry and bitter humor, that brings on a yellow color. It is one of the four that exist in the human body. It is found in the stomach and passes to the veins and the intestine: and according to the part in which it predominates, or disturbs, it causes different diseases, like vomiting and others. Its differences are varied, because it can be cold and dry, black in color or like a dead ember, or else it is composed of the aforementioned two attributes for which reason it is called Atrabilis: and thus many others that the doctors know and discern.)[26]

Melancholy, therefore, is a nearly all-encompassing term for excesses of sentiment, imbalance of mind and spirit, antisocial and / or obsessive behavior, and a variety of psychological and physiological aberrations. Under the wide category of melancholic imbalances are mania, epilepsy, lovesickness, lycanthropy, acedia, flatulent melancholy or hypochondria, and malcontentedness.

The renewed emphasis by the Florentine Neoplatonists upon the pseudo-Aristotelian notion that the melancholy mind is the more intelligent one of scholars, poets, and philosophers does not generally form the basis of European medical discussions. Most doctors writing about melancholy in the sixteenth and seventeenth centuries nevertheless acknowledge this viewpoint rather unquestioningly, though adhering to the negative Galenic view of melancholy as a diseased condition. Velásquez and Freylas among other doctors in

25. Ibid. Freylas is also mindful of the diverse usages of the word "melancolía" and prefaces a section of his detailed description of the numerous melancholy symptoms by saying: "convendra quitar primero la equivocacion, que en estos sujetos se suele hallar" (it would be best first to eliminate the errors that one usually finds regarding these matters); *Conocimiento, curacion y preservacion*, fol. 226r.

26. *Diccionario de Autoridades*, 412; see also Jackson, *Melancholia and Depression*, 7-10.

Spain are joined in this approach by other medical writers like Timothy Bright and Thomas Wright in England, Pierre Charron in France, and Levinus Lemnius and Andrew Boorde of the Netherlands—all of whom wrote their works on melancholy within a twenty-year period from the 1580s to 1601.[27] A social vogue of melancholy nevertheless developed out of the renewed awareness of melancholy as a positive component of mental acuity and led would-be greats to feign the most obvious symptoms of a melancholic personality in order to be considered brilliant.[28] These affected types became quickly conventionalized in literary portrayal and suggest the popularized quality of melancholy. The average citizen, therefore, could be expected to appreciate depictions and allusions to melancholy traits and their conflicting evaluations, not only because of social phenomena like the vogue of melancholy but also because humoralism had for centuries formed the basis of medical and pseudomedical practices. Thus, the dichotomy evident in the medical discourse of melancholy is further indication of the general transvaluation of the understanding of this humoral condition, a shift that enjoys a centrality within the philosophical, ideological, and epistemological struggle in sixteenth- and seventeenth-century Europe.

As is the case in England and other European countries, melancholy receives more medical, philosophical, and literary attention from Spanish writers than the other three humors. While such works as Burton's *Anatomy of Melancholy* (first edition 1621) and Bright's *Treatise of Melancholy* (1586) were appearing in England in the late sixteenth and early seventeenth centuries, Spanish physicians published similar books and treatises, many of whose titles attest to the parallel importance of and interest in melancholy in Spain—for example, *Libro de la melancholia* (*Book about melancholy*) by Velásquez (1585), *Discurso si los melancolicos pueden saber lo que esta por venir* (*Discourse on whether melancholics can know the future*) by Freylas (1605), or *Diagnostio et cura affectuum melancholicorum* (1624) by Alfonso de Santa Cruz.[29] These medical works

27. See Timothy Bright, *A Treatise of Melancholie;* Thomas Wright, *The Passions of the Minde in Generall,* 1601; Pierre Charron, *Of Wisdome,* 1601, trans. Samson Lennard; Lemnius, *The Touchstone of Complexions;* Andrew Boorde, *The Breviarie of Helthe.* See also Babb, *Elizabethan Malady,* 68–69; Lyons, *Voices of Melancholy,* 10.

28. See Babb, *Elizabethan Malady,* 73–75 and Jackson, *Melancholia and Depression,* 101–3 for further discussion.

29. Other Spanish medical works that include substantial information on melancholy and which have been useful in the preparation of this study are by Luis Mercado, *Opera;* Pedro Mercado, *Diálogos de Philosophia Natural y Moral;* Francisco López de Villalobos, *Sumario de la medicina,* ed. Luis S. Granjel; Christóbal Pérez de Herrera, *Proverbios morales y conssejos christianos;* Dionisio Daza Chacón, *Practica y teorica de cirugia en romance y en latin;* Juan Gutiérrez de Godoy, *Disputationes Phylosophicae, ac Medicae super libros Aristotelis de memoria, & reminiscentia, physicis utiles, medicis necesariae duobus libris contentae;* Gaspar Bravo de Sobremonte, *Resolutionum, & Consultationum Medicarum;* Cristóbal Acosta, *Tratado en contra y pro*

need not be considered source material for the literature of the Golden Age in the way some critics have argued.[30] Instead they should be read as simultaneous expressions of many of the same issues the authors of artistic literature examine and react to in their writings.

Pretentions to originality did not, it would seem, motivate the medical expository writers to produce their works on melancholy, for in most instances they recapitulate what had been written over the centuries. Unlike today's scientists and physicians, who struggle to keep abreast of new developments and discoveries, the Renaissance doctors, as did their predecessors over hundreds of years, continued to rely on the medical knowledge of the past. Even in the seventeenth century, when old ideas were beginning to cede to new medical theories, the strength of the accepted authorities still tended to dominate and the expository books must be understood as one of the stages in the steady production of such medico-philosophical works.[31] Their dependence on older texts and authors is obvious on nearly every page as these writers often carefully acknowledge their sources, a process through which they ratify or denounce issues being raised in a contemporary context. Velásquez asserts in his introduction, for example: "de mi ninguna cosa digo en todo este tratado, todo es . . . recopilado, de los mas graves authores que yo en esta materia he podido ver" (I say nothing on my own in this whole treatise, everything is . . . compiled, from the most important authors on this material that I have been able to see).[32] Constant references and quotations from Hippocrates, Galen, Plato, Aristotle, St. Augustine, and St. Thomas Aquinas, among many others, abound, and in these works the Latin quotations are often translated into the vernacular for further clarity. Many doctors openly declare their preference for composing their entire texts in the common language in order to ensure their usefulness to a wider reading audience.[33]

Indeed, having admitted that his work is merely a recapitulation of other texts, Velásquez explains his own contributions as follows: "assi he andado vagando por diversos authores, procurando de unos en otros raciocinando,

---

de la vida solitaria; Pedro Foresto, *Observationum et Curationum Medicinalium sive Medicinae Theoricae & Practicae;* and Pedro García Carrero, *Disputationes medicae super sen primam.*

30. For example, Green's study on *Don Quijote,* "El 'Ingenioso' Hidalgo," is premised on the assumption that Cervantes had Juan Huarte de San Juan's *Examen de ingenios* in mind when developing his famous protagonist.

31. In this regard, Heiple cites Philip II's personal physician, Francisco Vallés, whose treatise *Controversia* is an example of the scientific writing that predominates in Spain, in which philosophers and scientists "returned to the medieval habit of citing authorities and disputing abstract metaphysical questions" (*Mechanical Imagery,* 5).

32. *Libro de la melancholia,* fol. 9.

33. See assertions by López de Villalobos, *Sumario de la medicina,* xviii; Bernardino Montaña de Monserrate, *Libro de la anatomia del hombre,* 8; Daza Chacón, *Practica y teoria de cirugia,* n.p.

sacar esta verdad de que trato en limpio" (thus I have wandered through diverse authors, obtaining from some and thinking about others, to extract this truth of which I treat clearly).[34] In support of such efforts, Thomas Murillo y Velarde writes almost a century later, "y assi se ha de tener en mucho a qualquiera de los modernos, que a costa de su trabajo, y estudio procura de exponer las sentencias de los graves Doctores, tomando de uno, y de otro lo que a su proposito hace" (and so one has to think highly of any one of the modern scholars, who through his work and study tries to explain the opinions of the important doctors, taking from one and the other that which suits his purpose).[35] These works are therefore articulated within a self-referential framework: melancholy is examined by means of a process that requires the very melancholic activity of study and scholarship. Not unlike Burton's compendium of information on melancholy, some of the Spanish physicians likewise approach their subject in such a way that validates it simultaneously as process and product.

The diversity of source materials characteristic of these works is matched by the diversity of topics considered in them, for while their focus centers on humoralism in general and melancholy in particular, these are subjects which touch on all areas of human life. Thus the ages of a human lifespan, the individual's place among the animals in the universe, the proper relation of the rational and sensitive faculties, the limitations of human efforts without God's grace, the nature of angels, and the effects of geography and climate on human physiology and behavior are but some of the digressions included with the descriptions of melancholic symptoms, cures for melancholic diseases of the mind and body, and other more clinical medical advice. Their diversity, moreover, makes the expository works difficult to categorize, for, though principally scientific in nature and intention, they often cross the dividing line between medical tract and artistic literature. Metaphor and symbolism were useful in scientific discussions of melancholy, for example, a fact that Bridget Gellert Lyons comments upon:

> In the expository books, such concepts as the darkening of the mind by black melancholy humour, and the parallels that were drawn between outer and inner darkness in explaining the phenomenon of fear, had both a physiological basis and a connection with a complex of images derived from the original career of Saturn. The melancholy man was described as haunting dark places, as being shut up in caves and dens, and as fleeing the light of the sun. The heart that was oppressed by gross and heavy melancholy humours was imprisoned, just as the melancholic himself was. There was no

34. *Libro de la melancholia*, fol. 9.
35. *Aprobacion de ingenios, y curacion de hipochondricos, con observaciones, y remedios muy particulares*, fol. 4.

clear line of distinction between fact and image, or between the state of the melancholic's mind and the landscape that he inhabited or projected.[36]

In addition to such imagery, numerous entertaining stories of melancholic
individuals who believed themselves to be, among other things, chickens,
wolves, or the more famous figures of glass, are often found in the European
works and diminish the distance between them and creative literature of the
period.[37] The literary quality and the self-referentiality of many of these medical treatises further suggest the self-conscious melancholic framework within
which their authors present their clinical material, and the sympathy that many
of them feel for melancholics is articulated openly.[38] In his *Passions of the
Minde in Generall* (1601), Wright reiterates this sentiment in a discussion of the
multiple meanings of the word "melancholy" and the universality of the melancholic afflictions: "What Maladies grow by cares and heavinesse, many can
testifie, and few there bee, which are not subject to some melancholy humour,
that often assaulteth them, troubling their minds, and hurting their bodies."[39]
Lyons speculates that "[i]t may have been partly from such hints of identifica-
tion and sympathy with their subject on the part of some of these writers that
Burton created his literary *persona* of the melancholy man dissecting the subject
of melancholy and pitying its victims."[40]

The seeming maze of material on melancholy indicates its all-encompassing
nature as a medium of both malaise and greatness in the Europe of that time. In
his own book on melancholy, Murillo, in service to Philip IV, refers to his
subject as "materia tan dificultosa, donde ay tanta diversidad de opiniones"
(such difficult material, in which there is so great a diversity of opinion).[41] In
Spain, the contradictory nature of melancholy's evaluation is evident in a com-

36. *Voices of Melancholy*, 14–15; see also Jackson, *Melancholia and Depression*, 395–99.

37. Such passages can be found in Velásquez, *Libro de la melancholia*, fol. 79; Alfonso de Santa
Cruz, "Diagnotio et cura affectuum melancholicorum," in Antonio de Ponce de Santa Cruz,
Opuscula Medica, 102; André DuLaurens, *A Discourse on the Preservation of the Sight: of Mel-
ancholike diseases; of Rheumes, and of Old Age*, tr. Richard Surphlet, 101–4; Johann Weyer,
Ioannis Wieri de Praestigiis Daemonum, et Incantationibus ac Veneficijs Libri Sex, 424; Tommaso
Garzoni, *The Hospitall of Incurable Fooles*, 19; Robert Burton, *The Anatomy of Melancholy*,
464; and Pedro Mercado, *Dialogos de Philosophia Natural y Moral*, Uiii–Uv, among many others.
See also Babb, *Elizabethan Malady*, 42–47.

38. The self-conscious narration evident in the medical treatises on melancholy also has great
significance for the place of the picaresque texts within the tradition of the melancholy malcontent, as will be discussed in chapter 4. Also noteworthy is the obvious link between the discourse
of malcontentedness and Burton's presentation of material in the *Anatomy of Melancholy*, a topic
studied by Babb, *Elizabethan Malady;* Lyons, *Voices of Melancholy;* and Stanley Fish, *Self-Consuming Artifacts.*

39. *The Passions of the Minde*, 62.

40. *Voices of Melancholy*, 10.

41. *Aprobacion de ingenios*, fol. 2.

parison of Huarte's *Examen de ingenios* (*Examination of wits*) and the works of his contemporaries. The sixteenth-century Huarte not only posits a more generous view of the humoral eccentricities than was then usual, but he also proffers a biological determinism and numerous challenges to the ancient authorities that his contemporaries do not articulate. Huarte's *Examen de ingenios* is indeed an interesting study, and though it does not deal specifically or solely with melancholy, it does offer information on the humor, temperament, and related conditions identified by that term. Huarte stands historically as one of the few physicians (and certainly without match in Spain) "to show the circumstances under which the best 'wits' were formed, and [that] the best wits belonged to those who had left the beaten path in order to study nature and penetrate her mysteries."[42] Though he does follow medical tradition and writes of the different meanings of melancholy, he places special emphasis on the notion of melancholy genius that is found in the *Problemata XXX* and repeatedly singles out Aristotle from among the ancient philosophers as an important source of truth about melancholy.

Huarte's interest in the psychological effects of melancholy upon an individual, on the other hand, is not an unusual component of the medical treatises. From the beginning of its treatment by physicians, melancholy is indeed the humoral imbalance most associated with mental consequences for its victims. The mental faculties of memory, imagination, and intellect are thought from ancient times to be affected by the predominant physiological conditions, and Galen, in particular, discusses the supposed influence upon the faculties by the four qualities of heat, cold, moisture, and dryness, as well as their combined properties. Velásquez, among others, reiterates the analogical thought and the micro/macrocosmic sense of order that still validated such ancient tenets, explaining:

el temperamento no se ha de differir por los humores, sino por las calidades. Y assi, resulta su temperamento a todas las cosas, dela mezcla y union de las quatro calidades, que concurren a la generacion de todas las cosas, es el nativo temperamento en todas las cosas, y en cada una de ellas y assi toma la de nominacion de se llamar caliente o frio del que en la mixtion vino a exceder y tener predominio. Y este temperamento, es el autor en todas y en cada una de las partes, de las actiones y operaciones que cada una haze: como nos lo mostro Galeno declarando, que el temperamento nativo, resulta de la mezcla y y [sic] proporcion de las quatro calidades, frio, calor, humedad, y sequedad.

(One must not differentiate temperament by the humors, but by its qualities. And so,

42. Lyons, *Voices of Melancholy*, 11.

temperament results from all matters, from the mixture and union of the four
qualities that are present at the generation of all things; this native temperament is in
all things, and in each part, and thus is identified as hot or cold according to which
comes to surpass or dominate in the mixture. And this temperament controls the
whole in all parts and all actions and operations that each performs: as Galen showed
us, declaring that the natural temperament results from the mixture and proportion of
the four qualities, cold, heat, moisture, and dryness.)[43]

The explanation of the higher human faculties in the Middle Ages and
Renaissance rests upon the tripartite division of the soul into vegetative, sensitive, and rational categories. Human beings share with animals the vegetative
and sensitive souls which, respectively, direct the nonconscious physical processes and the processes of perception and motion. The rational soul sets
humans apart from other animals and is composed of the reason, the memory,
and will, through whose interrelated functions humans are capable of contemplation, self-conscious thought, judgment by means of intellectual comparisons, and ultimately of movement toward good or positive action and away
from evil. The human thought process depends upon the balanced interwork-
ings of the two rational faculties, the intellect and the memory, with the sensitive
faculty of the imagination. External information enters the mind via the five
external senses and is received through the imagination—or in some explanations by the "common sense," a term used to describe a conduit of apprehension
that then conveys its information to the imagination. The imagination is described in these early theories as the eye of the mind, since it is the internal
medium of reception for sensory images and knowledge of the outer world,
information it must receive before the intellect can begin to interpret.

Early distinctions between the imagination and the *phantasia* attribute to the
latter more freedom at a "higher" or rational level to recombine the sensory
images. The *phantasia* is nevertheless described as a faculty of reception of
external information, and its relative freedom also makes it more suspect and
error-prone.[44] The memory serves as a storehouse of the sensory images that
the imagination directs to it as well as a repository for information sent to it by
the intellect. The imagination is also able to retain the images it receives, but
only for a brief period[45] and thus accomplishes a retentive function at the
sensitive level similar to that of the memory at the rational level. Plato and

43. *Libro de la melancholia,* 51v.
44. See Murray W. Bundy, "The Theory of Imagination in Classical and Mediaeval Thought,"
266–67, for a discussion of the synonymous usage of *imaginatio* and *phantasia.*
45. See Babb, *Elizabethan Malady,* 3; Thomas Aquinas, *Summa Theologica: Basic Writings of
St. Thomas Aquinas,* ed. Anton C. Pegis, 2:742–43; Albertus Magnus in Bundy, "The Theory of
the Imagination," 187.

Aristotle comment on parallels between the memory and the imagination, and Avicenna contends that imagination functions as a sort of memory with respect to the common sense. Albertus Magnus likewise draws attention to the comparison between imagination and memory, and Roger Bacon goes so far as to subsume the notion of imagination and phantasia into that of memory.[46]

The intellect, then, operates by means of comparing the images it retrieves from the memory and the new sensory images received from the imagination (in either its apprehensive operation or its recombination of previously received images). In the *Summa Theologica,* Thomas Aquinas provides a model for the interdependent organization of the human faculties that later scholars generally followed. He says:

> for the reception of sensible forms, the *proper sense* and the common sense are appointed . . . for the retention and preservation of these forms, the *phantasy* or *imagination* is appointed, being as it were a storehouse of forms received through the senses. Furthermore, for the apprehension of intentions which are not perceived through the sense, the *estimative* power is appointed: and for their preservations, the *memorative* power, which is a storehouse of such intentions. . . . Now we must observe that as to sensible forms there is no difference between man and other animals; for they are similarly immuted by external sensibles. But there is a difference as to the above intentions: for other animals perceive these intentions only by some sort of natural instinct, while man perceives them also by means of a certain comparison. Therefore, the power which in other animals is called the natural *estimative* in man is called the cogitative, which by some sort of comparison discovers these intentions.[47]

A later Renaissance explanation of the faculties by Luis Vives reveals that the medieval notions were still held valid, for in *Tratado del alma* (*Treatise on the soul*) he describes the *voluntad* (will), the *inteligencia* (intelligence), and the *memoria* (memory) as faculties of the higher rational soul of humans and points out the interdependent operation of these with the faculties of the sensitive soul, much as does Aquinas:

46. On Plato and Aristotle, see Bundy, "The Theory of the Imagination," 73–75; on Avicenna, 183; on Magnus and Bacon, 191–92 and 198.

47. 2:742–43. Pero Mexía's sixteenth-century *Silva de varia leccion* contains information about the faculties. He describes the imagination as an interior sense "cuyo cargo y poder es rescebir y retener los simulacros e imágines que el seso común (que es el primero) recibió de los sentidos exteriores y enviarlas a la estimativa, y de ahí va a la fantasía; al cabo al arca y depósito que es la memoria" (whose duty and power it is to receive and to retain the simulacra and images that the common sense [which is the first] received from the exterior senses and to send them to the estimative faculty, and from here they go to the fantasy; finally the safe and depository that is the memory); 313.

Así como en las funciones de nutrición reconocemos que hay órganos para recibir los alimentos, para contenerlos, elaborarlos y para distribuirlos y aplicarlos, así también en el alma, tanto del hombre como de los animales, existe una facultad que consiste en recibir las imágenes impresas en los sentidos, y que por esto se llama imaginativa; hay otra facultad que sirve para retenerlas, y es la memoria; hay una tercera que sirve para perfeccionarlas, la fantasía, y por fin, la que las distribuye según su asenso y disenso, y es la estimativa.

(Thus as in the functions of nutrition we recognize that there are organs to receive food, to hold it, to prepare it and distribute it and apply it, so too in the soul, man's as well as that of the animals, there exists a faculty that serves to receive the images impressed upon the senses, and which for this reason is called the imagination; there is another faculty that serves to retain them, and it is the memory; there is a third that serves to complete them, the fantasy, and finally, that which distributes them according as it agrees or disagrees, and it is the estimative faculty.)[48]

These descriptions are repeated, implicitly or explicitly, in the sixteenth- and seventeenth-century medical treatises on melancholy, for the mental problems associated with the various recognized forms of melancholia involve imbalances primarily in the rational soul that were thought to be caused by the physical disproportion in the properties of heat, cold, moisture, and dryness which, as we have seen, characterize the numerous melancholy conditions.

Like the majority of ancient, medieval, and Renaissance authorities on psychological theories of the faculties, the sixteenth- and seventeenth-century doctors evince, as Babb puts it, "multitudinous differences concerning details." Throughout their psycho-philosophical and medical texts, nevertheless, the imagination is not generally presented as a "thinking" or creative faculty in the more modern sense of intellectual invention. The highest power attributed to it is its ability to conceive "circumstances and situations other than those existing at the moment and of forming synthetic images from disparate elements,"[49] but always by means of data obtained through the senses. In these somewhat more creative moments, however, the imagination remains dependent upon the memory for retrieval of its long-stored images, since its own retentive capabilities are short-term. Velásquez specifically insists: "la imaginación ha ganado voto entre doctos e ignorantes en ser efficaz, y de mucho poder. Pero no lo es de tanto como vemos . . . Porque aunque es verdad que es efficaz, y poderosa, es, en lo que puede, y tiene su licencia y mando. Y no es absoluta, sino limitada" (The imagination has been considered by scholars and the untrained as effective, and very powerful. But, as we see, it is not so powerful. . . . Because

48. Juan Luis Vives, "Tratado del alma (De Anima et Vita)," in *Obras completas,* ed. Lorenzo Riber, 1:x.
49. Babb, *Elizabethan Malady,* 2, 3.

although it is true that it is effective, and powerful in what it can do, and where it has freedom and authority, it is not absolute, but limited).[50] Freylas also disputes any extraordinary power attributed to, specifically, the melancholic imagination and does not accept the supposed prophetic abilities such individuals are sometimes said to have. The doctors generally maintain that it is the intellect that actively interprets and self-consciously uses the primary and secondary information stored by and obtained from the other two faculties. It is also the faculty to which physicians most frequently assign a privileged status in a melancholic individual because it functions best in a dry system without the greater heat thought necessary for the imagination or the moisture necessary for the memory. Freylas offers this contention: "los sujetos secos, como estos melancolicos . . . hazen con mayor perfeccion todas las obras del entendimiento" (Those who are dry, like these melancholics . . . perform to greater perfection in everything they understand).[51] Huarte concurs on this point and explains: "la melancholía es un humor grueso, frío y seco . . . es la melancolía más apropiada para el entendimiento" (Melancholy is a thick humor, cold and dry . . . melancholy is most appropriate for the intellect).[52]

What is significant in these Spanish medical texts is the simultaneity of their insistence upon certain claims concerning the intellect's ability to function properly in a melancholic system and melancholia's unsettling effects upon the internal visionary operation of the imagination. Such contentions reinforce the medieval appreciation of reason, which Bundy labels its "glorification," and which he explains as the basis of much of classical and medieval thought.[53] The medieval goal of balance and reason's guidance of the passions[54] is not discarded in the later theories of melancholy, but the highly contemplative brain of the melancholic does produce imbalances in terms of faculty psychology. The imbalance is often articulated with recourse to problems with the imagination but not in terms of its role as an active faculty. The imagination is instead consistently understood as a mediating faculty, a fact that often seems to be the source of twentieth-century misreadings of the cause and effect of melancholic disequilibrium and mental aberrations.

Under the system of faculty psychology, a breakdown or malfunction in the thought process is best explained by recourse to the interdependent organization of the faculties, avoiding altogether modern doctrines of the imagina-

---

50. *Libro de la melancholia*, fols. 41v–42r.
51. Alonso de Freylas, *Conocimiento, curacion y preservacion*, section not paginated.
52. Juan Huarte de San Juan, *Examen de ingenios para las ciencias*, ed. Esteban Torre, 137.
53. Bundy, "The Theory of the Imagination," 274.
54. See Babb, *Elizabethan Malady,* 4.

tion.[55] The scientific and philosophical writing of the period as well as the artistic literature propose such theories. Don Quijote, a frequently examined model of Golden Age characterization, offers a paradigmatic example of the transvaluation of melancholy and of the early seventeenth-century understanding of human thought. Numerous scholars have considered Cervantes's depiction of Quijote's mentality in terms of humoralism and/or faculty psychology and have claimed to rely on the seventeenth-century context of the work and its author. Juan B. Avalle-Arce, for instance, contends that

> es un inútil anacronismo, además de peligroso, el uso de los descubrimientos de Freud, discípulos y opositores, para tratar de penetrar los arcanos psicológicos que encerraban las mentes de edades anteriores, apuntadas a nortes muy distintos a los de la edad de Freud, que, al fin y al cabo, es la nuestra. Válida y efectiva, sin embargo, es la aplicación de textos psicológicos del Siglo de Oro español para explicar mentalidades de esa época, o bien textos literarios de la misma.

> (Besides being dangerous, it is a useless anachronism to use the discoveries of Freud, his disciples and opponents, as a means of penetrating the psychological mysteries found in minds from past ages, pointed toward objectives very distant from those of Freud's age, which, after all, is ours. Valid and effective, however, is the application of Spanish Golden Age psychological texts to explain mentalities of that period, or else its literary texts.)[56]

I concur with the contention that humoralism and Luis Vives's explanations of the cerebral faculties provide a basis for a reading of the *Quijote,* an approach likewise supported in varying degrees by Rafael Salillas and M. de Iriarte and authors of numerous later studies.[57] My conclusions about Don Quijote's humoral make-up, however, differ significantly from those reached in several of these current examinations.

Otis Green, for example, argues plausibly that an appreciation of the importance of the term "ingenioso," which Cervantes attaches to the protagonist in the book's title, is essential for critical sensitivity to that characterization. Focusing upon the physical attributes of Don Quijote and his surroundings, Green

55. For further discussion, see C. Christopher Soufas, Jr., "Thinking in *La vida es sueño.*"
56. Juan Bautista Avalle-Arce, *Don Quijote como forma de vida,* 99–100.
57. Rafael Salillas, *Un gran inspirador de Cervantes. El doctor Juan Huarte de San Juan;* M. de Iriarte, *El doctor Huarte de San Juan y su "Examen de ingenios";* Otis Green, "El 'Ingenioso' Hidalgo"; Daniel Heiple, "Renaissance Medical Psychology in *Don Quijote*"; Malcolm Read, *Juan Huarte de San Juan;* R. O. Jones, *A Literary History of Spain: The Golden Age Prose and Poetry;* Stephen Gilman, *Cervantes y Avellaneda;* William Melczer, "Did Don Quixote Die of Melancholy?" in *Folie et déraison à la Renaissance,* 161–70; Chester S. Halka, "*Don Quijote* in the Light of Huarte's *Examen de ingenios:* A Reexamination"; C. Christopher Soufas, Jr., "Thinking in *La vida es sueño*"; E. C. Riley, *Don Quijote,* 48–51 and 110–12. Also in this line, see Cyril A. Jones, "Tirso de Molina's *El melancólico* and Cervantes' *El Licenciado Vidriera,*" in *Studia Ibérica: Festschrift für Hans Flasche,* ed. Karl-Hermann Korner and Klaus Ruhl.

states at the outset that an interpretation of the crazed pseudo-knight based on Huarte's *Examen* allows one to follow "with clear understanding the course of Alonso Quijano's transition from a country gentleman of *choleric temperament* to an imaginative and visionary monomaniac." His intention is to show "that Alonso Quijano is a man primarily *colérico,* that his natural condition is exacerbated by a 'passion' and by 'lack of sleep,' which produce a hypertrophy of his 'imaginative faculty'" and that "Don Quijote's adventures could have happened only to a 'colérico', a man by nature *caliente* and *seco,* and that such a man was, according to Renaissance psychology, of necessity *ingenioso.*"[58]

Otis Green's exposition begins with an apparent misunderstanding of the term "cólera adusta," which he uses as a synonym for natural choler. The evidence he offers for such a judgment is based in part on Covarrubias's definition of *loco,* which includes the following information: "Entre loco, tonto y bovo ay mucha diferencia, por causarse estas enfermedades de diferentes principios y calidades. La una de la cólera adusta, y la otra de la abundancia de flema" (Among crazy, simple, and foolish, there is a great difference, because these illnesses are caused by different principles and qualities. The one by adust choler, and the other from the abundance of phlegm).[59] The medical writers indeed consider "cólera adusta" or "cólera flava" to be an origin of certain imbalances, among them the condition labeled "adust melancholy" or "atra bilis." Velásquez articulates such an explanation: "Demanera que, o quemandose la mesma melancholia natural, o el otro humor melancholico, que se engendra de lo mas gruesso dela sangre podresciendose ella, o asandose aquel genero de cholera, que llamamos flava, se haze y engendra, el humor atrabilioso" (So that either by the same natural melancholia burning itself, or by the other melancholic humor, which is produced from the dregs of blood, putrefying itself, or by that sort of choler, which is called flava, roasting itself, is the atrabilious humor made and engendered).[60] As has been mentioned, the overwhelming majority of Renaissance scientists, physicians, and philosophers associate insanity and mania with some form of melancholia, and even those doctors like Lobrera de Avila who associate mania, for example, with both "cholera adusta" and "melancholia adusta" distinguish between the two forms

58. Green, "El 'Ingenioso' Hidalgo," 176, 177; my italics. It is interesting to note that Velásquez, like many of his contemporaries, considers a certain amount of heat to be a proper attribute for some manifestations of the melancholic system, and he asserts at one point: "que los sugetos dispuestos naturalmente para engendrar muchedumbre de melancholia, son como avemos provado, calientes y secos" (that the subjects naturally disposed to produce an abundance of melancholy are, as we have proved, hot and dry); *Libro de la melancholia,* fol. 54r.
59. Sebastian de Covarrubias y Horozco, *Tesoro de la lengua castellana y española,* 770.
60. *Libro de la melancholia,* fol. 48v.

through descriptions that more readily link Alonso Quijano with the latter. Lobrera writes of mania:

> Conocese quando es la causa cholera adusta en que no tiene sossiego ninguno: y siempre esta rixoso . . . y si alguno le haze enojo o mal olvidasele presto que no le dura el enojo. Por el contrario quando la mania es de melancholia adusta esta mas callado y sossegado a ratos: pero quando comiença a hablar esta primero pensando: y despues no le pueden hazer callar: y esta muy flaco: y el color del cuerpo de negrido: y estos son los que suelen hazer malas burlas a los que no se guardan dellos: porque dizen palabras muy dissimuladas como si estuviessen en todo su seso: y quando se descuydan dellos hazen como dixe malos engaños.

> (It is clear when the cause is adust choler in that there is no composure: and also the person is quarrelsome . . . and if one makes the individual angry or wretched he forgets it quickly since his anger does not last long. On the contrary, when the mania is from adust melancholy the individual is rather quiet and calm at times; but when he begins to speak he is thinking at first; and later one cannot make him stop; he is very thin; and the color of his body is dark; and these are the ones who usually trick people who are not on their guard, because they speak very cunning words as if they were in full possession of their faculties, and when one disregards them, as I said, they play very bad tricks.)[61]

The typical imprecision in many Spanish treatises concerning the term "*cólera*" adds to the difficulty modern readers encounter when they compare these medieval notions and the literary representations of melancholy. Quijote is portrayed as a type of melancholic to whom we might apply the interchangeable terms "melancólico," "insano," "manico," or "loco," in accordance with the then accepted medical vocabulary. Green proceeds to base his essay on a reading of the Cervantine character as a choleric developed, as he claims, in keeping with medical teachings about choler and its hot, dry properties.[62] There is no textual evidence in *Don Quijote,* however, that Alonso Quijano is ever naturally choleric or that excessive heat characterizes his physiological condition before his period of excessive reading. There is every indication, on the other hand, that the country gentleman Quijano is a classic melancholic scholar, which means, following the medical teachings of Cervantes's day (and their classical and medieval underpinnings), that the Manchegan *hidalgo* (gentleman) is originally cool and dry, though a certain amount of heat is present in his brain for his studious activities. He is not a disastrously cold melancholic of fearful, despondent, and lethargic temperament. It is, moreover, the drying

61. Lobrera de Avila, *Remedios de cuerpos humanos,* fol. xl.
62. Green, "El 'Ingenioso' Hidalgo," 177.

effect of study and contemplation that is of particular medical concern. The medieval *Regimen Sanitatis Salerni,* for example, is a textbook widely used by students of medicine during the Renaissance, and it lists among the caveats for the melancholic temperament the following: "he that desireth health of body, must eschew and avoide . . . thought and care. For thought dryeth up mans body."[63] Lemnius writes in his sixteenth-century *Touchstone* about students and magistrates who "at unseasonable times sit at their Bookes and Studies." He goes on to explain: "For through overmuch agitation of the mynd, natural heat is extinguished, & the Spyrits aswell Animall as Vitall, attenuated and vanish away: whereby it commeth to passe, that after their vitall iuyce is exhausted, they fall into a Colde and Drye constitution."[64] Basing themselves on the same arguments, Bright and Freylas warn of these and other unpleasant effects of melancholy studiousness.[65]

The prevailing theories tend to stress a reciprocal link between melancholia and study, for the humoral condition inclines one toward an inactive, thoughtful way of life which, in turn, exaggerates the melancholy symptoms of mind and body. Though Huarte also links contemplation and scholarship with melancholy, he specifically stresses study as a means for therapeutically raising the temperature of an excessively cool brain and body.[66] He thereby reiterates his own high estimation of the melancholy scholar in the tradition of Marsilio Ficino, who explains in great detail the physical process of melancholy produced by study.[67] As Babb points out, the "association between pathological melancholy and intellectual activity . . . antedates Ficino by many centuries,"[68] for the first-century Greek doctor Rufus, the ninth-century Arabian Rhazes, and Constantinus Africanus in the eleventh century are among the earliest commentators upon this connection. Cervantes is clearly within a long-held tradition by depicting his scholarly reader as melancholic, and we are given to understand that in the book's prehistory, Quijano devotes himself to endless hours of studious endeavors, behavior which evinces his melancholic, not choleric, temperament.[69]

We know that Alonso Quijano spends a vast amount of leisure time in

63. In Babb, *Elizabethan Malady,* 24–25.

64. *The Touchstone of Complexions,* fol. 136v; see also Babb, *Elizabethan Malady,* 25.

65. Ibid. Bright, *A Treatise of Melancholie,* 243; Freylas, *Conocimiento, curacion y preservacion,* 227r.

66. Huarte, *Examen de ingenios,* 149.

67. Marsilio Ficino, *The Book of Life,* trans. Charles Boer, chapters 3–6.

68. Babb, *Elizabethan Malady,* 25 n. 29.

69. Heiple also considers Quijano a melancholy scholar of overly dry constitution and explains the dietary and physical effects upon his system that Cervantes includes in the novel; "Renaissance Medical Psychology," 68–69.

reading: "Es, pues, de saber, que este sobredicho hidalgo, los ratos que estaba ocioso—que eran los más del año—se daba a leer libros de caballerías" (It is, then, known that this aforementioned gentleman, during his periods of idleness—which were the most numerous of the year—took to reading books of chivalry).[70] This explanation in itself establishes a very firm link between Quijano and the tendency toward melancholia, for it is idleness and the opportunity to study, contemplate, and ruminate that the physicians blame for bringing on or worsening the melancholy characteristics of mind and body.[71] Lyons summarizes such notions, saying that melancholy is "frequently a product of idleness and exacerbated by it," and Babb includes with "arduous mental activities" the "sedentary life" as part of the "scholar's occupational disease."[72] The consequences of excessive *ocio* are linked traditionally with melancholic disorders—among them, religious melancholy (which causes despair and neglect of the religious duties on the part of the accidic clergy) and the dangers and discomforts of love melancholy (which were thought to be exaggerated by the softness and idle hours of court life).[73] These are conditions that physicians treat by prescribing measures to fill up the empty hours such as music, companionship, games, or activities to divert the patient's attention from the fixations bred by too much leisure time. Quijano's condition is presented initially as a standard case of unrelieved scholarly melancholia. It does not thus invite Green's interpretation of a choleric figure, for the primary symptom ("se le secó el celebro" [his brain dried up], p. 73) is the physical/mental outcome of bookishness. Quijano is much better understood as a melancholic whose adust melancholic condition is caused and/or intensified by an idle life and a fixation upon reading that alter his naturally melancholic system in an adverse way.[74]

The difference between my interpretation and that of others underscores the all-encompassing nature of melancholy in the Renaissance and the resultant

70. Miguel de Cervantes Saavedra, *Don Quijote de la Mancha*, ed. Martín de Riquer, 71. Subsequent in-text page references are to this edition.
71. For a different interpretation, see Heiple, "Renaissance Medical Psychology," 68–69.
72. Lyons, *Voices of Melancholy*, 28; Babb, *Elizabethan Malady*, 25.
73. See Babb, *Elizabethan Malady*, 48, 131.
74. Green, "El 'Ingenioso' Hidalgo," and Avalle-Arce, *Don Quijote como forma de vida*, make much of the fact that Quijano lives in La Mancha, a hot, dry region with an atmosphere and climate that would affect the physiology and temperament of the would-be knight. Such environmental influence is taken seriously by the doctors in their treatises. Freylas notes specifically that melancholia of a more positive nature can be brought on by one of a combination of conditions, including: "por abitar en region y lugar caliente y seco" (by living in a region and locale that is hot and dry); *Conocimiento, curacion y preservacion,* fol. 226v. This is a condition that corresponds to Alonso Quijano's situation, but Freylas offers this information in his description of a melancholic, not a choleric. Heiple, "Renaissance Medical Psychology," 66–67, also discusses this geography as one of the so-called six non-naturals that affect Quijote's humoral constitution.

imprecision in differentiating between descriptions of some of its manifestations and those of other temperaments and constitutions. Besides the dictionary definition of *cólera* cited earlier, another good example of such overlapping symptomatology appears in Freylas's treatise. His description of the choleric reads as follows:

> En esta complexion se entiende el sujeto caliente y seco . . . Tiene el color del rostro cetrino, el cuerpo enjuto, y delgado, moreno, y velloso; tiene gran promptitud y facilidad en sus obras, es de presto y agudo ingenio, y de mucha memoria, facil de ayrarse, y le dura mas el enojo que al sanguino por la sequedad, con la qual guarda las especies de la injuria recebida, tiene los pulsos ligeros y duros, grande y apresurada respiracion, es atrevido y determinado, y enojado temerario, inquieto, duerme poco, tiene los cabellos negros, recrease con lo frio, ofendese de cosas calientes, come poco, la boca seca, y libre de saliva, y de escrementos.

> (In this complexion the subject is hot and dry. . . . He has a yellow color to his face, a body that is dry, thin, dark, and hairy; he is quick and straightforward in his duties, his wit is fast and agile, he has a good memory, quick to anger, and the vexation stays with him longer than with a sanguine individual because of his dryness, which holds the received images of the annoyance; he has light but strong pulse, deep and fast respiration, he is daring and determined, bold when angered, worried, he sleeps little, he has black hair, he enjoys the cold, and takes offense at hot things, he eats little, has a dry mouth free of saliva, and has little excrement.)[75]

In his next chapter, he asserts that the melancholic is characterized

> por templanca adquirida con largos estudios, vigilias, y trabajos, gastada y resuelta la parte mas delgada de la sangre, y de la colera, o por demasiado calor requemada . . . Conocerse ha estos sujetos por el color moreno, las venas anchas y azules, el cuerpo enxuto, y velloso, los cabellos negros. Son prudentes, sagazes, de grande y sossegado ingenio, de firme y constante parecer.

> (by restraint acquired with extended studies, wakefulness, and work, the most delicate part of the blood being spent and settled, as well as that of the choler, or burned by too much heat. . . . These subjects are known by their dark color, their wide and blue veins, their dry and hairy bodies, their dark hair. They are prudent, wise, of great and composed wit and seem firm and steadfast.)

Among the symptoms of natural melancholia are also "color cetrino" (yellow color) and "seco de excrementos" (dry excrement).[76]

Since such similarities are not uncommon in the medical works, the general

---

75. *Conocimiento, curacion y preservacion*, 211r.
76. Ibid., 226v and 226r.

notions about humoralism make the ideological substructure of a literary characterization of humoral types all the more important for consideration. Bright, for instance, even proclaims: "Of all the other humours melancholie is fullest of varietie of passion, both according to the diversitie of place where it setleth . . . as also through the diverse kinds, as naturall, unnaturall . . . either of bloud adust, choler, or melancholie naturall."[77] The intellectual aspect of melancholia and the centrality of melancholy in the pseudo-science of the Renaissance as well as in the literary typology tended to broaden the already traditionally wide definition of the humoral syndrome to the point that it could account for many, if not all, unusual behavior patterns and physiological conditions. Huarte's definition of adust melancholy also provides a good example of the acceptance of ambiguities where melancholy is concerned: "la [melancholía] que se llama 'atra bilis' o 'cólera adusta', de la cual dijo Aristoteles que hace los hombres sapientísimos; cuyo temperamento es vario como el del vinagre; unas veces hace efectos de calor, fermentando la tierra, y otras enfría" (the [melancholia] that is called "atra bilis" or "adust choler," of which Aristotle said that it makes men most wise; whose temperament is varied like vinegar; some times it produces the effects of heat, fermenting the earth, and at others it chills).[78]

Another essential problem with several of the studies of Quijote's characterization stems from a failure to take into account fully the Renaissance understanding of the mental faculties, their specific functions within the "ánima racional," and their interdependence.[79] They tend to interpret the imaginative faculty of the Cervantine character as the cause of his madness rather than a contributory and affected component of his disorder. Don Quijote's imbalance is, according to this line of reasoning, rooted in a very active imagination, indeed, a "hypertrophy of his imaginative faculty."[80] Though Avalle-Arce does refer extensively to the Renaissance notions about the faculties with numerous quotes from Luis Vives, his resultant reading of Cervantes's portrayal of Quijote's mental aberrations seems to diverge from the evidence he offers. Recalling the perceptive function of the imagination, Avalle-Arce says: "Las imágenes que se perciben sólo pueden pasar de lo sensorial a lo anímico por la aduana de la imaginativa, y ésta don Quijote la tiene lesionada" (The images that are

77. Bright, A Treatise of Melancholy, 101. Babb notes: "Clearly the melancholic category is very indefinitely bounded. When one attempts to lay down its limits, he becomes involved in terminological difficulties"; Elizabethan Malady, 36.

78. Huarte, Examen de ingenios, 147. See Aristotle's "Problemata XXX," in Klibansky et al., Saturn and Melancholy, 18–29.

79. I refer to those studies by Green, "El 'Ingenioso' Hidalgo"; Avalle-Arce, Don Quijote como forma de vida; and Stephen Gilman, Cervantes y Avellaneda.

80. Green, "El 'Ingenioso' Hidalgo," 177.

perceived can only pass from the sensorial to the psychic region through the storehouse of the imaginative faculty, and it is in this faculty that Don Quixote has suffered damage). He does not, however, explain properly what "lesionada" means with regard to the imagination in Renaissance terminology, and thus he contends:

> En consecuencia, lo que registra el fuero más interno de nuestro caballero andante no responde un absoluto a la realidad que perciben sus sentidos. Pero es más grave aún, porque nuestro héroe tiene lesionada asimismo la fantasía . . . Y así llego al final de este aspecto de mi demostración: la venta es recibida por el alma de don Quijote como un castillo por el desajuste de su imaginativa, y una vez que se imprime en su alma la imagen de un castillo acude su lesionada fantasía a perfeccionarla 'con todos aquellos adherentes que semejantes castillos se pintan'.

> (Consequently, what registers on the most internal self of our knight errant does not really correspond to the reality perceived by his senses. But it is even more serious, because our hero as well has his fantasy damaged . . . And thus I arrive at the end of this aspect of my demonstration: the inn is received by Don Quijote's soul as a castle due to the disorder of his imaginative faculty, and once the image of a castle is imprinted on his soul his damaged fantasy comes to complete it "with all those adherents that similar castles represent.")[81]

Such an attribution of the active function of interpretation to the imagination (which is properly a function of the intellect through the process of apprehension and comparison of images) largely ignores the basis of thought in medieval and Renaissance terms.

I would argue that these exegetical studies of Quijote's humoral characterization are expressed in terms of a more modern concept of the imagination. In Cervantes's portrayal, the interpretation that Quijote's intellect makes of the images his imagination receives and his memory retrieves leads to his folly, but only because his memory is damaged by the dryness of his system. Renaissance doctors explain the necessity of systemic moisture for the proper functioning of the memory. Velásquez discusses this need and concurs with general Renaissance theory that childhood, the period of the most humid bodily conditions, is the age when the memory best retains the impressions sent to it by the other two faculties ("mas dispuesta para recebir las impressiones" [more disposed to receive the impressions]).[82] In the case of Huarte, for all his unorthodoxy with

---

81. Avalle-Arce, *Don Quijote como forma de vida,* 100. He applies this argument to his interpretation of other episodes as well (for example, that concerning the *yelmo de Mambrino*), claiming to base his interpretation on "la perspectiva de Vives y no la filosofía del siglo XX" (the perspective of Vives and not twentieth-century philosophy); 112.
82. *Libro de la melancholia,* fol. 35v.

regard to the humoral eccentricities he advocates, his explanations of physiology and psychology do rely on rather conventional tenets concerning the faculties and the effects of temperature and moisture. He, too, asserts that it is childhood "en la cual edad aprende el hombre más de memoria que en todas las demás, y en el celebro le tiene humidísimo" (at which age man learns more by memory than at any other, and when his brain is most wet). The special importance of the memory in the thought process is likewise noted by many doctors, and Huarte follows this tendency, arguing that "llamamos a la memoria potencia racional porque sin ella no vale nada el entendimiento ni la imaginativa. . . . Y el oficio de la memoria es guardar estos fantasmas para cuando el entendimiento los quisiere contemplar; y si ésta se pierde es imposible poder las demás potencias obrar" (We call the memory a rational faculty because without it neither the intellect nor the imagination are worth anything. . . . And the function of the memory is to hold these fantasms for a time when the intellect wants to contemplate them; and if this one [the memory] is lost it is impossible for the other faculties to function). He likewise declares, "los melancólicos adustos carecen de la memoria" (adust melancholics lack memory).[83]

Significant, then, is the fact that the desiccation of Alonso Quijano's brain, through a process accomplished by days and nights of consecutive reading, culminates with the cessation of his reading, the activity that has been supplying his imagination exclusively with images of the life of *caballeros andantes* (knights errant). Don Quijote's memory retains these images and, in fact, is inundated with them since the only thing Quijano does for an exceedingly long period is read his favorite books. This typical pastime of melancholics dries him out so completely that eventually his memory can store no new information. Babb notes that the "melancholy brain is dry and hard" and thus a "fancy which has found lodgement in a melancholy mind is very tenacious." He supports his contentions with such Renaissance arguments as the following from Du Laurens's *Discourse* about an impression on a melancholy brain which "suffreth not itselfe easily to be blotted out."[84]

Huarte, too, explains about the effects of dryness upon the memory and the intellect: "la memoria . . . depende de la humidad como el entendimiento de la

83. Huarte, *Examen de ingenios,* 126, 125, 147. A dissertation specifically on memory and written in Wittenburg in 1609 by Melchor Cruschius presents information on preserving the memory in early old age and stresses the importance of maintaining a proper degree of heat and avoiding too much moisture or dryness by means of a balance with regard to sleep, diet, and exercise ("De memoria bona conservanda," in Oskar Diethelm, *Medical Dissertations of Psychiatric Interest: Printed before 1650,* 108); see also Juan Velázquez de Azevedo, *El Fenix de Minerva, y arte de memoria.*
84. Babb, *Elizabethan Malady,* 42; Du Laurens, *A Discourse on the Preservation of Sight,* 97.

sequedad . . . de tal manera, que el hombre que tiene gran memoria ha de ser falto de entendimiento, y el que tuviere mucho entendimiento no puede tener buena memoria; porque el celebro es imposible ser juntamente seco y húmido" (Memory . . . depends on humidity as the intellect does on dryness . . . in such a way that the man who has a great memory must lack understanding, and he who may have much wisdom cannot have a good memory; because it is impossible for the brain to be dry and humid at the same time).[85] Velásquez lists the memory as the first faculty to be adversely affected by melancholy, though it is the cold of the humor and its resultant condition that he cites as a primary obstacle to memory's efficiency.[86] He concurs with such assertions as those of Du Laurens about the tenacity of images fixed in a dry, melancholy brain, which cannot receive new impressions easily. Explaining that a balance is needed with regard to dryness and moisture for the efficient reception and retention of impressions, he says: "Quanto mas que no ay tanta sequedad, ni esta tan perdida la humedad en ellos que no se reciba muy bien qualquiera impression. Porque aunque para la facil apprehension, es mejor tener cierta humedad, para la firmeza del retener, cierta sequedad. De donde entiendo yo que por la mayor parte los melancholicos, son memorativos . . . tenaces y perpetuos" (At least there is not so much dryness, nor is the humidity so lost in them that no impression is received at all. Because although for easy apprehension, it is better to have certain moistness, for the strength of retention, it is better to have certain dryness. From which I understand that for the most part melancholics have retentive and long-lived memories).[87] Thus, in Don Quijote's case (a character introduced to us as naturally "seco de carnes" [dry of flesh], p. 36), though his senses perceive and his imagination receives the information from his senses, his memory becomes too dry to assimilate the flood of new images or provide other, and correct, ones to the *entendimiento*.[88]

The end of his reading marks the point when Quijano's memory becomes too full of images from "los libros caballerescos." This is a process that Cervantes

85. Huarte, *Examen de ingenios*, 125–27.
86. *Libro de la melancholia*, fols. 62r–64r.
87. Ibid., 34v.
88. Curiously, Avalle-Arce also asserts that Quijote's senses function efficiently, but nevertheless attributes more than a mediating function to the imagination. At one point, he claims: "los sentidos no engañan a don Quijote en absoluto . . . Las imágenes que se perciben sólo pueden pasar de lo sensorial a lo anímico por la aduana de la imaginativa, lo que registra en fuero más interno de nuestro caballero andante no responde en absoluto a la realidad que perciben sus sentidos" (the senses do not deceive Don Quijote at all. . . . The images perceived can only pass from the sensorial to the psychic by means of the clearinghouse of the imagination, that which it records on the most internal register of our knight errant does not correspond at all to the reality that his senses perceive); *Don Quijote como forma de vida*, 109–10. For a viewpoint closer to my own, see Ruth El Saffar, "Cervantes and the Imagination."

carefully outlines for his readers. We are told that during his period of reading he begins to show signs of an impaired memory, for he starts to forget what is not directly a part of the world of *literatura caballeresca:* "se daba a leer libros de caballerías con tanta afición y gusto, que olvidó casi de todo punto el ejercicio de la caza, y aun la administración de su hacienda" (He took to reading books of chivalry with such relish and delight that he forgot almost completely the hunting activities, and even the administration of his household).[89] His intellect begins to make connections between the sensory information (still provided efficiently by his imagination) and the abundant images preserved in his memory. This is the normal rational process for thought, according to faculty psychology, but in Quijano's case it is accomplished through the offices of two functioning faculties and one damaged one. The impairment of his imagination is simply a secondary problem brought on by the damage to the whole interdependent network of faculty interaction. Retained images fill up his dried-out memory, which can retain no new impressions, and this flood of data overwhelms his imaginative faculty, as Cervantes makes clear: "del poco dormir y del mucho leer se le secó el celebro, de manera que vino a perder el juicio. Llenósele la fantasía de todo aquello que leía en los libros" (with little sleep and much reading his brain dried up, such that he went mad. His fantasy filled up with all that he read in the books [p. 37]). As traditional explanations regarding the imagination explain, these overabundant images are retained for brief periods in the imagination. Cervantes, therefore, is scientifically correct in his seventeenth-century context when he maintains: "y asentósele de tal modo en la imaginación que era verdad toda aquella máquina de aquellas sonadas soñadas invenciones que leía" (In this way it was established in his imagination that all the sensational and dreamed-of fictions of the books were true [p. 38]).

In addition to the numerous occasions when Quijote's thought subverts the reality he perceives through faulty comparisons (inns/castles, windmills/giants, etc.), this same process is exemplified in Quijote's discourse on the Age of Gold, which he delivers to the goatherds in part 1—a moment when those around him are inclined to admire his mentality, a trap that has ensnared some modern critics as well. After this speech, which segregates him further from the group with which he wants to interact, the narrator relates: "Toda esta larga

89. *Don Quijote,* 36; see also Lyons, *Voices of Melancholy,* 26; Bright, *A Treatise of Melancholie,* 30–31. With regard to the passage cited from *Don Quijote,* the secondary meaning of the Spanish verb *olvidar* found in the *Diccionario de Autoridades* is likewise applicable to melancholic mentality and behavior: "Se toma tambien por dexar el cariño que antes se tenia" (It is also understood as losing the fondness for something that one once had); 36.

arenga—que se pudiera muy bien escusar—dijo nuestro caballero, porque las bellotas que le dieron le trujeron a la memoria la edad dorada, y antojósele hacer aquel inútil razonamiento a los cabreros" (All this long harangue—which could easily have been avoided—our gentleman spoke, because the acorns that they gave him brought to his memory the age of gold, and made him feel like making that useless reasoning to the goatherds).[90] The sight of *bellotas* registers a sensory impression through his imagination, but the only image his intellect can compare it to, from among those obtainable from his dry and fixated memory, derives from the books he has read. His intellect interprets and on its strength Don Quijote expounds, but this is still the diatribe of a "loco melancólico." His later discourse on "armas y letras" in chapter 37 of part 1 is a complete blending of the elements of his obsession, for it is his scholarly melancholy that has brought him into contact with the books that suggest the images of knighthood and combat that obsess him.[91] It is to be noted that all of the incorrect interpretations that Quijote makes throughout both parts of the novel have their origin in what he has read and thus are products of an intellectual endeavor (his excessive reading) undertaken in isolation and withdrawal from society.

The author of *Don Quijote* goes to great lengths to explain the madness of his protagonist in terms of the intellectual imbalance that it is. An overindulgence in scholarly pursuits and thought produces a *loco* who thinks rationally insofar as his thought is the product of the interdependent operation of the faculties, a condition described as a "razón de la sinrazón" (reason of unreason) of one whose mind deceives him because that interdependence has become distorted. Cervantes emphasizes the intellectual nature of Don Quijote's madness by stressing that "thought" is the root of Quijano's problem: "En efeto, rematado ya su juicio, vino a dar en el más estraño pensamiento que jamás dio loco en el mundo" (In effect, his sanity completely gone, he hit upon the strangest thought that a crazy man had ever had [p. 38]). Having forgotten his true identity, his new name becomes the exemplary product of an overactive, overextended intellectual process: "y en este pensamiento duró otros ocho días, y al cabo se vino a llamar 'don Quijote'" (and he spent another week on this thought, and finally came to call himself "Don Quixote" [pp. 39–40]). Aldonza Lorenzo is also renamed "Dulcinea del Toboso" because "a ésta le

90. P. 106. The Age of Gold is, moreover, the legendary period of Saturn's reign, the god associated with melancholy whose significance will be examined in more detail in chapter 2.

91. Some of the other scholars who consider Quijote's humoral make-up judge these discourses as moments of exemplary lucidity on Quijote's part. See, for example, Heiple, "Renaissance Medical Psychology," 69; and Avalle-Arce, *Don Quijote como forma de vida*, 119.

pareció ser bien darle título de señora de sus pensamientos" (it seemed good to him to give her title as lady of his thoughts).[92]

It is as well erroneous to read Cervantes's novel as a literary espousal of Huarte's *Examen* or any other such pseudo-scientific work. The unorthodoxy of the *Examen* certainly brings Huarte attention, and the typing of persons adds to the popularity and public curiosity that the work enjoys.[93] His is, however, a highly personal rendition of humoralism and natural abilities, as he repeatedly makes clear with references to "mi doctrina."[94] A deterministic explanation of human capabilities cannot be reconciled with Catholic doctrines of divine grace and human free will, and Cervantes—a Catholic and a conservative Christian—does not challenge these theological tenets in *Don Quijote*. Whereas Huarte attributes to the imagination a somewhat more active role than it enjoys in the traditional philosophical and medical treatises, Cervantes merely depicts a man whose thought proceeds along the then contemporary rational organization but with abnormal consequences because of the problem with his memory.[95] The story itself, in fact, is framed by the narrator's act of willful forgetting: "En un lugar de la Mancha, de cuyo nombre no quiero acordarme" (In a village of La Mancha, whose name I do not want to remember [p. 35]), which parallels the rational process by which Don Quijote loses his memory.

Cervantes develops Quijote as an individual of eccentric wit out of place among his friends and acquaintances and who meets with defeat, or is ridiculed by his peers, because excessive thought and study have deranged him. Huarte's thesis about the suitability of the humoral types for the various professions is, in effect, parodied by Cervantes, who offers his readers a melancholic whose adust condition deranges him to the point that the man of letters tries temporarily to live the life of the man of arms. Through such a character, however, Cervantes mocks Huartian professional determinism, for Quijote is not suited for the military undertakings toward which his insanity inclines him. The point is just that: his humoral constitution renders him insane. Nevertheless, the

92. P. 41. The use of the words *imaginar* and *imaginación* in the studies by Green, "El 'Ingenioso' Hidalgo," Gilman, *Cervantes y Avellaneda,* and Avalle-Arce, *Don Quijote como forma de vida* is an apparent anachronism, for in the *Diccionario de Autoridades,* the verb *pensar* is defined as follows: "Imaginar, premediar, considerar y discurrir" (206). The use of the terms *imaginar* and *pensar,* interchangeable in their seventeenth-century context, can be a source of misreading for modern scholars who persist in attributing a creative, thoughtful, and inventive capacity to the imagination as depicted in Golden Age texts.

93. See Read, *Huarte de San Juan,* 27–31, on the enthusiastic reception of the *Examen.*

94. Arturo Farinelli, "Dos excéntricos: Cristóbal de Villalón. El Dr. Juan Huarte," 56.

95. See Iriarte, *El doctor Huarte de San Juan,* 229, 303, and Read, *Huarte de San Juan,* 106–14, on Huarte's ideas on the imagination.

parody comes full circle by virtue of the fact that Quijote/Quijano never really lives anything but the life of a man of letters. His quests are all part of the literary world that he has too completely embraced and that has brought him to his folly. Unlike the eccentric wits that Huarte admires, Quijote is not held up by Cervantes as a positive model. In order to merit salvation, spiritually and intellectually, Quijote must remember at last that he is Quijano: "ya yo no soy don Quijote de la Mancha, sino Alonso Quijano, a quien mis costumbres me dieron renombre de 'Bueno'" (I am no longer Don Quixote of La Mancha, but rather Alonso Quijano, to whom my habits gave me fame as "the Good" [pp. 1063–64]), something he does in time to confess and make his will. He dies as a Christian, as a fully reintegrated member of society, as a participant in the still-reigning order of thought.

Much of the evidence presented in behalf of the argument that Huarte's *Examen* serves as a basis for the characterization of Quijote rests on very selective quotations about the clinical and scientific explanations of the humors. The majority of the material in the *Examen* can be found in many other Renaissance studies of melancholy and general humoralism written in many European languages and representing information that dates back to the earliest physicians. Cervantes's use of the word "ingenioso" in his title, for instance, is offered as evidence by Salillas, Iriarte, Green, and Hutchings, among others, that the *Examen de ingenios* is the inspiration for the seventeenth-century masterpiece.[96] Precisely this word, however, calls into question Cervantes's opinion of Huarte's deterministic notions, for in the *Examen* the doctor ponders what he considers to be Aristotle's fallacious attribution to "la fortuna ciega" (blind fortune) that "por la mayor parte, las riquezas están en poder de los malos y la pobreza en los buenos" (for the most part, riches are in the control of the wicked and poverty belongs to the good). Huarte contends that the true answer to such a problem is that "los malos son muy ingeniosos, y tienen fuerte imaginativa para engañar comprando y vendiendo, y saben granjear la hacienda y por dónde se ha de adquirir; y los buenos carecen de imaginativa" (the evil are very ingenious, and they have strong imaginations to deceive through buying and selling, and they know how to win property for themselves and where to acquire it; and the good folk lack imagination).[97] The contention of many Hispanists that the choleric Quijote excels through his imaginative faculty as an *ingenioso* thus renders him, in Huarte's terms,

96. See especially C. M. Hutchings, "The *Examen de ingenios* and the Doctrine of Original Genius."
97. *Examen de ingenios*, 267–68.

malo.[98] But, of course, even Cervantes's most casual readers know simply from the epithets bandied about in the novel that the melancholic *hidalgo* Don Quijote, the "Caballero de la Triste Figura" (the Knight of the Sad Figure), is finally and definitively recognized as Alonso Quijano el Bueno. Rather than celebrating the ideology presented in the *Examen,* Cervantes, it seems, goes about undermining and parodying that work by means of Huarte's very vocabulary. For the majority of the novel the pseudo-knight is indeed an outstanding wit in the sense of an individual "off the beaten path," but he is, of course, insane and shown to be mistaken. He is thus not *ingenioso* in any sense that Huarte intends. The fact that he neglects and sells off his land and estate only to buy *libros de caballería* (something Cervantes carefully notes) sharply contradicts Huarte's description of the mercenary craftiness of the *ingeniosos.*[99]

Textual evidence offered in *Don Quijote* and interpreted within the context of the transvaluation of melancholy, then, tends to refute the contentions that Quijote is choleric. The lists of descriptive choleric characteristics provided as attributable to Quijote raise further questions. Green, following Iriarte's lead, comments upon Huarte's recourse to the ancient connection between *ingenio* and *mania,* for example.[100] As has been noted here, the term "mania" is actually synonymous with melancholy in medical literature written well before the Renaissance, and the sixteenth- and seventeenth-century physicians, among them Huarte, uphold this terminological parallel.[101] Avalle-Arce bases his notions of Quijote's choleric temperament upon the definition of "colóricos" found in the *Corbacho.* Among those qualities applied to Quijote are "yrados" (angry), which is also a characteristic listed in the same work under the category of "ombre malencónico."[102] Avalle-Arce likewise connects the term "fuerte" (strong) with Quijote on the basis of the passage in part 1 (chapter 43) when Quijote brags to Maritornes and her companion, showing them his hand "para que miréis la contextura de sus nervios, la trabazón de sus músculos, la anchura y espaciosidad de sus venas; de donde sacareis qué tal debe de ser la fuerza del brazo que tal mano tiene" (so that you look at the constitution of the nerves, the

98. Elsewhere Huarte lists the vices "soberbia" (pride), "gula" (gluttony), and "lujuria" (lust), as those most problematical for imaginative *ingenios* who have great "habilidad para hacer mal" (great ability for evil); *Examen,* 201.

99. Acknowledging Cervantes's parody of the *Examen* in the *entrems* entitled *La elección de los Alcaldes de Daganzo,* Iriarte nevertheless claims that though the tone is one of mockery, the author praises the source: "glorificó el pensamiento nuclear del *Examen de Ingenios,* parodiándolo en su entremés" (he glorified the nuclear thought of the *Examen de ingenios,* parodying it in his *entremés*); *El doctor Huarte de San Juan,* 314. See also Green, "El 'Ingenioso' Hidalgo," 183, for his reading of this passage.

100. Huarte, *Examen de ingenios,* 433; Green, "El 'Ingenioso' Hidalgo," 176–78.

101. *Examen de ingenios,* 109; see also Babb, *Elizabethan Malady,* 36.

102. Alfonso Martinez de Toledo, *Arcipreste de Talavera o Corbacho,* ed. Michael Gerli, 208.

consistency of the muscles, the width and spaciousness of the veins; from which you can judge how strong the arm connected to such a hand must be [pp. 446–47]). This is, of course, the boast of a madman, and it is well proven throughout the novel that the knight is no worthy physical match for his adversaries.

Other characteristics like "vindicativos al tiempo de su cólera" (vindictive at the time of their rage) can find a parallel in the description of melancholics who are, for example, "sañudos" (furious), "irados" (angry), and "riñosos" (quarrelsome).[103] The ability to be "sueltos en fablar" (talkative) is associated with Quijote's two famous discourses on "la edad dorada" and on "las armas y las letras," which, as has been argued, are products of his dried-out melancholy faculties. Other medical texts closer in date of composition to Cervantes's novel, moreover, often connect great discursive abilities with melancholia. Sir John Elyot, for one, claims in his *Castel of Helth* that melancholics are given to "sodayne incontinencie of the tongue."[104] The Spanish physician Lobrera de Avila concurs and writes in his description of the individual whose "mania es de melancholia adusta" (mania is from adust melancholy) that "quando comiença a hablar esta primero pensando: y despues no le pueden hazer callar" (when he begins to speak he is thinking at first: and later one cannot make him be quiet).[105] Other descriptions in Avalle-Arce's list are applicable only if we accept the notion that Quijote is a natural choleric whose depiction is based on a fifteenth-century description that does not acknowledge the category of adust melancholy, a category that, by the sixteenth century, includes the rest of the characteristics cited.[106]

That Don Quijote claims in chapter 6 of part 2 to be a man of "armas" born under the sign of Mars is no less absurd than are his pronouncements about the identity of windmills or barbers' basins. This notion is also part of the vast body of material he has read, and his dried-out, badly functioning memory can only serve up these images and recollections of the written word for interpretation by the intellect. A Cervantine dialectical note also sounds here, however, if one asks the question, what if Alonso Quijano were really a man born under the influence of Mars? No surer proof can be offered for Cervantes's rejection of Huarte's biological determinism or Ficino's assertions about astrological influence, since the unofficial *caballero* is time after time defeated or tricked until finally he is forced to abandon the life of arms as a condition of surrender.

103. *Corbacho*, 208–9.
104. Elyot, *Castel of Helth*, fol. 73r.
105. Lobrera de Avila, *Remedios de cuerpos humanos*, fol. xl r.
106. See Babb, *Elizabethan Malady*, 33–34.

Slowly over the course of the novel, a gradual but steady moistening of Don Quijote's brain occurs,[107] effected by the extended periods of sleep the protagonist experiences after his two returns home and his time spent in the Cueva de Montesinos.[108] In part 2 Don Quijote's imagination is still functioning efficiently, as it has from the outset, providing him with sensory information about the reality with which he interacts. Since his system is still overdry, however, his memory cannot yet store new images and facilitate proper comparisons, and thus process correct interpretations. Though in chapter 10 he sees the three "labradoras" (peasant women) as untidy rustics, smells the garlic on their breath, and hears their unrefined speech, Don Quijote persists in his quest for adventures, just as he does after being victimized by the Duke and Duchess. Nevertheless, as the book proceeds, Quijote must progressively rely upon the convenient notion of enchantment to explain to himself what is happening, for the gradual moistening of his brain is allowing him to compare and interpret more sanely. When this happens the images of *caballería* lose their primacy and the fixations weaken. To continue as Don Quijote, he must renounce the rational interpretations of his improving mind and consciously operate outside a viable mode of thought. The "razón de la sinrazón" thus acquires a further dimension. Throughout these experiences, he is marginalized and excluded from the ranks of normal society.

Quijote's final defeat forces him to return home and coincides with the culmination of the process that has made his memory more pliable and moist. His obsession with the life of knight errantry, for example, cedes to a new one

107. Heiple concurs in "Renaissance Medical Psychology," 69–70.
108. Even the therapeutic ministrations of his housekeeper, niece, and friends who ply him with foods help to counteract the unbalanced system, following the tradition of "contraria contrariis curantur." Within such a tradition, Huarte, in fact, acknowledges: "el sueño de la noche pasada ha humedecido y fortificado el celebro, y la vigilia de todo el día lo ha desecado y endurecido" (the sleep of the past night has moistened and fortified the brain, and the wakefulness during the day has dried and hardened it); *Examen,* 127. This is in keeping with standard medical theory, and Huarte offers this explanation in the context of clarifying why the memory is faulty in old age to the benefit of the *entendimiento* while the opposite is true in childhood. He later claims, moreover, that "el entendimiento y la memoria son potencias opuestas y contrarias" (the intellect and the memory are opposed and contrary faculties); 129. This explanation can have further application to Quijote since he is approaching old age by the standard of his day (around fifty years of age). It is interesting that Huarte proposes this explanation as "mi doctrina" (my doctrine), 128, though many other doctors certainly articulate the same argument (see Babb, *Elizabethan Malady,* 58–67). Furthermore, he states his theory as a rebuttal of the Aristotelian response to the question "¿qué es la causa que siendo viejos tenemos mucho entendimiento, y cuando mozos aprendemos con más facilidad?" (what is the cause of the fact that when we are old we understand a great deal, and when we are young we learn with greater ease?); 126. He does, however, invoke Aristotelian authority about the effects of sleep as well as a Hippocratic aphorism: "Los que de noche tienen gran sequía, durmiendo se les quita" (Those that at night are very dry, sleeping relieves them of this); 127.

about the pastoral life—still a literary product stemming from his overabundant reading, but a sign that different images are surfacing for estimation by his intellect. After being reminded by his housekeeper's vivid recollections of her own long and difficult "pastoral" life ("Mire, señor, tome mi consejo; que no se le doy sobre estar harta de pan y vino, sino en ayunas, y sobre cincuenta años que tengo de edad" [Look, sir, take my advice; for I do not give it to you glutted on bread and wine, but rather clearheaded after fasting, and with fifty years of experience], p. 1061), he begins to rethink his new plan to go and live the life of a literary shepherd. It is significant that Don Quijote then asks, "Llevadme al lecho" (Take me to bed). After he "durmió de un tirón, como dicen, más de seis horas" (he slept six hours straight, as they say, without a break), he awakens to reaffirm a sane mode of thinking (p. 1063). Able to make valid comparisons, he remembers who he is and is able to assume his proper place in the hierarchical system upon which his society bases its thinking and moral values. He is once again able to recognize universal interconnections and abandons the tendency toward hypertrophic thought that has made him an advocate of thinking as a "reasoning practice upon the world," a crazed undertaking indeed.

Cervantes's transvaluation of melancholy is fully evident as the novel concludes. Quijote's madness is the result of his melancholy scholarship. He is, during his adventures, a manic melancholic, but when Quijote/Quijano regains the normal functioning of his faculties and steps back into the traditional epistemology to recognize his proper place within a "chain of being," he does so also as a melancholic. His system has mediated to the degree that he can again remember more than the stories he has read and can understand the proper connections between the objects of the universe. His normal and natural systemic melancholy returns as does his normal identity, but the melancholy of his sane moments is also what is killing him: "Llegó su fin y acabamiento cuando él menos lo pensaba . . . o ya fuese de la melancolía que le causaba el verse vencido, o ya por la disposición del cielo" (His end arrived when he least expected . . . either it was due to the melancholy that finding himself defeated caused or to the will of heaven); "Fue el parecer del médico que melancolías y desabrimientos le acababan" (It was the opinion of the doctor that melancholy and depression finished him off [p. 1062]); "— Ay!— respondió Sancho, llorando—. No se muera vuestra merced . . . porque la mayor locura que puede hacer un hombre en esta vida es dejarse morir, sin más ni más, sin que nadie le mate, ni otras manos le acaben que las de la melancolía" ("Ah," responded Sancho, crying. "Don't die, your grace . . . because the greatest insanity that a man can commit in this life is to let himself die, without further ado, without anyone killing him, nor other hands finishing him off than those of melancholy"[p. 1063]). In some of the earliest texts on melancholy, ancient physicians like Rufus of Ephesus warn of the consequences of prolonging pathological symptoms of melancholy and urge early treatment in order to effect healing.[109] Quijote's melancholia, of course, has been of long duration.

In the end, Quijote lapses back to the colder, more sedentary melancholia of the book's prehistory. Quijote comes full circle in his alternations from contemplative melancholic to active, manic adust melancholic and then back to the colder, sadder, inactive melancholia. Green recounts this humoral composition of the dying *manchego,* but considers it "an acute attack of melancholy."[110] It is instead the means by which Cervantes effects his own representation of melancholia's transvaluation, giving us a melancholic whose melancholy is the cause of both his madness and his sanity. Cervantes is perhaps the prime example from among the ranks of the Spanish Golden Age authors who, by means of a melancholy character, recognize the secular mind's power and autonomy while consciously advocating the continued validity of a system of thought and values that is being threatened by others also intent upon performing "reasoning practices" upon the world. As the dying melancholic Quijote reasserts his place among the members of his society and the still reigning order of thought, he does so as the confessed melancholic who has also recanted of his sins of the intellect.

109. See Jackson's discussion of Rufus's writings on melancholy in *Depression and Melancholia,* 35–39.
110. Green, "El 'Ingenioso' Hidalgo," 188.

2

Religious Melancholy (Tirso)

In truth it was melancholy that the devil breathed into Adam at the time of his fall: melancholy which robs a man of his ardour and faith.

St. Hildegard of Bingen

he epigraph above calls attention to the importance of melancholy in the religious and the moral teachings against sin. St. Hildegard of Bingen concentrates on the origin of melancholy, which she describes as simultaneous with the commission of Original Sin. In her account, the twelfth-century saint focuses on the moment when Adam ate the forbidden apple and the melancholy humor in his blood curdled, "as when a lamp is quenched, the smouldering and smoking wick remains reeking behind. . . . the sparkle of innocence was dulled in him, and his eyes, which had formerly beheld heaven, were blinded, and his gall was changed to bitterness, and his melancholy to blackness."[1] Hers is a description of melancholia that represents an important medieval articulation of the link between the humoral condition and the spiritual, ethical, and moral issues which continue to be raised 450 to 500 years later by the Renaissance doctors and scientists in their multifaceted treatises on melancholy. The beliefs that began to emerge in the later sixteenth century and blossomed full-blown in the seventeenth echo her insistence upon the moral responsibility incumbent upon the melancholic and those administering to him or her to seek relief and/or cures through medical and theological means.

The Renaissance expository writers reiterate as well St. Hildegard's insistence upon the all-pervasive quality of melancholy as a nearly universal affliction. In her view, melancholia is Adam's punishment and thus the "incurable hereditary evil" to which all human beings are vulnerable, while in the early seventeenth century, Burton likewise writes: "thou shalt soon perceive that all the world is mad, that it is melancholy."[2] Such notions reinforce the tradition of

1. In Jackson, *Melancholia and Depression*, 326. See also Jean Starobinsky's discussion of St. Hildegard's writings on melancholy and original sin, in *History of the Treatment of Melancholy*, 35.
   2. Burton, *Anatomy of Melancholy*, 28.

melancholy as a concern in moral teachings and associate it with the pride and thirst for forbidden knowledge as the basis of humanity's Fall. This is a dimension that finds an almost full reverberation in the intellectual scope of the literary representation of melancholy in the seventeenth century, when emphasis was placed on the melancholic's illicit use of the mind in both secular and spiritual matters.

The religious melancholic is an individual whose depiction in Renaissance literature evinces his or her ties to ethical and medical notions that date back to the early centuries of Christianity. That depiction reaches a height of scientific focus in the late sixteenth and early seventeenth centuries, when the medico-scientific writers like Alfonso de Santa Cruz and Pedro Mercado include references to it or provide related case histories.[3] Burton's examination of the syndrome in his *Anatomy of Melancholy* is the first extensive secular coverage of the subject, and it serves as a compendium of an age-old topic frequently written about by officials of the Christian Church. Burton's chapter on religious melancholy appears in the *Anatomy* from its earliest edition (1621) and, though certainly not widely circulated in Spain, it is coextensive with certain Spanish dramatic representations of the same spiritual/humoral condition. I choose to concentrate on one such work, Tirso de Molina's *El condenado por desconfiado,* for two reasons. First, its range of possible dates of composition has been postulated between 1615 and 1625.[4] These dates situate the drama in that period of heightened literary interest in melancholy when Tirso and other writers had more frequent opportunities for exposure to notions about aspects of religious melancholy and its evolution from the earlier sinful condition known as *acedia* that Burton also summarizes during approximately the same period. Second, *El condenado por desconfiado* is a play in which its author scrutinizes the majority of the questions surrounding the topic of religious melancholy, including the complex and varying elements of despair, neglect, idleness, delusions, and vulnerability to the Devil's persuasion that melancholics were believed to suffer and that continued to characterize the notion of *acedia* from the Middle Ages through the Renaissance.[5]

As a character clearly defined within the framework of the seventeenth-century understanding of religious melancholy, Tirso's ascetic hermit Paulo in *El condenado por desconfiado* has much in common with such diverse figures

3. Santa Cruz, "Diagnostio et cura affecctuum melancholicorum," 35–36 and Mercado, *Dialogos de Philosophia,* fol. Xiiii.

4. Henryk Ziomek, *A History of Spanish Golden Age Drama,* 93.

5. Babb, *Elizabethan Malady,* 47–54; Jackson, *Melancholia and Depression,* 72. A particularly accessible sixteenth-century Spanish account of the dangers of melancholia for members of monasteries and convents written by one from their ranks is found in St. Teresa of Avila's *Las fundaciones,* ed. Guido Mancini (Madrid: Iter Ediciones, 1970), 86–90.

of history and fiction as the gods of Olympus, the fourth-century monks living with Evagrius in the Egyptian desert, and countless other historical and literary personalities believed to suffer from a pathological melancholy system. Part of the background of Tirso's characterization of Paulo involves the terminological evolution of *acedia,* a word used very early to describe the tedium afflicting the monks of Alexandria as a consequence of the monotony of their routine, which causes, among other things, restlessness, dejection, and a wish to leave the monastic life altogether. Lyman looks back even further to the Homeric stories about the Olympian life, in which the literal definition of *acedia,* "uncaring," had been "inadvertently institutionalized in the leisure world of the Greek deities" whose hedonistic life gave way to gloomy disillusionment and immoral pursuits that contaminated as well the mortals with whom they interacted.[6] Through the writings of John Cassian, the monastic vice of *acedia* was introduced into the Latin West and passed through transformations during the Middle Ages, becoming associated and even interchangeable with the deadly sin of sloth. Thus it was eventually a danger for persons of any profession.

A new emphasis was placed on the internal mental state and emotions as causes of *acedia;* now seen as a weakness of the spirit, religious melancholy was likewise connected to *tristitia,* thereby gaining a psychological basis as well, as Siegfried Wenzel explains. He further contends: "In this process *acedia* came to be understood as man's culpable aversion against the divine good—a conception with which the emphasis on the vice's mental aspects and the more 'spiritualized' view reached its culmination."[7] Paralleling this cycle was another, for the Scholastics characterize *acedia* as a sin occupying a position between sins of the spirit and those of the body. Other moralists group *acedia* with the carnal vices of lust and gluttony because of its pathological connection to one's need for rest and sleep, exaggerated in the physical listlessness often evident in the melancholic. The demonasticization of *acedia,* its internalization, and its categorization as a "vice of the spirit" as well as a "vice of the flesh" occurs, nevertheless, over the whole of the Middle Ages, and Wenzel ultimately concedes a tripartite categorization—"monastic, Scholastic, and popular"—which, he tells us, "can be localized with some accuracy in time, and even more, in literary genre." He adds, however, that "never did a later form completely replace an earlier one. The laicization . . . of the vice in the twelfth and thirteenth centuries did not entail the total loss of monastic elements . . . and the concept of *acedia* one meets in the fourteenth and fifteenth centuries is a comprehensive one, embracing elements from all stages of *acedia*'s past life."[8]

6. Standford M. Lyman, *The Seven Deadly Sins,* 14–15.
7. Siegfried Wenzel, *The Sin of Sloth: "Acedia" in Medieval Thought and Literature,* 174–76.
8. Ibid., 170–71, 179; see also Starobinski, 31–35, 325–41 and Jackson, *Melancholia and Depres-*

As is the case with scholarly melancholics, their religious counterparts are also solitary thinkers, and Tirso depicts his accidic monk as prideful in his contemplation. The emphasis on the "mental aspects" involved in one's "culpable aversion against the divine good" to which Wenzel refers is at the heart of what Tirso portrays in *El condenado por desconfiado*.[9] The play dramatizes the dialectical response on the part of its author to the epistemological struggle over the perceived strength or danger inherent in the active melancholy mind. The play also addresses a related point made by Sullivan concerning the composite nature of Golden Age dramatic presentations that encompass "the basic antagonisms of the Counter Reformation itself, i.e., Renaissance liberation in conflict with a medievalizing reaction; the *comedia* was a theater that restated medieval values, but explored the scope of human freedom without being able to help itself."[10] Tirso's transvalued treatment of the melancholy mentality portrays Enrico the bandit as a counterpart to the religious melancholic Paulo, for Enrico exhibits numerous traits of melancholy criminality that were also thought to plague the religious melancholic once he or she had despaired of salvation. Like two complementary character studies of distinct but related melancholic disorders, Paulo and Enrico dramatize what the more scientific writers record in their treatises, but these two diverge in their eventual responses to their afflictions. Understanding the context of melancholy within which Tirso develops the action, theme, imagery, and characterization in this play provides a means of reading the work that accounts for its canonicity in seventeenth-century terms.

In the nonliterary studies of *acedia*, the authors comment upon the concept in its more secular context through its connection to humoral melancholy. Those pseudo-scientific writers of the sixteenth and seventeenth centuries who

sion, 65-77, 325-41.

9. Henry W. Sullivan discusses what he considers Tirso's consistent depiction of the privileged status accorded the individual will and its freedom in the pursuit of personal goals. He asserts: "This subordination of intellect, energy and ethical nicety to the attainment of an end determined by the individual will may be termed an ethical voluntarism. . . . Tirsian *voluntad* desires ends and employs manipulative, intelligent cunning to obtain that end" (*Tirso de Molina and the Drama of the Counter Reformation,* 171). I would, nevertheless, argue that the intellect is not subordinated to the will in melancholy characters such as Paulo, for in Tirso's straightforward representation of the faculties of the rational soul—the reason, the memory, and the will—it is the reason or the intellect that contemplates and interprets what is good and what is evil and then informs the will of its determination. The will, which desires the good and rejects the evil, causes physical action toward the good through the sensitive passions and thus functions as the primary controlling agent in the human soul. It is, however, important to understand the essential role of the intellect in the determination of good toward which the will moves. As in all cases of melancholy, the reasoning process of the mind is disrupted in various ways, and the manipulative energies of the religious melancholic, like those of the scholar, are better understood as originating in the overly contemplative intellect. Certainly, the ends sought by Paulo are very much products of his melancholic intellect.

10. Ibid., 63.

do address the topic of religious melancholy as a discrete type describe it as marked by despair over one's salvation and failure to pursue or to finish good works. Certain characteristics became associated with the religious individuals whose melancholy symptoms were either the result or, conversely, the cause of their devout lifestyle; insufficient or unfit diet, fasting, and other such hardships of a strict religious life were thought either to produce or to exacerbate the physiological symptoms of the disorder. So, too, the solitude which melancholics are said to seek as well as the darkness of a cave or a monastic cell are part of the hermit's ambience. Cristóbal Acosta asserts in his late sixteenth-century *Tratado en contra y pro de la vida solitaria* (Treatise against and for the solitary life) that "melancholía no os faltará, que allende la vuestra natural, la divina scriptura llama triste al que vive solo y sin compañía" (you will not lack melancholy, for besides your natural melancholy, divine scripture labels sad the one who lives alone and without company).[11] The study and meditation associated with melancholy is often described as a cause of heightened anxiety and a weakening of faith and convictions in the religious. In their melancholic states, they convince themselves of their own eternal damnation and the impossibility of ever receiving God's grace and redemption.

Murillo, in particular, regards the religious as especially susceptible to melancholia. With references to Pliny, he includes those "dados a los estudios, y a la Religion" (those given to study and to Religion) in the category that also encompasses the "Insanos, Melancholicos, y Maniacos" (Insane, Melancholics, and Maniacs), adding that these individuals are known popularly as "alumbrados" (illuminati) and are "callados, tristes, y excordes" (quiet, sad, and mentally unbalanced). The blending of medical and moral notions evident in the majority of the expository works is clearly articulated in Murillo's study, as certain sections dealing with the cure of melancholy diseases attest. He posits, for example, "que los Medicos no curen el cuerpo, antes que este curada el alma con el Santissimo Sacramento de la Penitencia, y Sagrada comunion, y confession Sacramental . . . y es gran desdicha lo que en esto passa, que muchos Medicos . . . por dezir a los enfermos que se confiessen en tiempo, se hallan con ellos muertos, no sin grande cargo de sus conciencias" (that the Physicians do not cure the body, before the soul is cured with the Holy Sacrament of Penitence, and Holy communion, and Sacramental confession . . . and it is very unfortunate what happens in this matter, for many Doctors . . . by telling the sick people to confess, find that they die, not without great charge to their consciences). He further counsels physicians that they recognize the link between disease and sin (an echo of St. Hildegard's account of the origin of

11. *Tratado*, not paginated.

melancholy) and so the doctor must consider "si acaso la enfermedad que se padece es causada, y le vino al enfermo por sus pecados: porque es de Fe Catolica, que por nuestros pecados enfermamos muchas vezes" (if by chance the illness suffered is caused and comes to the patient through his sins: because it is part of the Catholic Faith that due to our sins we become sick many times). He adds, however: "Mas aunque el Demonio pueda causar enfermedades innumerables, puede el Medico, como instrumento de la Divina Iusticia, o qualquiera otro varon de vida inculpable, (pie & devote), ahuyentar a los Demonios" (But although the Devil may cause innumerable diseases, the Doctor, as an instrument of Divine Justice, or any other man of guiltless life, "devoutly," can drive away Devils).[12] The physician's task is thus diverse and combines both ethical and scientific fields.[13] Murillo cites the exhortation *nosce teipsum* as an important moral underpinning to his arguments about the religious melancholics, explaining: "el que fuere perfectamente sabio, se conocera perfectamente a si mismo . . . y assi, como se puede afirmar que se cognosca perfectamente el Melancholico, o Maniaco, que con sus propias manos se quita la vida" (he who may be perfectly wise, will know himself perfectly . . . and so, as one can affirm that the Melancholic or the Maniac knows himself perfectly, for with his own hands he ends his life).[14] The despair and self-destructive tendencies (in both a physical and spiritual sense) are therefore an inherent danger in the melancholy self-contemplation that needs to be tempered and redirected by means of theological and medical ministering.

Tirso's characterization of Paulo in the play undeniably entails the traditional conception of *acedia*. The isolated life based on a routine of meditation and sparse diet, the latter highlighted through the complaints of Paulo's servant Pedrisco, is indeed what has occupied the hermit for ten years. His initial attack of despair, moreover, follows a period of sleep, and his subsequent rancor and neglect of his duty to God are, as Daniel Rogers asserts, in keeping with the vices that St. Thomas associates with *acedia*.[15] The blending of the accepted notion of *acedia* with that of the humoral disorder of melancholy must, however, be considered. What Paulo does and says and the visual and poetic imagery attendant upon his behavior reflect this blend of psychological, physiological, and ethical factors.

As the play begins, Paulo expresses his preference for solitude and darkness:

---

12. Murillo y Velarde, *Aprobacion de ingenios,* fols. 21v, 29r, 28r, 33v.

13. Babb, *Elizabethan Malady,* 19, views medicine and psychology as interconnected in the Renaissance.

14. *Aprobacion de ingenios,* fol. 21r.

15. Daniel Rogers, "Introduction" to *El condenado por desconfiado,* by Tirso de Molina, 24.

¡Dichoso albergue mío!
Soledad apacible y deleitosa,
que en el calor y el frío
me dais posada en esta selva umbrosa.

(My happy refuge!
Peaceful and delightful solitude,
that in the heat and the cold
gives me shelter in this dark forest.)[16]

In the medical books, as in their artistic literary counterparts, an affinity for solitary darkness is often mentioned in descriptions of melancholy characteristics. The associated metaphorical suggestions link melancholy with that darkness of mind which the dark humor brings about as well as that physical darkness in which melancholics prefer to stay or which might worsen their already fearful nature. Murillo writes, for example:

espantanse, y assombranse estos melancholicos, como lo hazen los muchachos en las tinieblas, y obscuridades, y entre los crecidos, y mancebos, los indoctos, y rudos; porque de la manera que las tinieblas exteriores, casi a todos los hombres les dan pavor, y miedo, si no es que son muy ossados, o enseñados: assi de la misma manera, el color del humor melancholico viene a hazer tener temor con tinieblas, y obscuridad, cubriendo con sombra, o assombrando el celebro, demanera, que lo que parece que se colige de Galeno, es, que la causa destos sympthomas, miedo, y tristeza, mas es el color del humor, que no la destemplança de las qualidades.

(These melancholics become frightened and startled, as do children in the shadows and in darkness, and among older people and youths, the uneducated and the uncultured; because in the way that external darkness shocks and frightens almost all people, if they are not very brave or educated: thus the color of the melancholic humor causes fear by shadows, darkness, covering with shade, or by startling the brain, so it seems that what we can summarize from Galen is that the cause of these symptoms, fear, and sadness, is the color of the humor rather than the irregularity of the qualities.)[17]

The tradition of *acedia* and the vulnerability of religious persons, in particular hermits, to melancholia makes the references to solitude and darkness significant in the case of a figure purportedly living such a reclusive life. St. Hildegard's references to the darkness of the descent of sin and melancholy on humanity are also recalled by such passages.

Thus, although Paulo's monologue seems to express the *beatus ille* topos, it more appropriately indicates to the audience the melancholic condition that

16. Tirso de Molina, *El condenado por desconfiado,* ed. Ciriaco Morón and Rolena Adorno, act 1, verses 1–4. Subsequent references (act and verse) will be cited in the text.
17. *Aprobacion de ingenios,* fol. 98v.

afflicts him. The intensity of Paulo's statements builds through the first four stanzas of his speech to the point where he shouts:

> ¿Quién ¡Oh celeste velo!
> aquestos tafetanes luminosos
> rasgar pudiera un poco
> para ver . . . ?
>
>   (1.21–24)

> (Who, Oh celestial veil!
> could tear a little bit
> these luminous curtains
> in order to see . . . ?)

Again, there is an echo of Hildegard's metaphorical explanation of melancholy, which posits Adam's loss of innocence as an inability to look into heaven, a privilege that had formerly been his. Paulo suggests his parallel experience of wishing to duplicate the prelapsarian privilege that nevertheless cannot be reclaimed by humanity, whom he figuratively represents in this moment of blasphemous pride. He hastens to add, however, "¡Ay de mí! Vuélvome loco" (Woe is me! I am going crazy [1.24]), thereby identifying his own underlying instability and linking himself from the beginning of the play with the state of *locura* which, like *manía,* the sixteenth- and seventeenth-century scientists use as a synonym for *melancolía,*

His outburst displays as well the ecstatic state that melancholia was thought capable of triggering in the religiously devout, for as Lawrence Babb asserts: "Melancholy symptoms of a religious character include many rapturous fancies."[18] As is typical of religious melancholics, Paulo's thoughts turn to the question of his own meriting of salvation and to the threatening "puertas del profundo" (doors to hell [1.36]). Furthermore, his last sentence before leaving the stage ("Ved que el hombre se hizo / de barro vil, de barro quebradizo" [Understand that man was made of common clay, of fragile clay]; 1.75–76) carries with it the traditional biblical teaching but also hints at the connection between the humor melancholy and the earth, its mate among the natural elements.

The hermit's words end with his entrance into one of the mountain grottoes and are followed by the vociferous complaints of his only servant and companion Pedrisco. The *gracioso* bemoans specifically the bad diet that robs him, and

18. Babb, *Elizabethan Malady,* 48.

presumably his master, of sound health. Outlining the regimen the two men follow and the emotional consequence it has for both at times, he says:

> Aquí penitencia hacemos,
> y sólo yerbas comemos,
> y a veces nos acordamos,
> de lo mucho que dejamos
> por lo poco que tenemos.
>   (1.112–16)

> (Here we do penance,
> and we only eat herbs,
> and at times we remember,
> how much we left behind
> for the little that we have.)

Pedrisco's complaints, though comical in presentation because of their stress on his interest in creature comforts, nevertheless emphasize repeatedly his sadness, "triste fin me pronostico" (I predict a sad end for myself [1.81]), and lamenting further ("memorias me hacen llorar" [memories make me cry]; 1.124): "ya está todo perdido" (now everything is lost [1.132]). Pedrisco thus sets the mood for Paulo's next monologue, which itself begins "¡qué desventura! / Y ¡qué desgracia, cierta, lastimosa!" (What misfortune! / And what certain and regrettable bad luck! [1.139–40]). It is this frame of mind which dominates Paulo throughout the rest of the play, and this scene, moreover, subtly suggests that the entryways through which the hermit and his servant pass into their respective caves are analogous to the doors to hell ("puertas del profundo") which Paulo dreads in his first speech. The dark abyss, however, is a mental and emotional one, linked nevertheless to the physical world through his melancholy physiology but leading to eternal spiritual damnation because of the obsessive despair upon which he seizes.

The immediate cause of Paulo's fear and sadness, the two emotions most characteristic of melancholia, is his nightmarish dream vision of "la muerte cruel" (cruel death) and the final judgment upon his condemned soul. Having described the unsettling images, Paulo relates his concerns in terms that reinforce his identity as a religious melancholic: "Con aquella fatiga y aquel miedo / desperté" (I awoke with that fatigue and that fear [1.177–78]). He emphasizes at once the physical weariness associated with *acedia* and the fright of melancholia. He then goes on to describe the classical traits of one so afflicted:

> . . . aunque temblando, y no vi nada
> si no es mi culpa, y tan confuso quedo,

que si no es a mi suerte desdichada,
o traza del contrario, ardid o enredo,
que vibra contra mí su ardiente espada,
no sé a qué atribuya.

(1.178–83)

(. . . although trembling, and I saw nothing
if not my guilt, and so confused do I remain,
that if it is not to my wretched luck,
or trick, ruse, or intrigue of Satan,
who moves his burning sword against me,
I do not know to what to attribute it.)

His doubts and self-recrimination are accompanied by repetitive despairing questions: "¿Heme de condenar, mi Dios divino, / como ese sueño dice, o he de verme / en el sagrado alcázar cristalino?" (Am I to condemn myself, my divine God, / as that dream says, or will I find myself / in the sacred crystal palace? [1.185–87]); "¿qué fin he de tener?" (what end must I have? [1.189]); "¿He de ir a vuestro Cielo, o al infierno?" (Will I go to your Heaven, or to hell? [1. 192]).

Of particular interest to Renaissance expository writers are the powers ascribed to melancholics who are said to be able to see into the future and experience rapturous visions. In Spain, most treatises on melancholy reflect their authors' refusal to accept such purported powers, and express instead another popular Renaissance notion that the devil preys more frequently upon melancholic individuals and is responsible for their visions of damnation. In his appended section about these supposed prophetic powers, Freylas directly addresses the connection between the devil and melancholy, saying, "es cierto que se junta el demonio con el humor melancolico, porque halla en el muy grande disposicion para hazer grandes danos, como es persuadir a que se ahorquen, o desesperen de la misericordia de Dios" (it is certain that the devil joins himself to the melancholy humor, because he finds in it a very great disposition to do great harm, like persuading melancholics to hang themselves, or to despair of God's mercy).[19] Murillo likewise writes "el Demonio se alegra con el humor Melancholico" (the Devil rejoices in the Melancholic humor). He goes into great detail in his arguments meant to discourage belief in the purported abilities of melancholics to prophesy and to speak languages never studied (particularly Latin), citing many ancient and contemporary sources about the devil's intervention in such cases.[20] These sorts of expressions by

19. Freylas, *Conocimiento, curacion y preservacion,* section not paginated.
20. *Aprobacion de ingenios,* fols. 31r, 30r–33r.

Spanish expository writers are commonplaces in the tradition of melancholy as the *balneum diaboli* that many of their European contemporaries also record.

In his discussion of this phenomenon, Babb includes references to similar statements by Philip Barrough, Johann Weyer, Robert Burton, André Du Laurens, and others.[21] Jackson, who devotes an entire chapter in his study to beliefs about the purported supernatural powers enjoyed by melancholics and their presumed sources, explains that the issuing of prophesy by melancholy persons had varyingly been through a transformation of the Platonic theory of divinely inspired madness in combination with the Aristotelian theories about the superior capabilities of the melancholic mind. Numerous medical writers acknowledge the strength of such a tradition, but they often relegate the prophetic visions to the realm of pathological delusion.[22] Certainly, the Spanish physicians who are more generally Galenic in their approach to melancholy support this kind of assessment.

Dramatizing a similar view of such melancholic abilities of prophecy, Tirso represents the devil's sway upon Paulo's diseased melancholy mind. Like several of the physicians, however, Tirso makes plain that God allows the devil's trickery. The devil in *El condenado por desconfiado* is able to influence Paulo, but only after the experience of his frightening dream, which intensifies the connection between the hermit and melancholia. Freylas, for instance, writes: "el que [tiene abundancia de] melancolia visita con los suenos los muertos, y sepulcros, y . . . cosas negras y tristes" (he who [has an abundance of] melancholy visits the dead in dreams, as well as graves, and . . . dark and sad things).[23] In addition, Murillo discusses at length the melancholy fixations and obsessions that befall an overly melancholy mind because of both fear and the devil's intervention. The effects he describes seem particularly applicable to Paulo:

> Ay algunas personas tan escrupulosas por razon de la complexion melancholica, y fria, que estan dispuestas para el temor, y assi las mugeres melancholicas, y los hombres que padecen esta enfermedad estan mas sugetos a esta passion, porque el temor, y la frialdad aprietan el corazon, y de alli se dispone la imaginacion a concebir el mal que esta por venir, y por flaqueza de la cabeça quando esta con lesion, como sucede en los melancholicos, o el Demonio los despierta, y atiza, el que puede mover los humores melancholicos, con permision de Dios, y la imaginacion puede ser enganada, y tener demasiadamente alguna cosa, o por abstinencias, vigilias, y asperezas, o compania de personas escrupulosas.

21. Babb, *Elizabethan Malady*, 48–49.
22. On the supernatural powers of melancholics, see *Melancholia and Depression*, 325–41; on pathological delusion, see 327–28.
23. *Conocimiento, curacion y preservacion*, section not paginated.

(There are some persons who are so scrupulous because of their cold and melancholic makeup that they are disposed to fear. Thus many melancholic women, and the men who suffer from this disease, are quite subject to that passion, because fear and coldness press upon the heart. In this way, one's imagination is prepared to conceive some future evil. And, as happens with melancholics, either some weakness in the head as when it has been wounded, or the Devil, with God's permission, wakes and stirs in them that which can move the melancholic humors and the imagination can be deceived, putting excessive emphasis on some thing: abstinence, vigils, mortification, or the company of pious people.)[24]

So it is that, in his monk's routine, Paulo is overly susceptible to cold fear and even more so once his body is affected by what was thought to be the cooling influence of sleep. The devil, who has received permission from "el Juez más supremo y recto" (the most supreme and just Judge [1.230]) to deceive, and thus test, Paulo, has been able to exacerbate his fearful thoughts about the future. The consequences are dire, for, not availing himself of the suggested remedies for his pathological condition—described, for example, by Murillo as confession, medical advice, and, in particular, recourse to God's grace—Paulo does not reverse the process.[25] The devil appeals to him through his senses in a physical visitation as well. The hermit's imagination receives this sensory information, but his overly active melancholy intellect is not able to interpret correctly the information offered. The natural tendencies he has toward pride and rumination become symptoms of his disease, and he progressively takes on more and more of the most negative qualities of pathological melancholia whose sufferers are "soberbios, altivos, renegadores, astutos, doblados, injuriosos, y amigos de hazer mal, y vengativos, y los que tienen el ingenio mas agudo, suelen ser acedos, colericos, y malcontentos" (prideful, haughty, ill-tempered, crafty, deceitful, insulting, vengeful, and fond of doing evil, and those who have the most astute wit, are usually disagreeable, angry, and malcontent).[26] On the authority of numerous Renaissance discussions of religious melancholy, Babb asserts: "Such [persons] often develop a dreadful melancholy which provokes them to commit monstrous crimes."[27]

Upon learning from the devil in angel's guise that his fate is to be that of the stranger Enrico, Paulo makes clear that he is experiencing the "impious delusions of divine favor" that many expository writers label as the devil's inspiration.[28] The hermit declares: "Algún divino varón, / debe de ser: ¿quién lo

24. *Aprobacion de ingenios*, fols. 73v–74r.
25. Ibid., fol. 29r.
26. Ibid., fol. 38r.
27. Babb, *Elizabethan Malady*, 48.
28. Ibid., 49.

duda?" (He must be some saintly man, / who can doubt it? [1.289–91]), and "¡Gran santo debe de ser! / Lleno de contento estoy" (He must be a great saint! / I am full of happiness [1.321–22]). His statement about contentment should, of course, be taken ironically, since his words and behavior provide evidence instead of his religious melancholia. La Puerta de la Mar, the site to which Paulo is directed in order to observe Enrico, is, moreover, symbolically linked to melancholy through connection with Saturn and one of his realms of influence, the sea. It also recalls the "puertas del profundo" that Paulo earlier dreaded.

The result of the devil's message is in the short run a more hopeful, though deluded, discourse on Paulo's part, rhetoric that lasts only until he observes Enrico and learns that this man is a hardened criminal with a record of multiple crimes. Other melancholy symptoms then begin to become evident in Paulo's demeanor. Abandoning all hope of salvation, he yields to the more violent side of his melancholy nature and suffers alternations between the so-called hot and cold characteristics that the pathological melancholic can experience as a consequence of a strong show of emotion. The result is a series of alternating cycles of violence, overwhelming fear, and incapacitating sadness that plague him during the rest of the play. The fires of hell which Paulo anticipates thus correspond to the more manic and violent activities upon which he embarks, though he heads for the mountains, made of earth and therefore symbolic of melancholy. He declares to Pedrisco: "En el monte hay bandoleros: / bandolero quiero ser" (In the mountains there are bandits: / I want to be a bandit [1.979–80]), adding further that in comparison to Enrico "[t]an malo tengo de ser / como él, y peor si puedo" (I want to be as bad / as he, and worse if I am able [1.984–85]). The inner heat of his agitated pathological adust state is apparent and he exclaims at one point: "Rayo del mundo he de ser" (I will become a thunderbolt of the world [1.998]), while at another, "Fuego por la vista exhalo" (I exhale fire through my eyes [2.1427]). He likewise continues to express his pride, describing the course his villainy will take: "Más que la Naturaleza / he de hacer por cobrar fama" (In order to gain fame / I must outdo Nature [2.1438–39]).

Following his intentions to lead the evil life that corresponds to the eternal damnation he expects, Paulo dramatizes the perversion of his will's action by means of his unhealthy intellect. He never completely relents in his certainty of condemnation and proves that his melancholy susceptibility to the devil's suggestion is more profound than is his faith in God's grace. He listens to but does not believe the angelic messenger sent to advise him to repent and accept God's forgiveness. Paulo's adherence to a conviction that his fate is predetermined is, of course, an unacceptable stance from the point of view of the Zumelian theology that Tirso follows.[29] The potential for physiological determinism inherent in humoralism is likewise rejected by the ethical notions of the physicians writing on melancholy, for measures to relieve the various melancholy disorders are nearly always aimed at restoring the patient to a state of balance (Huarte, of course, is a notable exception), physically and mentally, and overcoming the effects of the offending humor. Indeed, the humoral tendencies that render Paulo prone to melancholic despair, criminality, emotional imbalance, and excessive pride are aspects of his personality which Renaissance medicine teaches can be controlled. As Tirso presents him, then, there is no reason to assume that Paulo is inherently unable to break out of his cycle of religious melancholy. It is, however, a mistake to assume that the hermit needs merely to exercise reason's control over his passions, for like other melancholy characters in Spain's Golden Age, Paulo is a figure whose thought process is depicted as dangerous because he thinks too much.

The ruminations of a melancholy mind that the expository writers warn against are thus very much a part of Paulo's traits. The deeper and more pathological his melancholy, the more powerful becomes his tendency to think, and the more profound becomes his despair. His arguments for turning to the life of crime that Enrico leads, for example, are evidence of his consciously made decision to do so:

> si su fin he de tener,
> tenga su vida y sus hechos;
> que no es bien que yo en el mundo
> esté penitencia haciendo,
> y que él viva en la ciudad
> con gustos y con contentos,
> y que a la muerte tengamos
> un fin.
>
> (1.970-77)

> (If I must have his end,
> let me have his life and deeds;
> for it is not right that
> I do penance in the world,
> while he lives in the city
> with pleasures and happiness,
> and that in death we have
> the same end.)

He pursues his goal of evil with full conviction, affirming at one point: "Pues

29. For a cogent discussion, see Sullivan, *Drama of the Counter Reformation*, 13-69.

hoy verá el cielo en mí / si en las maldades no igualo / a Enrico" (Well then today heaven will see in my actions / if I do not equal Enrico / in evil [2.1424–26]). Paulo is thus cognizant of what he does and even reasons through his rejection of salvation. His melancholy temperament, of course, predisposes him to his initial despairing reaction to the dream in his cave, but Tirso, with Renaissance sensibility, develops him as an individual whose physical and psychological natures are interdependent and whose moral shortcomings cannot be categorized as merely the results of uncontrolled emotion or weak rationality.

The other important character in *El condenado por desconfiado* who is portrayed within the broad context of melancholy is Enrico. He initially exhibits the extreme violence, cruelty, and treachery associated with the melancholy villains who populate so many of the Elizabethan works examined by Babb and Lyons. Enrico's characterization is manipulated by Tirso to trace this bandit's evolution from destructive behavior in the first two acts to the fearful and sad melancholy contemplation of a captured prisoner in act 3. Enrico thus provides a significant figure against which to measure Paulo. The young villain begins the play in the same sphere of violence into which the hermit moves, but at the end, he is in a frame of mind which approximates that of Paulo in his earlier ascetic existence. Paulo dramatizes the consequences of despair and religious melancholy that culminate in violence and damnation. Enrico enacts the positive outcome that remains a possibility for Paulo and for any sinner who undertakes a contemplative self-examination for the correct reasons and accepts the limitations of the human intellect in comparison with God's grace. Tirso's transvaluation of melancholy thus provides two characters whose respective melancholy imbalances lead eventually to two completely different kinds of contemplation, one that brings about the damnation of a figure of devotion and the other the salvation of a murderous criminal.

Lyons describes melancholy villains as "plotting revengers" who derive "great enjoyment from [their] villainies." This is the case with Enrico in Tirso's play, for in act 1 he makes a festive occasion of the recounting of crimes among his band of accomplices (scene 11). Lyons further explains that "[d]isenchantment with the world and disillusionment over their failure in it are understood to make such characters amenable to any kind of villainy."[30] Babb adds that in Elizabethan England writers regarded the melancholic's criminal bias as very dangerous "because melancholy sometimes endows men with great acumen,

---

30. Lyons, *Voices of Melancholy*, 23, 35.

which presumably may be turned to evil uses."[31] Though Tirso does not refer to the birth of his bandit as having occurred under Saturn's astrological influence, as do some of the English playwrights with regard to their villainous characters,[32] Enrico claims "Yo nací mal inclinado, / como se ve en los efetos / del discurso de mi vida" (I was born with bad tendencies, / as is seen in the effects / of the passage of my life [1.724–26]). Tirso nevertheless suggests the connection between Enrico's criminality and the disposition with which he is born, elements that reinforce the characteristics of Saturnine melancholy as then understood as well as the melancholic's ability to overcome such inclinations.

Enrico proceeds to deliver a long monologue on his evil deeds, which encompass his entire life: ". . . haciendo / travesuras cuando niño, / locuras cuando mancebo" (. . . committing mischief as a child, / folly as a youth [1.737–39]). During the play his sustained criminality is depicted through descriptions of his robberies, swindles, and even murders. In accord with the definitions of melancholy villains, Enrico likewise expresses his misanthropy in terms of a reaction against his failures: "Quedé pobre y sin hacienda, / y como enseñado a hacerlo, / di en robar de casa en casa" (I was left poor and without property, / and having learned how to do so, / I turned to robbing house after house [1.748–50]). His evil, like Paulo's, is also consciously undertaken, a fact that he emphasizes with such boasts as: "Por hacer mal solamente / he jurado juramentos / falsos, fingiendo quimeras" (Only in order to do evil / have I committed perjury / inventing fantastic ideas [1.828–30]). He adds further:

> No digo jamás palabra
> si no es con un juramento,
> con un "pese" o un "por vida",
> porque sé que ofendo al cielo.
>   (1.844–47)

> (I never say a word
> if it is not with a curse,
> with a "may the Devil take me" or "God damn me"
> because I know that I offend heaven.)

Enrico continues with the claim that he has never been to Mass nor, finding himself in danger, has he ever confessed "ni invocado a Dios eterno" (nor invoked the eternal God [1.851]). His rejection of good and his embrace of

31. Babb, *Elizabethan Malady*, 84.
32. Some of the examples of this practice are noted in Babb, *Elizabethan Malady*, and include Robert Greene's Duke Valdracko in *Planetomachia* and Conrade in Shakespeare's *Much Ado About Nothing*. See Babb's discussion of melancholy villains (85–91).

wrongdoing and violence are similar to the course of action the despairing Paulo will soon undertake at the end of act 1 with the determination: "Los pasos pienso seguir / de Enrico" (I plan to follow the footsteps / of Enrico [1.1010–11]).

Neither man, however, denies a belief in God. Paulo even prays "Señor, perdona / si injustamente me vengo" (Lord, forgive me / if I avenge myself unjustly [1.1002–3]), just before he heads into the mountains to become a *bandolero*. Enrico declares his underlying hope of eventual salvation when he addresses Paulo and chides him for his lack of faith: "Desesperación ha sido / lo que has hecho, y aun venganza / de la palabra de Dios" (What you have done / is desperate, and even vengeance, / against the word of God [2.1971–73]). He adds, furthermore:

> mas siempre tengo esperanza
> en que tengo de salvarme;
> puesto que no va fundada
> mi esperanza en obras mías,
> sino en saber que se humana
> Dios con el más pecador,
> y con su piedad se salva.
>   (2.1996–2002)

> (But I always have hope
> that I will be saved;
> although my hope is not
> based on my works,
> but rather on knowing that God
> is humane with the greatest sinner,
> and through His pity he is saved.)

Tirso therefore uses his reprobate Enrico as the mouthpiece of the most positive message in the play. Through the melancholy villain, the dramatist underscores the hope for all sinners who must understand that salvation is a gift bestowed on unworthy recipients by a loving and forgiving Deity.

An important point also to be made in comparing Enrico and Paulo involves an issue addressed by the scientists and moralists who consider religious melancholy and its characteristic despair—as opposed to a genuine sense of sin—akin to the distinctions made by ascetic writers between "a positive and a negative kind of tristitia, the former leading to penance and salvation, the latter to death."[33] This is the very issue upon which the Englishman Timothy Bright

---

33. Jackson, *Melancholia and Depression*, 68; see also Babb, *Elizabethan Malady*, 52.

focuses in his *Treatise of Melancholie* and is the difference eventually enacted by Enrico and Paulo and the ends to which they progress. The lifelong criminal finally acknowledges his sins and asks for forgiveness while the one-time holy man is seen burning in the flames of hell because of his despair. Unlike Enrico, Paulo recognizes too late his error in relying solely upon his own interpretation of deceptive evidence and not enough upon God's promises.

Tirso clearly depicts a physiological and mental shift in Enrico once the young man is apprehended by the authorities and put into prison for the murder of the governor. Though in the beginning of his stay in jail he exhibits more violent tendencies, even killing one of the guards and threatening his former lover with renewed abuse because she has married another rogue, his surroundings come to reflect and enhance the internal changes in him brought about by the physical conditions as well as the thoughts and emotions he is experiencing. This depiction also recalls another notion about *acedia* and anger. As Lyons points out, "[i]n schemes of the sins, anger was a cause of *acedia*."[34] Her references to Chaucer and Dante call attention to two passages that seem to announce the association Tirso subtly insinuates through the feelings and behavior of Enrico. In the "Parson's Tale," Chaucer writes: "Envye and Ire maken bitternesse in herte, which bitternesse is mooder of Accidie."[35] Dante likewise pairs "l'anime de color cui vinse l'ira" (the souls of those whom anger overcame) in the Fifth Circle of Hell with those "che sospira, / e fanno pullular quest'acqua al summo" (who sigh and make the water bubble on the surface). This group explains to their observer: "Tristi fummo / nell'aere dolce che dal sol s'allegra, / portando dentro accidioso fummo" (We were sullen in the sweet air that is gladdened by the sun, bearing in our hearts a sluggish smoke) and they are sunk in black sludge—an appropriate reminder of the connection between *acedia* and melancholy.[36]

After his angry outbursts, Enrico finds himself removed from his cell to a deeper dungeon chamber, a place that physically intensifies a growing inner coldness that is presumably caused by the adustion of the humors from his outburst of anger, jealousy, and violence. The stage directions indicate that he is now in "Un calabozo" (a dungeon [p. 180]), and whereas he had earlier shared a cell with Pedrisco (now a member of Paulo's band of marauders) Enrico is, at present, in solitude. He begins scene vi with a speech that evinces his increasingly fearful melancholy state:

34. Lyons, *Voices of Melancholy*, 63.
35. In *The Canterbury Tales*, ed. A. C. Cawley, 575.
36. *The Divine Comedy: Inferno*, ed. John D. Sinclair, 104. The English translations provided in the text are Sinclair's.

En lóbrega confusión
ya, valiente Enrico, os veis,
pero nunca desmayéis;
tened fuerte corazón.

(3.2232-35)

(In gloomy confusion
now, brave Enrico, you find yourself,
but do not lose heart;
keep a strong heart.)

Almost immediately he hears the voice of the devil, who chooses this moment, when Enrico is his most melancholically contemplative and suggestive, to try to win another victory by delusion and persuasion. Enrico's initial reaction is one of heightened fear: "Esta voz me hace temblar. / Los cabellos erizados / pronostican mi temor" (This voice makes me tremble. / My hairs stand on end / and foretell my fear [3.2241-43]). Fear begins to dominate him, as he repeatedly makes clear: "tanto temor me da" (I am so afraid [3.2253]); "¡qué confuso abismo! / No me conozco a mí mismo, / y el corazón no reposa" (What a confusing abyss! / I do not recognize myself, / and my heart does not rest [3.2258-60]); and "Un sudor frío / por mis venas se derrama" (A cold sweat flows / through my veins [3.2271-72]). His ultimate response at this point is an intellectual one as he calls upon his own mental powers for answers: "¿Qué me dices, pensamiento?" (What do you have to say to me, thought? [3.2285]).

Unlike Paulo, who privileges the devil's messages above even those from an angelic shepherd, Enrico listens and heeds the counsel of a heavenly second voice that opposes the devil's urging to escape through an apparent breach in the prison wall. Though the bandit wavers in his decision when he learns that he will soon be hanged for his crimes, he eventually does confess his sins. His aged father Anareto rebukes him for, among other things, his "loco pensamiento" (insane thinking [3.2465]), but in the old man's presence Enrico dies a Christian death. Paulo, on the other hand, dies unconfessed and unsaved, and Pedrisco comments upon the outcome:

Las suertes fueron trocadas.
Enrico, con ser tan malo,
se salvó, y éste al infierno
se fué por desconfiado.

(3.2899-2902)

(Their fates were switched around.
Enrico, although so bad,

saved himself, and this one went to hell
because of his lack of faith.)

An important link between the characterization in *El condenado por descon-fiado* and the melancholy imbalance at the heart of the drama's theme and action relies on the many aspects of Saturn that are incorporated into the play as part of the imagery of melancholy. The subject of Saturn's relationship to melancholy has been explained with great clarity by Klibansky, Saxl, and Panofsky in their comprehensive study. Among the Renaissance texts cited in the present study, Foresto's provides a good example of the scientific reliance upon such a correspondence in order to describe the humoral temperaments.[37] Drawing upon a number of such works, Lyons gives a succinct rendition of these accepted associations between the planet, the mythological deity, and the humor, saying:

> The contradictory qualities that were attributed to Saturn the planet were a result of the diverse mythological origins of Saturn the god. As the ancient Kronos, he was king during the Golden Age and a beneficient god of agriculture, but he was also deposed, castrated and exiled by his son, and sent to live in a dark prison beneath the earth. He was associated with sea journeys and travel because of his own journey to Latium. A further confusion that entered into the character attributed to Saturn was the frequent identification of Kronos with Chronos, the god of time, who was naturally associated with old age and death. . . . In his most maleficient aspect [Saturn] was associated with dark prisons, drownings and suicide.[38]

To this list of traditional attributes and characteristics of Saturn can be added his eventual association with God the Father by means of his incorporation, along with other principal pagan deities, into the Christian system and symbolism during the Middle Ages and the Renaissance, a point made by Jean Seznec in his discussion "The Reintegration of the Gods."[39]

The mythographers and expository writers of Spain also record these associations in their works. Juan Pérez de Moya writes in his *Philosophia secreta* (Secret philosophy, first published in 1585) the following about the mythological figure Saturn:

Pintan a Saturno viejo, en cuanto Saturno significa el tiempo . . . dicen los astrólogos

---

37. In his *Observationum et Curationum Medicinalium,* see fols. Bii-Biii and L.
38. Lyons, *Voices of Melancholy,* 4.
39. Jean Seznec, *The Survival of the Pagan Gods,* trans. Barbara F. Sessions, 184-215.

que Saturno es frío y seco y de complexión melancólica, que son cosas que se hallan en los viejos, o porque con el tiempo las cosas se envejecen y corrompen.

(They describe Saturn as old, in that Saturn means time. . . . astrologers say that Saturn is cold and dry and of melancholic complexion, which are characteristics found in the elderly, or because things age and deteriorate with time.)[40]

He continues with more descriptive material that links the ancient god with the planet and ultimately with melancholics:

Píntanle perezoso en cuanto a planeta, porque es el que más tiempo gasta en cumplir su revolución . . . Decir que traía el gesto triste, le conviene en cuanto planeta, porque él hace los hombres sobre que tiene dominio, tristes, por ser Saturno de complexión fría y seca y melancólica, cosas que repugnan a la alegría. (1:62)

(As a planet they depict him as lazy, because it is he who spends the most time in completing his revolution. . . . It is said that he has a sad expression, which suits him as a planet, because he saddens those men over whom he has power; this is due to Saturn's being of cold, dry, and melancholic complexion, characteristics that are in opposition to happiness.)

As is typical of this period, Pérez de Moya also recognizes the Aristotelian notion of heightened mental acuity in the melancholic, saying: "Otrosí, hace [Saturno] a los hombres de gran pensamiento" (Besides, [Saturn] makes men great thinkers). He considers Saturn "sabio" (wise) though the long passage of time associated with him suggests problems with the memory: "los que son saturninos son cerrados, de pocas palabras y de gran consejo . . . apenas de ellos se puede entender lo que en su voluntad tienen . . . que esconde las cosas por su largura [de tiempo], y las trae en olvido" (Those who are saturnine are uncommunicative, of few words and of great counsel. . . . one can hardly understand what is their will . . . for it hides things due to the length [of time], and forgets them).[41]

Baltasar Vitoria likewise begins his *Teatro de los dioses de la gentilidad* (Theater of the heathen gods) with a lengthy section on Saturn and concurs with the traditional descriptions. With reference to a passage in Ovid's *Metamorphosis*, Vitoria asserts Saturn's authority over the "siglo dorado" (golden age). His fifth chapter describes how Saturn founded agriculture, but in this same section, the negative characteristics of planet and deity are also examined. Not only is Saturn "el primer Planeta de todos" (the first of all Planets) and "el mas alto de

40. Juan Pérez de Moya, *Philosophia secreta*, ed. Eduardo Gómez de Baquero, 1:62.
41. Ibid., 1:62, 63.

todos, y les precede . . . tratando de la prudencia, y mayoridad de los Planetas"
(the highest of all, preceding the others . . . with regard to prudence and age of
the Planets) but its influence is nevertheless "maligna" (malignant). In addition,
"su calidad es destemplada en frialdad, y sequedad, y assi es muy nocivo, y
enfermo" (its quality is unpleasant because of its coldness, and dryness, and
thus it is very harmful, and sick). The list of items, professions, individuals, and
characteristics associated with Saturn is lengthy in Vitoria's account. He tells
us, for example:

> Significa carceles, prisones, caminos largos, trabajos, tardanças, y aflicciones. Tiene
> su dominio sobre los solitarios, y viejos, labradores; sobre los avaros, usureros,
> çapateros, y sobre los que tienen por oficio hazer sepulturas, y enterrar muertos, sobre
> los siervos, cautivos, hombres viles, y de humildes pensamientos, y curradores, y
> tambien sobre los agoreros hechizeros, y nigromanticos . . . sobre las cuevas, y
> lugares tenebrosos, y obscuros.

> (He is associated with jails, prisons, long roads, toils, delays, and afflictions. He has
> dominion over the solitary, and the old, the workers; over the miserly, moneylenders,
> shoemakers, and over those whose job is gravedigging and undertaking, over servants,
> captives, villainous men, and those of lowly thoughts, and medical quacks, and also
> over witches, fortunetellers, and necromancers . . . over caves, and places that are
> gloomy and dark.)[42]

In his medical treatise, Freylas likewise describes the more negative type of
melancholic in similar terms, saying: "Son los tales Saturninos, frios y secos
desde los primeros principios de su generacion" (Such Saturnines are, cold and
dry from the beginning of their formation).[43] These views are conventional, as
examination of other sixteenth- and seventeenth-century works on medicine,
astrology, mythology, and other scientific or pseudo-scientific material shows.
Dariot, for example, describes Saturn as "[c]old and drie, melancholick,
earthie, masculine . . . malevolent, destroyer of life."[44] On the basis of this
quotation, Babb asserts that "'Saturnine' and 'melancholic' are virtually synonymous."[45]

The references to the sea in *El condenado por desconfiado* are some of the
most obvious formal elements suggestive of Saturnine influence. Not only is the
Puerta de la Mar (Gateway to the Sea) the site where Paulo first observes and

42. Baltasar de Vitoria, *Teatro de los dioses de la gentilidad*, fols. 17, 22, 23.
43. *Conocimiento, curacion y preservacion*, fol. 226v.
44. Claude Dariot, *A Briefe and Most Easie Introduction to the Astrologicall Judgement of the Starres*, trans. F. W., fol. D2r.
45. Babb, *Elizabethan Malady*, 10.

listens to Enrico, but throwing his victims into the sea is one of Enrico's seeming favored means of killing them. He threatens to do so to male visitors at Celia's house ("Que los arroje en el mar, / aunque está lejos de aquí" [Let me throw them in the sea, / though it is far from here; 1.488–89]) and later reports having committed such an act against a beggar (". . . cogíle en brazos, / y le arrojé en el mar" [. . . I caught him in my arms, / and I threw him in the sea; 1.666–67]). In act 2, he likewise declares that were he not restrained, he would administer the same death sentence to Paulo, his captor: "ya yo le hubiera arrojado / de una coz dentro del mar" (I would have thrown him / with one kick into the sea [1841–42]). Earlier in the same act, his own escape from the authorities is described by Enrico himself in terms that recall not only the melancholy imagery of the sea but also counterpose it to references to the element earth:

> Ya aunque la tierra sus entrañas abra,
> y en ella me sepulte, es imposible
> que me pueda escapar; tú, mar soberbio,
> en tu centro me esconde: con la espada
> en la boca tengo de arrojarme.
>
> (1349–53)

> (Now although the earth may open its bowels,
> and bury me within, it is impossible
> for me to escape; you, proud sea,
> hide me in your center: with my sword
> in my mouth I will throw myself in.)

The sea seems to be his means of escape, but wet with sea water, he is soon taken prisoner by Paulo's band of men, literally and figuratively trapped by the internal and external manifestations of his humoral imbalance and its medium of representation.

Tirso's play also abounds in references to fathers—literal and symbolic, earthly and spiritual. The relationship between the biological father and son, Enrico and Anareto, has been studied by Hispanic critics, and, in particular, by Parker, who contends that Anareto serves as a symbol of the authoritative God and that the son's loving and submissive behavior toward his flesh-and-blood father assures his reconciliation with the divine Father.[46] Rogers views the loving relationship between these two as a contrast to that between Paulo and a

---

46. Alexander A. Parker, "Santos y bandoleros en el teatro español del Siglo de Oro."

God of anger.[47] Enrico is indeed repeatedly identified as "hijo del noble Anareto" (son of the noble Anareto) and these two characters do constitute an exemplary view of devotion between father and son. Anareto can thus be associated with Saturn the father in the latter's positive role much as he is depicted by Fray Luis de León in "Noche serena" (Peaceful night) as "padre de los siglos de oro" (father of the golden centuries).[48]

As a figure analogous to the Christian God, Anareto appropriately leads his son to the confession of his sins that, in his last moments of life, assures the young criminal of eternal life of the spirit. This positive aspect of fatherhood is counterbalanced by Paulo the monk, often addressed in the play by others as "padre" but representing in his melancholy characterization the pernicious side of Saturn's paternal role. In his pride, Paulo parallels Lucifer's sinful wish to usurp God's power, thereby recalling the mythological situation that led, inversely, to Saturn's murderous plan to outwit the projected succession to his throne. Paulo is the dangerous father but is as well a parallel to Saturn's children. By patterning his behavior after the criminality of Enrico, Paulo figuratively fathers for himself a new identity and simultaneously retains the role of filial usurper. He prepares his own physical and spiritual destruction by adhering to his despairing decision not to seek divine mercy and thus acts as God and judges himself presumptuously. In this dual process he completes the destructive cycle of Saturn who, as the attempted murderer of his progeny, effectively attempts suicide at the same time. It should also be remembered that Saturn's one remaining son, Zeus, retaliated against his father's act by imposing exile after castrating him, thus killing before the fact any future issue.

The two aspects of Saturn are therefore suggested in the character development of Paulo and Anareto, a duality supported near the end of the play when "dos padres de San Francisco" come to visit Enrico in prison. His refusal to meet them (". . . que en los padres . . . / he de vengar mis pesares" [. . . for on these fathers . . . / I must avenge my distress; 3.2404–5]) is met with Pedrisco's admonition that "Tú te vas, Enrico mío, / al infierno como un padre" (You, my Enrico, are going / to hell like a certain father [3.2414–15]), presumably a reference to Paulo. That Enrico very soon does reject the monk's fate through the insistence and intervention of Anareto, draws more sharply the distinction between these two *padres* and thus underscores the dual nature of Saturn's paternity and the dual nature of melancholy in general as it was understood in the Renaissance.

47. "Introduction," 1–46.
48. Fray Luis de León, "Noche serena," in *Renaissance and Baroque Poetry of Spain,* ed. Elias Rivers, 99–101.

Indeed, the Renaissance mythographers record the filial and paternal violence that make up an important part of the Saturn legend. Pérez de Moya, among others, reports that the ancients believed that Saturn "cortó los miembros genitales a [Cielo]" (castrated Heaven), his own father.[49] Saturn as well subsequently endeavored to murder all of his sons in exchange for the privilege of ruling in the place of his older brother Titan: "que Titán hubo de darle el reino, con aditamento que Saturno matase los hijos varones que le naciesen, a fin de que, no habiendo Saturno hijos, tornase a los suyos el reino" (for Titan had to give him the kingdom, with the provision that Saturn kill any male children born to him, so that, with Saturn having no sons, the kingdom would return to [Titan's] own children).[50] The sense of competition expressed by Paulo concerning his emulation of Enrico's life of crime in *El condenado por desconfiado* suggests the struggle expressed in the mythological accounts of jealousy, subversion, and usurpation in the Saturn myth. Paulo does not succeed in transcending the negative aspects of this myth, whereas Enrico and his father do. In some versions of the myth of Jupiter's victory over his father, there are elements that more closely approximate the relationship Anareto and his son enjoy. Pérez de Moya writes, for instance, about the consequences of the actions of Saturn's wife, Opis. Having saved her son Jupiter from his father's destructive plan, she violates the horrendous agreement made with Titan:

Andando los tiempos (descubridor de las cosas secretas), supo Titán que Saturno, su hermano, tenía hijos, contra el concierto y pleitesía con el puesta, por lo cual enojado juntó grandes compañías de sus hijos, llamados Titanos, y quitó a Saturno el reino, y a él y a su mujer púsoles en prisiones. Sabidas estas cosas de Iúpiter, que era ya valeroso mozo, vino con gran ejército de cretenses a favorecer a sus padres; y habida cruda batalla contra su tío y los Titanes, los venció y libró a sus padres; y restituídos en su reino, se volvió a Creta, según Lactancio.

(With the passage of time [discoverer of all secrets], Titan found out that Saturn, his brother, had sons, against the agreement and the pact made with him, because of which, angered, he brought together his own sons, called Titans, and took away Saturn's kingdom, and put him and his wife in prison. Once Jupiter, who was a very brave young man, knew of these things he came with a great army of Cretans to aid his parents; and there was a great battle against his uncle and the Titans; he defeated them and liberated his parents; and having restored the kingdom to them, he returned to Crete, according to Lactancio.)[51]

These are the sort of protective feelings toward his earthly father that Enrico

49. *Philosophia secreta*, I:57.
50. Ibid., 51.
51. Ibid., 52.

displays throughout *El condenado por desconfiado*. Though he has squandered Anareto's modest wealth during his younger years, Enrico expresses the guilt he feels, both in words and in deed: "y tengo piedad con él, / por estar pobre el buen viejo, / porque soy causa" (and I have pity for him, / because the good old man is poor, / which is my fault [2.878–80]). Guilt is, moreover, a melancholy emotion—and one particularly associated with religious melancholy.[52] Enrico thus mirrors as well this element of Paulo's affliction, but the behavior he displays in consequence is only positive to the extent that he provides for his father's needs and shows the old man love and respect. It is, however, his ill-gotten money that he uses to support the bed-ridden Anareto: "De lo que Celia me da, / o yo por fuerza le quito, / traigo lo que puedo acá" (From what Celia gives me, / or from what I take by force, / I bring what I can here [2.1060–62]).

Eventually, it is Anareto who is moved to save his son spiritually, fulfilling the benevolent role of Saturn as protector and nurturer, though he persuades his son to surrender his earthly life. The reward for such an act, however, is eternal salvation. Together Anareto and Enrico transcend the destructive competition and violence of the myth. Paulo, on the other hand, suffers the eternal punishment that the yielding to his Saturnine condition merits. In Tirso's dramatization of these two processes, the true father/son pair overcomes the negative Saturnine pattern whereas the Paulo/Enrico relationship reenacts it. In their case, the older man sets out to take the place of the younger one, but ends by destroying himself. Melancholy and allusions to Saturn are at the center of *El condenado por desconfiado,* and though Tirso is not the only Spanish playwright of his age to dramatize accepted notions about religious melancholy, his portrayal is more thoroughly grounded in the epistemological context that encompasses the religious struggles of the seventeenth century. Other dramatists do suggest, for example, the devil's powers of persuasion upon scholars. In Calderón's *El mágico prodigioso* (The prodigious magician), the protagonist Cipriano begins the play as a student who prefers his books to the company of his friends and servants and his scholarship to participation in a festival to honor Jupiter in nearby Antioch. Though a pagan, he is deep in philosophical consideration of a weighty religious matter, "la definición de Dios" (the definition of God). The devil appears to Cipriano and offers false answers and ensnares him in a pact that, unknown to the young man, is part of the devil's plan to win from God the soul of the virtuous and devout Justina. Typically, Calderón makes clear the element of divine permission for such an undertaking. In an aside, the devil says: "Pues tengo licencia / de perseguir con mi rabia

52. Jackson, *Melancholia and Depression,* 328–29.

/ a Justina" (Well I have license / to pursue Justina with my / wrath).[53] In *El José de las mujeres* (The Joseph of women) Calderón presents a female protagonist, Eugenia, whose studiousness has kept her in contemplation of religious matters. Having rescued from destruction by her pagan father one volume of Christian writings, she finds the philosophical material difficult to understand, and exhibits the melancholy scholar's discomfort over dedication to a difficult task. As her frustration reaches a climax and she throws her pen across the room, two supernatural figures appear to her to offer answers to the question that perplexes her. They are the Demonio and the monk Eleno—two figures easily recognizable within the tradition of religious study.

Tirso's *El condenado por desconfiado,* however, is a more fully developed portrayal of the then current notions about religious melancholy and represents in dramatic form much of the same information that Burton includes in his unique section devoted to this condition. In addition, among the pictures that make up the frontispiece of the *Anatomy of Melancholy* is a figure that corresponds to the religious melancholic. Labeled Superstitiosus, he is described in the corresponding verse as "Tormented hope and fear betwixt: / For hell perhaps he takes more pain, / Than thou dost Heaven itself to gain." Such is Paulo's distress and consequent perdition. Though Burton and Tirso, separated linguistically and geographically, can in no way be considered collaborators in their writings about religious melancholy, they do reveal much about the widespread Renaissance understanding of the distressing condition and the general transvaluation of melancholy. Both record or represent the heightened intellectual activity and prophetic ability of the melancholic individual in a religious context, but they each reinforce the belief in the devil's influence upon and intervention in the thought process of such a victim. Through the spiritual victory of Enrico, Tirso portrays the human capability to resist the devil's sway by means of turning to the higher power of divine forgiveness and grace. Paulo's damnation represents the alternative defeat through continued reliance upon the melancholic intellect that is corrupted by satanical manipulation. Pérez de Moya recounts, furthermore, that in the metaphorical cosmic scheme of antiquity "a la mente primera de Dios llamaron Saturno" (they called the first mind of God Saturn).[54] Such a notion reiterates the association of the highest mentality with melancholy yet within a framework which recognizes that the only legitimate source of wisdom and understanding is a divine one.

53. Pedro Calderón de la Barca, "El mágico prodigioso," in *Obras completas,* vol. 1, ed. A. Valbuena Briones., 609, 611.
54. *Philosophia secreta,* 32.

3

Love Melancholy (Lope, Calderón)

It will not be out of place here to join love to the affections of the brain, since it consists of certain cares.

Paul of Aegina

Mentis quoque malum est in amore furere, & ita amorem inter affectus cerebri annumerant medici: qui plerumque tragico luctu, in maniam aut melancholiam definit.

Pedro Foresto

The melancholia peculiar to lovers also boasts a long history of recognition by physicians and literary authors, and Burton actually considers religious melancholy to be a species of love melancholy whose object is God.[1] Since antiquity, love melancholy is categorized as a primarily mental imbalance with marked and varied physical and emotional symptoms that include fluctuations of pulse and temperature, alternations from warm, moist stages and feelings of joy to cold, dry stages of despondency, fearful reactions, or violent destructiveness.[2] Love as a pathological condition contributes to the dialectical nature of the relationship between melancholy's so-called admirable and detested effects, for the discourse of love that encompasses the dangerous and destructive emotional malady and mental characteristics of jealousy as well as the lighthearted fun of the self-consciously counterfeit lover provides a useful set of conventions that flourish in dramatic and poetic expression in sixteenth- and seventeenth-century Europe.

John L. Lowes and Scott C. Osborn provide further clarification of this contextual framework in their examinations of the meaning of the expression "heroical love."[3] The etymological evolution of the term "heroical" to its modern sense, which lacks its earlier, fuller significance, can lead twentieth-century scholars to misread Renaissance works. On the basis of such texts as Burton's *Anatomy* and John Dryden's plays as well as numerous medieval and Renais-

1. Burton, *Anatomy of Melancholy*, 593.
2. Babb, *Elizabethan Malady*, 128–29, and Jackson *Melancholia and Depression*, 352–56.
3. John L. Lowes, "The Loveres Maladye of *Hereos*," *Modern Philology;* Scott C. Osborn, "Heroical Love in Dryden's Heroic Drama."

sance fictional and scientific works, Lowes and Osborn make convincing cases for accepting the coexistence in thought and art of the positive qualities of love and the negative symptoms of lovesickness, the latter being a condition associated with melancholia and known in English as "heroical love" or the "malady of *hereos*." Tracing the development of the definition of the word "heroical," Lowes and Osborn find its roots in the Greek "ἔρως," which underwent transmogrification of form and meaning during the Middle Ages and Renaissance, when Arabic and Latin words and associations were combined with the original Greek. The effect was a bifurcation in the English word "heroical" so that our contemporary definition was, during the Renaissance, accompanied by its usage as a label for the "'lover's malady' . . . an affliction, moreover, to which the aristocratic or the great in heart were peculiarly subject."[4]

The medieval Catalan doctor Arnaldus de Vilanova affirms such an accepted notion in his work *De amore heroico*. Diego de San Pedro does likewise in *Carcel de amor* (Prison of love) through the figure Deseo (Desire), who claims: "siempre me crié entre hombres de buena criança" (I was always brought up among men of good breeding). In the same work, the superiority of the *entendimiento* of lovers is likewise indicated as a sign of their greatness and of their vulnerability to suffering:

> Bienaventurados los baxos de condición y rudos de engenio, que no pueden sentir las cosas sino en el grado que las entienden; y malventurados los que con sotil juizio las trascenden, los cuales con el entendimiento agudo tienen el sentimiento delgado; plugiera a Dios que fueras tú de los torpes en el sentir.

> (Fortunate are those of lowly condition and simple minds, who are unable to feel things except to the degree that they understand them; and unfortunate those who with delicate reason transcend those things, who with a sharp intellect have fine sentiment; would to God that you were among the sluggish of feeling.)[5]

The Spanish term equivalent to heroical love, "amor eroico," is found in Peninsular medical works such as Murillo's seventeenth-century treatise on melancholy, in which he likewise explains lovesickness as a form of melancholia: "El herotico afecto, o amor, es genero de melancholia, llamase vulgarmente heroico, y tiene peculiar curacion y conceleridad" (The erotic affect, or love, is a

4. Osborn, "Heroical Love," 481.
5. Diego de San Pedro, *Obras completas, II: Cárcel de amor*, 173, 82. De Vilanova is cited in Keith Whinnom's "Introducción crítica" to the same edition, 15. See also Lowes's discussion of Arnaldus within the context of the historical evolution of the medical understanding of heroical love, "The Loveres Maladye," 5–7.

category of melancholia, commonly called heroic, and it has a peculiar cure and progress).[6]

The above brief statement of the syndrome echoes other much longer scientific accounts written in the earlier part of the same century that also articulate the dialectical quality of the notions about the melancholic brain. Daniel Sennert, for example, discusses lovesickness among the melancholy disorders he studies in his *Practical Physick,* contending:

> This Dilirium from Love may be referred to the Melancholy before mentioned, but because it hath something peculiar, and is more vehement than the rest, we shall speak of it in this Chapter. . . . It is a melancholy doting from too much love, for most Lovers by a blind sort of love, are carried from right Reason diversly, and sometimes it is so vehement that [it] deprives a man of Reason, and causeth a Delirium.[7]

Such an account reiterates some of the earliest definitions of lovesickness as one of the "diseases of the head."[8]

The sixteenth- and seventeenth-century theorists writing on lovesickness are thus part of a long-standing tradition that links lovers with the melancholy mentality that is both superior and deranged. Explanations are often provided about the intellectual and emotional characteristics in terms of their effects on the rational faculties. During his tenure of service to Charles V, López de Villalobos recorded the following explanation:

> Esta imaginativa adolesce algunas veces de un género de locura que se llama alienacion, y es por parte de algun malo y rebelde humor que ofusca y enturbia el espíritu do se hacen las imágines, fórmase allí la imágen falsa . . . Los enamorados son desta materia: que la imágen de su amiga tienen siempre figurada y fija dentro de sus pensamientos, por donde no pueden ocupar jamás la imaginacion en otra cosa; en esta imágen, y en las cosas anejas y tocantes á ella, están trasportados y rebatados todas las horas; con ella hablan, della cantan y della lloran, con ella comen y duermen y despiertan, á ninguna cosa responden á propósito, ni piensan que puede hablar nadie en otra manera sino aquella.

> (This imaginative faculty suffers at times from a sort of insanity that is called mental derangement, and it is due to some bad or uncontrollable humor that clouds and stirs the spirit where the images are made. There the false image is formed. . . . The lovesick are of this kind: for they have formed and set the image of their beloved always within their thoughts, whereby they can never occupy their imagination with any

6. Murillo y Velarde, *Aprobacion de ingenios,* fol. 137v.
7. Daniel Sennert, *Practical Physick,* trans. N. Culpeper and Abdiah Cole, 1:157.
8. Jackson, *Melancholia and Depression,* 354; see also Paul of Aegina, *The Seven Books of Paulus Aeginata,* trans. Francis Adams, 1:383 and 390–91.

other thing; in this image, as well as in the things tangential and pertaining to it, the lovesick are transported and bemused at all hours; they speak with her, they sing of her and cry over her, they eat, sleep, and awaken with her, they respond to nothing appropriately, nor do they think anyone can speak of anything but her.[9]

Sennert later also explains the cause of the lover's disease in a similar manner:

> The first Cause is a strong impression of an amiable thing not good nor profitable, but lascivious by which men are mad with Reason; for if the species of a man or woman received by sight or discourse be strongly imprinted upon the memory, and presented often to the imagination and mind, there is such a desire of the thing loved, that it changeth the party much, so that he can neither eat nor sleep, but is much troubled.[10]

It must be stressed again, however, that in these passages, the writers comment upon the damaged imagination but still in terms of its capabilities for image projection and not in the modern sense of its creativity. As is typical in the general discussions of melancholy disorders, excessive dryness is often identified as a problem once the despondent melancholic stages of lovesickness have developed. Du Laurens contends: "See here how love corrupteth the imagination, and may bee the cause of melancholie or of madnes. For in thus busying both the bodie and minde, it so drieth the humours, as that the whole frame of temperature, especially that of the braine, is overthrowne and marred."[11] The wild fancies that he and other physicians describe in their anecdotes and case histories of love melancholics are, like Quijote's, the products of highly active minds that are out of balance. The images that obsess the victims are frequently those of the beloved that have been too firmly imprinted in the dried brain.[12] Many physicians list in Ovidian fashion numerous remedies for this melan-

---

9. López de Villalobos, "Anfitrion, Comedia de Plauto," in *Biblioteca de Autores Españoles,* 36:489. He also explains the "imagen falsa" which is, as described in other texts on faculty psychology, a product of badly reconstructed images retrieved from the memory: "Que si tú piensas en caballos, es porque en la imaginacion tienes entonces formadas las imágines de aquellos caballos, et si piensas en la mar ó en la tierra, en las mercadurías ó en la guerra, allá están hechas las imágines, así las piensas; que si están al proprio de como acá son, la imaginacion es verdadera, y si están compuestas y falsas, tu pensamiento es vano y falso" (For if you think of horses, it is because in the imagination you have then formed the images of those horses, and if you think of the sea or the earth, of material things, or of war, the images are made there, and thus you think them; and if they are the same as they are here, the imagination is truthful, and if they are invented and false, your thinking is vain and false [489]). See John Dagenais's comments on this passage in "The Imaginative Faculty and Artistic Creation in Lope," in *Lope de Vega y los orígenes del teatro español: Actas del I Congreso Interacional Sobre Lope de Vega,* ed. Manuel Criado del Val, 322.

10. *Practical Physick,* 1:157-59.

11. Du Laurens, *Discourse of the Preservation of the Sight,* 120.

12. See Du Laurens, *Discourse of the Preservation of the Sight,* 117-21; Santa Cruz, "Diagnostio et cura affecctuum melancholicorum," 33-35; and Juan Bautista Aguilar, *Teatro de los dioses de la gentilidad,* 253.

choly condition, and among the Spanish doctors, López de Villalobos provides a particularly complete accounting, with ten categories of relief that range from hunting expeditions to separation from the woman in question and drinking great quantities of wine.[13]

The simultaneous reiteration of the psycho-pathology of love in medico-scientific expression and literary articulation is an indication of the persistence of analogy as the traditional basis for communication about life and the world within a systematic unity.[14] Marjorie Hope Nicolson has proposed, nevertheless, that the metaphor of the circle of unity broke down during the seventeenth century with the dominance newly assumed by the Cartesian paradigm. She sees a separation of the language of science from that of poetry as a result of the intellectual shift.[15] It may instead be closer to the mark to consider the benefit of a semantic revision in this respect, for what seems to occur, at least in the literary discourse of love under present consideration, is a redefinition of the entire framework into which the varied fields could fit. If melancholy is transvalued, then the Renaissance and Baroque poetic humanism that intuited the rupture of thinking and feeling can still accommodate a synthesis by extending its appreciation of the difference between appearance and reality. This is possible through a promotion of the dialectical tension between divergent attributes of the humoral condition and an insistence upon the transgression of the inner and outer realms of manifestation in order to present a new and broader homogeneity and maintain for a while longer the symbiosis between scientific and poetic expression. Thus, it is not surprising to find in Lope's *Los locos de Valencia* (The insane of Valencia) a poetic description that parallels Murillo's medical one of *amor hereos*:

> llamaron este mal de vuestra Fedra
> Erotes, que es un género de tristes
> que sólo del amor están enfermos;
> el frenesí conturba los sentidos,
> levanta en ellos furia y fiera cólera,
> hácese cuando acaso el que la tiene
> percibe dentro en sí vanas imágenes.
>
> (they call this illness of your Fedra
> Erotes, which is a type of sadness
> in which they are sick only because of love;
> frenzy disturbs their senses,

13. *Sumario de la Medicina*, fol. 7.
14. Daniel L. Heiple, "The 'Accidens Amoris' in Lyric Poetry."
15. Nicolson, *The Breaking of the Circle*.

> fury and fierce choler rise in them,
> it happens when by chance he who so suffers
> perceives within himself foolish images.)[16]

The pathological qualities of love inform amorous poetry throughout the Middle Ages and the Renaissance and claim authority from the classical descriptions of such writers as Ovid. As is the case in the medical treatises, the malady of *hereos* is portrayed in two differing ways in Renaissance and Baroque literature.[17] It is a truly serious and devastating condition that endangers the sanity and even the very life of the afflicted party, since the melancholy desperation and madness of lovesickness lead to suicidal thoughts and actions. This is the realm of the Petrarchan conventions that is certainly familiar literary territory for Spanish Golden Age authors. Green has traced, for example, Garcilaso's depiction of heroical love and its negative characteristics in *Egloga I, Egloga II,* and *Canción IV* (Song IV [1.152–60]).[18] The shepherd Albanio of the second *Egloga* is a particularly good portrayal of one afflicted with this disorder.[19] His unrequited love for Camila drives him into the insanity of lovesickness and twice he tries to commit suicide but is saved, once by a fortuitous gust of wind that prevents his fatal leap from a cliff, and later by his friends, who stop him from drowning himself. The potential means of death contrived by Albanio do suggest Saturn's earth and water symbolism, and he describes himself at one point as a man "a quien la tierra / a quien la mar s'enclina" (whom the earth / whom the sea persuades [v. 553]). His symptoms are as well quite clinical and parallel the medieval descriptions of melancholy lovesickness: "mi rostro y color" (my face and complexion [v. 427]); "mi grave pensamiento" (my serious thought [v. 460]); "Quedé yo triste" (I was sad [v. 485]); "sin comer y dormir bien cuatro días" (without eating or sleeping well for four days [v. 504]); ". . . mi rostro triste, / mi temerosa voz y húmedos ojos" (. . . my sad face, / my fearful voice and moist eyes [vv. 570–71]); "locura debe ser" (it must be madness [v. 808]); "yo me daré la muerte" (I will kill myself [v. 878]); "cierto tiene trastornado el seso" (it is certain that his mind is unhinged [v. 884]). Albanio's friends Nemoroso and Salicio talk about his illness and its possible remedies ("¿Parécete que puede ser curado?" (Do you think he can be cured? [v. 1034]) and consider beating him, one of the standard treatmens for frenetic and manic melancholia: "Probemos así un rato a cas-

---

16. In *Obras de Lope de Vega*, 12:434.
17. See Du Laurens, *Discourse on the Preservation of the Sight*, 117–20.
18. Otis Green, *Spain and the Western Tradition*, 1:152–60.
19. Garcilaso de la Vega, "Egloga II," in *Poesías castellanas completas*, ed. Elias L. Rivers. All subsequent references (verse) are given in the text.

tigalle; / quizá con espantalle habrá algún miedo" (Let's try punishing him a while; / perhaps we can awaken fear by frightening him [vv. 1013–14]). They ultimately decide on a visit to the pseudo-scientist/magician Severo, who "aplicará contrarias calidades" (will apply opposite qualities [v. 1854]) to the suffering Albanio in support of the standard medical practices of remedying through opposites.

Cases of this dangerous sort of love melancholia can be found in Golden Age drama as well. Calderón's depiction of Apeles in *Darlo todo y no dar nada* (To give all and to give nothing), for example, presents a man whose passion for Campaspe, the woman he loves, drives him to frenzy when he believes her lost to him because King Alejandro finds her desirable.[20] Apeles's classic case of heroical love is depicted with all the usual symptoms that such seventeenth-century doctors as Pedro Foresto cite in discussions of love as a melancholic disease.[21] Even in a play like Lope's comical *La dama boba* (The foolish lady), Clara's question: "¿Qué es amor, que no lo sé?" (What is love, for I do not know?) is answered by Pedro with a list of love's devastating effects that also suggests the most unsettling aspects of melancholia: "¿Amor? ¡Locura, furor!" (Love? Insanity, frenzy!)[22]

Tirso's *El melancólico* presents the same imbalance by means of the main character's affectation of the symptoms he displays. This is the other mechanism that is particularly important in the dramatic transvaluation of love melancholy in the seventeenth century. What had long been a more seriously depicted syndrome of the rejected lover became the more consistent focus of a comic reworking of the self-conscious suitor. This is also a popular phenomenon in sixteenth- and seventeenth-century English drama, and, with references to such Shakespearean figures as Romeo before his first encounter with Juliet (1.1.138–61), Armado in *Love's Labour's Lost* (1.1.233–37), and Valentine in *Two Gentlemen of Verona* (1.1.15–28), Lyons explains:

> Although the feelings connected with rejected love, seriously explored, were central to the Petrarchan conventions of so many Renaissance love lyrics, the male love-melancholic on the stage was almost always . . . a figure of fun . . . made to express, through . . . standardized costumes and the patterned ways in which [he] behaved, a certain amount of self-indulgence.[23]

20. In *Obras completas*, ed. A. Valbuena Briones, 1019–67.
21. *Observationum et Curationum Medicinalium*, 351–54; see also Alfonso de Madrigal, *Tractado por el qualse prueba por la Santa Escriptura como al ome es necessario amar, é el que verdaderamente ama es necessario que se turbe*, 241; Jacques Ferrand, *Erotomania or a Treatise Discoursing of the Essence, Causes, Symptomes, Prognosticks, and Cures of Love, or Erotique Melancholy*, trans. Edmund Chilmead, 10; López de Villalobos, *Sumario*, fol. 7; Aguilar, *Teatro de los dioses*, 283; and Geronimo Mercurial, *Medicina Practica*, 33.
22. In *Obras escogidas*, ed. Federico Carlos Sainz de Robles, 1.811–12.
23. *Voices of Melancholy*, 25.

Explored seriously or by means of comic representation, lovesickness focuses upon the transvalued melancholic mentality that becomes deranged in the one case because of a depth of feeling or, in the other case, is mimicked in order to gain attention and admiration. Both manifestations call into question the value of the mentality under scrutiny. Spanish Golden Age authors in more than one case transcend the conventions and offer a more complex transvaluation of love melancholy in their stage depictions. Examples of the most firmly canonized representations of such epistemologically conservative and artistically brilliant portrayals are found in Lope's *El caballero de Olmedo* and in Calderón's wife-murder trilogy *A secreto agravio, secreta venganza* (Secret vengeance for secret offense), *El médico de su honra* (The physician of his honor), and *El pintor de su deshonra* (The painter of his dishonor). Love melancholy, in general, which Babb, Lyons, and Jackson have explained particularly well from a literary as well as a scientific perspective, has likewise been carefully considered with regard to Lope's play by the Hispanists William C. McCrary and Diego L. Bastianutti, who are sensitive to the humoral issues that inform the characterization and imagery of *El caballero de Olmedo*.[24] By readdressing the depiction of love melancholy in this work, however, I propose a readustment in our understanding of Lope's dramatization of the syndrome which is not, as McCrary and Bastianutti argue, a paradigmatic depiction of a melancholy, suffering lover. Lope's play is instead a masterful subversion of the conventions of both the classical notion of the malady of *hereos* and a sophisticated and conservative critique of the melancholy intellect. Lope coincides with his countryman Calderón in a representation of the dangers inherent in a character's self-isolation from the surrounding community by virtue of an inappropriate intellectual response to being in love.

Since the medical writers teach that the lover is not in a strict sense a melancholic figure to begin with because "his condition [is] neither humoral nor 'causeless', but easily cured by obtaining the object of his desire,"[25] the doctors often suggest that sexual satisfaction be obtained to ameliorate the effects of being in love. López de Villalobos lists this with other remedies for lovesickness in his *Sumario*.[26] Indeed, the element of rejection by the beloved is the overriding cause listed for the onset of the cold, dry physiology and despondent mental condition of the typical love melancholic.[27] The early stage of lovesickness,

24. See William C. McCrary, *The Goldfinch and the Hawk: A Study of Lope de Vega's Tragedy "El caballero de Olmedo"*; Diego L. Bastianutti, *"El caballero de Olmedo:* sólo un ejercicio triste del alma."

25. Lyons, *Voices of Melancholy*, 25.

26. Fol. 7.

27. See Jackson, *Melancholia and Depression* for a good summary of the history of medical notions about lovesickness with references to Erasistratus, Aretaeus, Galen, Oribasius of Per-

however, is marked by a rise in blood, the humor believed to exacerbate amorous feelings and even lasciTvity. Ferrand writes: "Abundance of Blood of a good temperature, and full of spirits" is a "Cause of Love." The so-called hot, moist passions can induce amorous feelings, and Ferrand goes on to list joy as an important example of just such a forerunner of love.[28]

Babb's summary of the physical and psychological symptoms of being in love, as the Renaissance understood them, is a particularly clear one. Emphasizing the shift from the hot, moist stage of desire to the melancholic stage after rejection or lack of satisfaction, he, too, recalls the contemplation that is usually a problematical characteristic of this and any melancholic disorder: "The lover's mind is constantly and anxiously intent upon his mistress' charms and upon his hopes, fears, and despairs." Relying on Du Laurens's description of the drying effect of such active thought, Babb concludes: "The lover's melancholy is in some degree due to the same causes as the scholar's."[29]

Lope's Alonso in *El caballero de Olmedo,* therefore, does not fit the category of rejected lover, for even as the play opens, he and Inés have fallen in love mutually and have reached a silent understanding through the medium of the eyes that pledges the one to the other. In his initial speech, Alonso describes their first encounter:

> De los espíritus vivos
> de unos ojos procedió
> este amor que me encendió
> con fuegos tan excesivos.
> No me miraron altivos,
> antes, con dulce mudanza,
> me dieron tal confianza,
> que, con poca diferencia,
> pensando correspondencia,
> engendra amor esperanza.
>
> (The love that inflames me
> with such excessive fire
> proceeded from one living
> spirit of a pair of eyes.
> They did not look at me arrogantly,
> but instead, with sweet exchange,
> they gave me such confidence,

---

gamon, Paul of Aegina, Rhazes, Haly, Abbas, Avicenna, Felix Platter, Sennert, Ferrand, and Burton, among others, 352–72.

28. *Erotomania,* 64, 61.

29. Babb, *Elizabethan Malady,* 134.

> since, with little difference,
> thinking of communication,
> love engenders hope.)[30]

Acknowledging his heated, amorous stage of the lover's disease but reporting as well the reciprocal feelings expressed by Inés, Alonso identifies himself as a lover but not a rejected one. His references to the importance of the eyes in the communication of amorous attraction are commonplaces as well in the literature on love.[31] What ensues in the play's first two acts, however, consists of Alonso's carefully planned and self-conscious performance as pining suitor, a pose through which Lope allows his audience to laugh for a while at the affectations of the voguish lover and his recourse to the overt literary conventions.

Indeed, Inés readily accepts the first written message of love from Alonso and by act 2 has declared her devotion to him:

> . . . yo
> diré a todo el mundo no,
> después que te dije sí.
> Tú solo dueño has de ser
> de mi libertad y vida;
> no hay fuerza que el ser impida,
> don Alonso, tu mujer.
>
> (2.1030–36)

> (. . . I
> will tell all the world no,
> now that I told you yes.
> You alone will be the master
> of my liberty and my life;
> there is no force that impedes my being
> your wife, Don Alonso.)

This is no courtly lover spurned by an unattainable lady. Alonso and Inés are quite simply two young people mutually in love, but the errors they commit by playing at and affecting unnecessary aspects of courtly love do, in turn, cultivate the onset of melancholy symptoms both in a progressively more meditative Alonso and in his rival Rodrigo, a clearly identifiable sufferer of authentic

---

30. Lope de Vega, *El caballero de Olmedo,* ed. Joseph Pérez, 1.11–20. Subsequent quotations (act and verse) are from this edition and are cited in the text.

31. See, for example, Sennert, *Practical Physick,* 1:157–59 and Du Laurens, *Discourse of the Preservation of Sight,* 118.

heroical love. Lope thus uses the humoral imbalance in a manner very different from that explained heretofore by McCrary and Bastianutti.[32]

Alonso's employment of the Celestinesque Fabia and the explicit and implicit patterning of his courtship of Inés upon the love affair between Calisto and Melibea make clear his own posturing as a love melancholic. Frederic A. de Armas has demonstrated that the *Celestina* itself is a story premised on Calisto's love melancholy and the consequences of melancholic vulnerability to diabolical influence, represented in that work by the evil bawd and her manipulation of the two young lovers.[33] Lope's treatment, however, begins with the lighthearted characterization of his protagonist, who adheres to the well-known literary conventions of heroical love evident in the *Celestina* and countless other works. The theatricality of Alonso's performance is supported by various elements. First, such a self-conscious stage figure as he, for example, is often overly preoccupied with his clothing and appearance,[34] and Lope's knight indeed is famous as the "gala de Medina" (adornment of Medina). Clothing in general receives much attention throughout the play: Inés exchanges her bright clothing for a brown nun's habit in her charade to avoid marrying Rodrigo, and Tello receives his pick of his master's fine clothing as recompense for delivering messages between Alonso and Inés. The play opens in the aftermath of the festival, during which the costuming of Medina's citizenry is in keeping with the carnival traditions, and Inés's disguise as a *labradora* is carefully described by Alonso in his first long speech. Both he and Inés also show great concern over the clothing they will wear to the games around which much of the action centers in the final act.

In addition, another aspect of Alonso's lovesick posturing is evident in his preference for expressing amorous sentiments in verse—an element that also connects him to the literariness of the melancholic obsessions that Quijote evinces. Lyons makes a point relevant to the play: "Because the medieval lover or Renaissance sonneteer had voiced his complaints in poetry, the love melancholic on the stage was ridiculed for his penchant for literature; the writing of sonnets . . . or the love of poetry or melancholy love songs were his inevitable, and therefore, comic marks."[35] There seems to be, of course, no ground for quarrel that Alonso's expressions of love, in his poetry or otherwise, are sincere, but the verses he writes to Inés are indeed part of comic scenes. It is Tello,

32. See, respectively, *The Goldfinch and the Hawk,* 113–24 and "*El caballero de Olmedo:* sólo un ejercicio triste."
33. Frederic A. de Armas, "*La Celestina:* An Example of Love Melancholy."
34. Lyons, *Voices of Melancholy,* 25.
35. Ibid., 26.

for instance, who recites Alonso's love *glosa* (gloss) to Inés in act 2 amid much ado about the knight's continued declarations of his passion to the flowers and *rábanos* (radishes) of Olmedo. As Tello reiterates: "que un amante suele hablar / con las piedras, con el viento" (for a lover usually speaks / to rocks and to the wind [2.1073–74]), another element that the authors of the scientific works on love melancholy also record. Sennert includes it among the sorts of problematical behavior of love-melancholics in his section on the syndrome, saying:

> The remote causes are all things causeing love, as the knowledge of the object by sight or hearing; but the first cause is a fair Object, real, or appearing so . . . Lovers keep no decorum in their actions, speech and gesture; they speak and act many things without any gravity.[36]

The comicity of Alonso's exaggerated and self-conscious pose as a lover-poet is reinforced by the frequency with which Lope mocks the art of verse composition by laughable types throughout his dramas. It is the *gracioso* Chacón in *La niña de plata* (The girl of silver), for instance, who recounts his experiences as a poet and the punishments and/or rewards his efforts have earned him. His exemplary sonnet recited before his lovesick master is the noteworthy "Un soneto me manda hacer Violante" (Violante demands of me a sonnet).[37] Similarly, Tello in *La noche de San Juan* (The eve of Saint John) is another clown who parodies the amorous poets, and Don Bela in *La Dorotea* likewise says: "Dale este papel; que también a mí me haze el amor poeta" (Give her this paper; for love also makes of me a poet) and Fernando in that same work claims "amar y hazer versos todo es uno" (loving and composing poetry are one and the same); and Don Juan in *Las bizarrías de Belisa* (The verve of Belisa) claims the authority of love as the principle upon which he has turned to the writing of poetry:

> ¿Quién, señora,
> no ha hecho malos o buenos
> versos amando, que Amor
> fue el inventor de los versos?
>
> (Who, my lady,
> has not composed bad or good

36. Sennert, *Practical Physick,* 1:157–59.
37. "La niña de plata," in *Obras escogidas,* ed. Federico Carlos Sainz de Robles, 1.647–87.

verses when in love, for Love
was the inventor of poems?)[38]

So, too, in *El caballero de Olmedo* the role-playing and representation that Alonso's pretense to heroical love suggests is further exaggerated in this scene since it is Tello who stands in for and thus represents his master by reciting the *glosa* to Inés. He begins his recitation with the mocking assurance, "Que es buena jurarte puedo / para poeta de Olmedo" (I can swear to you that it is good / for a poet from Olmedo [2.1107–8]).

Later, within the plot that Inés has devised to forestall any wedding plans with Rodrigo, Alonso's love note to her becomes the focal point of her charade, much like her first note to him is converted temporarily into a laundry list when Fabia must hide it from Rodrigo early in act 1. With obvious inherent implications for performances as melancholics, Fabia and Tello disguise themselves for the drama-within-the-drama in act 2, as, respectively, nun and scholar, and pretend to teach Inés Latin from Alonso's amorous text.

Tello later reports to Alonso on the success of that ruse in a scene that not only emphasizes Alonso's laughable affectation but also the theatricality of his behavior. The section begins with the young nobleman's delivery of a *romance* (ballad) that appears as well in various forms in *La Dorotea*,[39] in which the lover bemoans in typical courtly love fashion the absence of the beloved. It does not, however, decry the lady's rejection of her admirer, for near the end Alonso proclaims through the poetry of the love song:

> Bien sabe aquella noche
> que pudiere ser mía;
> cobarde amor, ¿qué aguardas,
> cuando respetos miras?
> (2.1651–54)

> (Well you know that that night
> she might have been mine;
> cowardly love, why do you await,
> when you look at the conventions?)

As Alonso finishes, Tello enters with Inés's most recent missive, which his master proceeds to read in sections with the explanation: "Porque manjar tan suave / de una vez no se me acabe" (So as not to finish all at once / a delicacy so

38. Lope de Vega, *La Dorotea*, ed. Edwin S. Morby, 259 and 297; "Las bizarrías de Belisa," in *Obras escogidas*, ed. Federico Carlos Sainz de Robles, 1.1685.

39. See *El caballero de Olmedo*, 110 n. 94.

sweet [2.1670–71]). Tello's description of the enactment of Inés's Latin lesson is then continually interrupted by Alonso—"Espera que leo / otro poco, que el deseo / me tiene fuera de mí" (Wait for me to read / a little more, for desire / has me beside myself [2.1682–84]); "Espera, que ha mucho rato / que no he mirado el papel" (Wait, for it has been a long time / since I have looked at the paper [2.1703–04]); "Perdonadme, manos bellas, / que leo el postrer ringlón!" (Forgive me, beautiful hands, / for I am reading the last line! [2.1723–24]). The theatrical posing of this overtly comical scene is underscored by Tello, who declares, "[e]n fin, / le has leído por jornadas" (in short, / you have read it by Acts [2.1727–28]).

Tello's words here highlight as well another important fact about Alonso's behavior and about the dual nature of the *tragicomedia* that Lope presents to his audience. Once again the polarity of melancholy is an essential ingredient, for within this drama the laughable lover does indeed become a more seriously afflicted pathological melancholic precisely because Alonso's playacting and his propensity to ruminate rather than act prolong the courtship unnecessarily. Such behavior further insinuates the knight's dramatization of love melancholia, for in Sennert's work on the disorder, he records among its most typically recognized characteristics these elements: "now idleness is a great cause why love taken by sight or hearing should insinuate it self into the mind, also solitariness, reading of love books, love discourse, and often converse with the Object."[40] Though Alonso does make continuous trips back and forth between Medina and Olmedo during the course of the drama, these periods of physical activity present opportunities to indulge his penchant for the discourse of love and the composition of his poetry, as Tello informs Inés. Thus Alonso's activity does not bring about a resolution of his desire to wed the woman he loves. Instead, it extends the waiting period and makes him vulnerable to the onset of authentic melancholy feelings.

Another important point concerning Alonso's behavior involves his very conscientious fulfilling of duty to his parents, as demonstrated by the constant trips back to his home. Unlike the distraught rejected lovers described in the medical books and depicted in literature, who neglect all facets of their normal activities and routines, Alonso does not display this level of derangement. He executes all undertakings with responsibility and care, not only his filial duties but also his participation in the aristocratic spectacle of the games, where he entertains the king whom he has already impressed. The monarch, in fact, has decided to honor him with "la primera encomienda" (the first land concession [2.1606]). Alonso consistently shows himself to be in control of his behavior,

40. *Practical Physick*, 1:157–59.

and his artificial adoption of symptoms of heroical love indicates the care with which he manipulates his responses. This comportment, however, reveals him to be a self-isolated thinker as well, and his role as Inés's lover / suitor ensures his continued separation from those around him in Medina's society who in effect function as the spectators of his performance.

Alonso's self-conscious fulfilling of literary and traditional symptoms of love melancholia leads him to extend the period before he and Inés declare to her father their wish to marry and thus to communicate their love. In spite of the arguments put forth by critics about hypothetical and extratextual barriers to their union, Inés and Alonso easily obtain her father's blessing, even after Don Pedro has already drawn up a formal marriage contract with Rodrigo. The ease with which Pedro abandons the other candidate for his daughter's hand once he knows her true feelings reiterates his anxiety for her simply to marry a suitable man, hence the lack of necessity for all of Alonso's contrivances to complicate and protract their courtship. Twice Tello points out the need for directness on Alonso's part: "Sólo te falta decir: / 'un poco te quiero, Inés'" (The only thing that you need to say: / "I love you a little, Inés" [2.997–998]) and "¿Qué te puede suceder / en una cosa tan llana / como quererte casar?" (What can happen to you / in something so easy / as wanting to get married? [2.1751–53]).

Rumination and excessive contemplation represent Alonso's nemesis, just as in the majority of conservative presentations of the melancholy mind in Golden Age Spain. Superimposed upon all aspects of this play, furthermore, is the element of time and its passing, which suggest Saturn's negative threat to balance and well-being. As time goes by, Alonso's lack of direct action to accomplish what he longs for is accompanied by his ever more active cerebration, and his pretended love melancholy cedes to a true melancholia. As act 2 closes, Alonso's premonitory dream about the yellow *jilguero* (goldfinch) killed in front of its mate by an *azor* (hawk) suggests the heightened state of a melancholy mind that is able to surmise what is to come. His premonition, however, need not be attributed to supernatural / divine origins like those that religious melancholics are said to experience. Alonso's dream is a composite of images suggested by the individuals encountered and the events experienced during the represented time in Medina. Lope's treatment of this episode complements Freylas's account of melancholy dreams, which itself repeats ancient and medieval beliefs about this subject: "podremos juzgar con principios naturales, que durmiendo un hombre . . . aviendo tomado de parte de noche con vehemente ymaginacion, principio de algun gran discurso de lo que no se sabe, ó está por venir, naturalmente continuando el tal discurso con las especies recebidas en la ymaginacion, en la vigilia, podria durmiendo entender algo de lo que está por venir" (We will be able to judge according to natural principles, for while a man is sleeping . . . having spent part of the night violently imagining the beginning of some great discourse about which nothing is known, or about the future, [and] naturally continuing said discourse with ideas received during wakefulness in his imagination, he could understand during sleep something of what is to come).[41]

The terrible dream visions that are said to plague melancholics are topics frequently addressed in the treatises on humoral medicine and related matters. The physician Gaspar Navarro, for example, explains dreams on the basis of one's predominant humor, and asserts of a melancholic that "sueña cosas negras, obscuras, tristes, y de muertos" (he dreams about black, dark, sad things and of the dead), adding also that "quando los Medicos curan de algunas enfermedades, preguntan al enfermo, si ha dormido, y que es lo que ha soñado: y de alli coligen el humor que reyna en el, y assi saben como lo han de curar" (when the Physicians cure some diseases, they ask the patient, if he has slept, and of what he has dreamed: and from that they infer the humor that predominates in him, and so know how they must cure him).[42]

McCrary's conclusion that the bird of prey in Alonso's dream represents Fabia, whom he, like some other Hispanists, interprets as a witch with strong black magical powers, is not supportable based on textual evidence.[43] Fabia offers no proof of such diabolical capabilities. Unlike her predecessor, Celestina, she does not need to convince her client's beloved of anything, since Inés is already in love with Alonso before the play begins. Fabia's rhetoric about spells and incantations should be given little credence since there is no reference to any instance of the efficacy of her purported magic. Indeed, her goal is to aid Alonso in his suit to marry Inés, and she fails miserably. Even her effort to frighten him into staying in Medina on the night of his death by means of the hired *labrador* (peasant) who sings the foreboding song is not successful. The *labrador* explains clearly the source of his song:

> No puedo
> deciros deste cantar
> más historias ni ocasión
> de que a una Fabia la oí.
> Si os importa, yo cumplí
> con deciros la canción.

41. *Conocimiento, curacion y preservacion,* section not paginated.
42. *Tribunal de supersticion ladina,* fol. 72r; see also Herónimo Cortés, *Lunario nuevo perpetuo y general y pronostica de los tiempos universales,* 6.
43. *Goldfinch and the Hawk,* 119–24.

Volved atrás; no paseis
deste arroyo.
              (3.2400–2407)

(I cannot
tell you more stories nor the origin
of this song except that
I heard it from a certain Fabia.
If it is important to you, I complied
by singing the song to you.
     Go back; do not pass
     this stream.)

This is not the work of an enchantress. Alonso himself rejects the notion of Fabia's magic powers, saying early in act 2: "No creo en hechicerias, / que todas son vanidades" (I do not believe in spells, / for they are all vanities [983–84]).

Fabia is then merely part of the literary conventions of the lover's imbalance that Alonso self-consciously gathers about him in order to adhere to an artificial standard in his courtship of Inés. The literary quality of his interaction with Fabia is emphasized precisely in the scene where he delivers the lines above, for he immediately makes his Calisto-like declaration of love in terms that the audience cannot help but identify with the fifteenth-century work (2.987–96). Tello and Inés's maid Ana complete the allusion with the following interchange:

> TELLO: ¿Está en casa Melibea?
>   Que viene Calisto aquí.
> ANA: Aguarda un poco, Sempronio.
>   (2.1002–4)
>
> TELLO: (Is Melibea at home?
>   For Calisto comes here.
> ANA: Wait a moment, Sempronio.)

Alonso shares much, therefore, with Don Quijote, who adheres to a literary model for his undertakings. Alonso, however, feigns his melancholy to begin with, which his pseudo-knightly predecessor does not do, but like the elderly Manchegan, he is a more classically despondent melancholic at the end.

The portentous quality of the dream at the end of act 2 is thus valid only to the extent that it is premised on Alonso's recognition of the threat that his melancholy rival Rodrigo poses. Tello has commented to him earlier upon Rodrigo's ominous jealousy: "pues a don Rodrigo veo / tan cierto de tu deseo /

como puedo estarlo yo" (Well, I see Don Rodrigo / as certain of your desire / as I myself am able to be [2.928-30]). Alonso acknowledges this notion as part of what seems to be the lover's code he strives to fulfill:

> Tello, un verdadero amor
> en ningún peligro advierte.
> Quiso mi contraria suerte
> que hubiese competidor
> y que trate, enamorado,
> casarse con doña Inés.
>   (2.975-80)
>
> (Tello, a true love
> takes notice of no danger.
> My adverse fortune wished
> that I have a rival
> and that he try, lovesick,
> to marry Doña Inés.)

He has thus already considered the ramifications of Rodrigo's presence and feelings. His imagination— the faculty still active in dreams, as the philosophical and psycho-medical works teach[44]—reorganizes the sensory information, and without the guidance of the dormant intellect, fashions the dream vision of the birds, which parallel the human characters and their potential for violent interaction. Alonso suspects the premonitory nature of the dream but is unable to interpret it fully and can only complain of his uneasiness over his vision of the yellow bird's death.

Lope's color symbolism in this episode is in keeping with the traditional notions and depictions of love melancholy.[45] Though it is common to find the color red stand for the heated and sanguine stage of the lover's imbalance, it is yellow that is most commonly associated with love melancholy in literary discourse. This is a tradition with a long literary history which the Siglo de Oro authors often use to represent or to mock the lovesick characters they create. A much earlier expression of this association is found in the *Cárcel de amor,* in which the prison is topped by three statues whose garb is colored symbolically to suggest melancholy and lovesickness: "Las tres imágines que viste encima de la torre, cubiertas cada una de su color, de leonado y negro y pardillo, la una es

---

44. See, for example, Murry W. Bundy, "The Theory of Imagination," 51-52, 76-78, 134.
45. See Teresa S. Soufas, "The Transvalued Discourse of Heroical Love in Francisco de Rioja's 'A una rosa amarilla'"; Herbert A. Kenyon, "Color Symbolism in Early Spanish Ballads"; Griswold S. Morley, "Color symbolism in Tirso de Molina"; W. L. Fichter, "Color Symbolism in Lope de Vega."

Tristeza y la otra Congoxa y la otra Trabajo" (The three images that you saw on top of the tower, each one covered in its color, of yellow and black and brown, the one is Sadness and the other Grief and the other Toil). The figure who attacks the prisoner is a black man dressed in yellow who "se llama Desesperar" (is called Desperation), a clearly melancholic disposition. Among the allegorical figures described as present or attendant upon the prisoner are Cuidado (Care), Mal (Evil), Pena (Pain), Dolor (Sorrow), Desdicha (Misfortune), and Desamor (Indifference).[46] These, of course, are standard afflictions of melancholia, found in a site (the prison) that is suggestive of Saturn. The god's own color symbolism is also captured in this and a multitude of other depictions in medieval and Renaissance literature of love, for the darkness of his sinister, oppressive, and filicidal reputation is represented in the discourse of lovesickness always with the yellow hues that at the same time suggest his benevolent reign over the Age of Gold.

Similarly, among the symptoms of the second stage of lovesickness found in the later Renaissance medical treatises is a sallow complexion.[47] In his dictionary, Covarrubias also explains yellow as follows: "Entre las colores se tiene por la más infelice, por ser la de la muerte, y de la larga y peligrosa enfermedad y la color de los enamorados" (Among the colors it is considered to be the most unhappy, because it is the color of death, and of long and dangerous illness and the color of lovers).[48] Numerous dramatic and poetic works of Renaissance and Baroque Spain include this association, and among the plays by Lope in which it is found are *El dómine Lucas* (Schoolmaster Lucas), *El remedio de la desdicha* (The remedy of misfortune), *La esclava de su hijo* (The slave of her son), *Amores de Albanio y Ismenia* (The loves of Albanio and Ismenia), and *El caballero de Olmedo*.[49] In the latter play the yellow feathers of the *jilguero* and the dark color of the *azor* in Alonso's dream call attention to the figuratively lighter and darker manifestations of the malady of *hereos* that result in the eventual dominance of the latter.

Though Alonso ultimately discounts the dream, he does reiterate his recognition of the danger Rodrigo's jealous ill-will poses to him. He displays further symptoms of genuine melancholia as the play progresses, and fear and sadness are the melancholic traits of which he speaks openly to Inés at their last meeting:

46. Diego de San Pedro, *Cárcel*, 90, 91.
47. See, for example, Ferrand, *Erotomania*, 121; Lemnius, *Touchstone of Complexions,* fol. 146; and Freylas, *Conocimiento, curacion y preservacion*, fol. 226r.
48. *Tesoro de la lengua*, 110.
49. See Kenyon, "Color Symbolism"; Morley, "Color Symbolism in Tirso"; and Fichter, "Color Symbolism in Lope."

La envidia de mis contrarios
temo tanto que, aunque puedo
poner medios necesarios
estoy entre amor y miedo
haciendo discursos varios.
                                    (3.2195–99)

(I fear the envy of my enemies
so much that, although I can
take the necessary measures
I am giving changeable speeches
on both love and fear.)

It is precisely this "haciendo discursos varios" that both contributes to and becomes a consequence of melancholy. As Babb, Lyons, and others explain, those young lovers who burn in the early sanguine stage of love can often experience a degenerative melancholic stage if consummation of their love is delayed or impossible. Alonso is not a genuine melancholic in the first two acts since textual information shows that the standard melancholy imbalance he exhibits late in the play is a direct result of his artificial prolongation of playacting and inactive contemplation. All of this helps him certainly to accomplish his unnecessary affectation of heroical love, but success in that area leads to his downfall at the hands of a jealous rival as well as to his own obsessions, fear, uneasiness, dreams, and finally hallucinations.

Upon his departure from Medina in act 3, Alonso sees and speaks to what appears to be his own *sombra* (ghost), and remarks: "¡Que un hombre me atemorice, / no habiendo temido a tantos!" (That one man can frighten me, / not having feared so many! [3.2256–57]). His immediate suspicion is "Es don Rodrigo" (It is Don Rodrigo [3.2258]), but he eventually quells his fright by means of the logical notion that the vision is due to his melancholic state: "Todas son cosas que finge / la fuerza de la tristeza, / la imaginación de un triste" (All are things that / the force of sadness fabricates, / the imagination of a sad person [3.2270–72]). A little further on he rationalizes, "O embustes de Fabia son, / que pretende persuadirme / porque no vaya a Olmedo" (Or they are tricks of Fabia, / who is trying to persuade me / not to go to Olmedo [3. 2277–79]) and convinces himself, moreover, ". . . ya no puede ser / que don Rodrigo me envidie, / pues hoy la vida me debe" (. . . it cannot now be / that Don Rodrigo envies me, / since today he owes me his life [3.2285–87]). He relies here on the significance of his rescue of Rodrigo in the day's bullfight. When Alonso is seen on stage again, however, he is midway on the road between Olmedo and Medina and once again extremely frightened: "Lo que jamás he temido, / que es algún recelo o miedo, / llevo caminando a Olmedo" (That which I never dreaded, / which is some reluctance or fear, / I carry with me to Olmedo [3.2341–43]). He is correct in apprising "Pero tristezas han sido" (But they have been sorrows [3.2345]) though he soon proclaims, in true melancholic fashion, "¡Qué escuridad! Todo es / horror" (What darkness! Everything is / horror [3.2357–58]).

The intricacies of Lope's masterful *tragicomedia* encompass the composite nature of that very art form, represented and articulated in this play in terms of the dialectical appreciation of the link between love and melancholy. His noble and admirable protagonist Alonso is not the paradigm of heroical love. That is a role assigned to the secondary character Rodrigo. The conventions of love and courtship that Alonso so carefully cultivates, therefore, are at every turn undermined by Lope, who, like his character, reveals his own awareness of the literary tradition of the syndrome he manipulates. Alonso, however, does not recognize the danger in choosing a melancholic disorder as his standard, whereas Lope communicates his understanding of that risk by means of the negativity of the portrayal of such a figure. The playwright offers his audience a principal character who, on the strength of his identity established before the play begins, is honorable, deeply in love, and intending to marry the young woman who reciprocates his affection. This protagonist nevertheless behaves from the play's opening lines in accord with the description of various stages of melancholy love, and while he contrives more and more to emulate those characteristics, Lope just as consistently invalidates them.

Alonso's love notes and poems themselves masquerade as the laundry list in act 1 and the sham Latin text in act 2, or function as the center of comic scenes when recited by Tello the clown or with exaggerated theatricality by Alonso himself. The protagonist's recourse to Fabia is a problematical element within the play unless understood as part of his adherence to the literary symbols of love melancholy based primarily upon the *Celestina*. Lope carefully shows Fabia to be only this—a powerless imitator. The act most suggestive of her black magic is the attempt to steal a tooth from the corpse of a hanged criminal. Tello is her accomplice, and his comical complaints and reticence amplify the lack of authenticity in Fabia's supposed powers. The level of parody that she embodies is significant in this very undertaking when she insists that the grumbling Tello carry the ladder to the gallows for her. This object, which recalls Calisto's means of access to his beloved as well as the instrument of his death, is hilariously mocked when it is recounted that Tello has fallen, only to soil himself at the base of Fabia's ladder.

While Alonso has portrayed the more comic stage lover whose procrastination eventually brings about his true melancholia, Rodrigo stands in opposition to the lighter side of the lovesickness affected by his rival. His own authentic love melancholy is the result of being rejected by Inés and is likewise exacerbated by the prolongation and the public theatricality of Alonso's courtship of her. From the beginning of the play, Rodrigo is presented as the spurned, though persistent, suitor of Inés. Upon his first appearance at her house, he says: "Si me vio por la ventana, / ¿quién duda que huyó por mí?" (If she saw me through the window, / who doubts she fled because of me? [1.426–27]). The darker and more sinister quality of love melancholia dominates Rodrigo, and the effects of melancholy jealousy are what cause him to turn his unbalanced homicidal madness toward the elimination of his rival. Speaking to Fernando about Alonso, Rodrigo says: "El talle, grave rostro, lo severo, / celoso me obligaban a miralle" (The physique, grave countenance, the severe demeanor, / obliged me to look at him jealously [3.1333–34]). His friend responds:

> Efetos son de amante verdadero
> que, en viendo otra persona de buen talle,
> tienen temor que si le ve su dama
> será posible o fuerza codicialle.
>
> (2.1335–38)
>
> (They are effects of a true lover
> who, upon seeing another person of fine figure,
> is afraid that if his lady sees the other
> she will possibly or inevitably desire him.)

This interchange suggests an interesting and important fact, that is, Rodrigo and Alonso have come to function in what may be understood as a tandem representation of the dialectical nature of Golden Age Spain's understanding of love melancholy. While laughable in his voguish theatricality, the melancholy poser models himself on a syndrome that must, as Lope demonstrates, be taken seriously because of the threat that the mentality of such a model conveys. Fernando's description of Rodrigo as the "amante verdadero" thus does not imply that Alonso is a false lover. Rather he emphasizes the standard connection between mental/emotional imbalance and love that Rodrigo embodies throughout the play and that Alonso initially imitates and later suffers authentically.

Early in the first act, Rodrigo refers to his own intentions to marry Inés. Even during his initial appearance, however, his statements are couched in terms of dissatisfaction because of Inés's coolness to him: "¿Hasta casarme con ella /

será forzoso que pase / por estos inconvenientes?" (Until I marry her will it be necessary to endure / these inconveniences? [1.397–99]). From that moment forward, he suffers one rebuff after another and becomes progressively more aware of the signs that he has lost Inés to Alonso. Complaining at various moments of her disdain and hoping for a remedy for his pain and distemper (1.461–62), Rodrigo rails against the emotional mistreatment he receives and even against what he perceives to be scorn from his own home region because of the general admiration of Alonso:

> Me esperan para que yo
> haga suertes que me afrenten
> o que algún toro me mate
> o me arrastre o me maltrate,
> donde con risa lo cuenten.
>   (3.1874–78)
>
> (They await me so that I
> take chances that dishonor me
> or that some bull kills me
> or drags me or mistreats me,
> which they will recount with laughter.)

There is much in this speech that sounds like the sentiments of the melancholy malcontent, another sort of melancholic with a social reality and a literary popularity during the late Renaissance (see chapter 4 for a complete discussion). Rodrigo combines that figure's feeling of spurned superiority and bitter misanthropy with his negative characteristics of the rejected lover, a combination Babb assures was a social and literary phenomenon as well in contemporary England:

> Representations of despondent love, moreover, contain many indications of the current interest in melancholy and of the ideas popularly associated with it. In Elizabethan literature "melancholy" is used in connection with love much more often than before. Englishmen have begun to think of the melancholy lover as a type related to the malcontent . . . Pining lovers are sometimes called malcontents.[50]

As Rodrigo's love melancholy manifests itself through the dark and threatening signs of jealousy and homicidal insanity, Fernando warns his disturbed friend: "Son celos, don Rodrigo, una quimera . . . / un pensamiento que a locura inclina" (Jealousy, Don Rodrigo, is a fancy . . . / a thought that inspires insanity [2.1357–61]). Indeed, Rodrigo very soon declares, "perderé el sentido"

---

50. Babb, *Elizabethan Malady*, 157.

(I will lose my reason [2. 1377]), and though Fernando tries to distract him from his obsessive jealousy with talk of the upcoming festivities for La Cruz de Mayo ("Menos aflige el mal que se entretiene" [The evil that is diverted afflicts less]; 2.1378), Rodrigo cannot free himself from thoughts of Alonso. Fernando finally warns, "¡Que está loco!" (He is insane! [2.1390]) to which Rodrigo replies, "Amor me desatina" (Love unhinges me [3.1382–83]), affirming again his heroical melancholy and thus his identity as a figure whose highly active intellect is dangerous.

Unable to combat his negative impulses and feelings, Rodrigo becomes by act 2 a melancholy villain, prompted by his jealous, lovesick obsessions.[51] Having fallen from his horse during the games in act 3, only to be rescued by none other than Alonso, Rodrigo complains in an ominous, melancholy declaration: "Mala caída, / mal suceso, malo todo" (Dreadful fall, / wretched incident, bad everything [2029–30]). He shortly begins an important speech with the affirmation "Estoy loco" (I am crazy [2039]) and ends with his first avowal to kill Alonso on the road between Olmedo and Medina. The next time he appears on stage, it is in the company of the men whom he has hired to ambush his rival. In a conversation with Fernando he expresses his anger over Don Pedro's broken word of consent to a marriage and over the trickery about Inés's religious calling. He likewise rails against Fabia's dealings with Inés, and he seems to consider the young woman a victim of the *alcahueta*'s (go-between's) black magic. This very assertion and his descriptions of all the spells and conjurations he attributes to Fabia stand in direct contrast to Alonso's final act of reasoning. Away from Medina, the knight from Olmedo can see Fabia for what she is—an old procuress and nothing more. Rodrigo, on the other hand, affirms the link between the desperate melancholic's vulnerability and demonic suggestion. He is about to order a murder. His blatant cowardice (though he assures all present that were he to fight Alonso fairly he would win) and his jealousy reveal the extent of his melancholia just as his irrational susceptibility to a belief in the nonexistent powers of Fabia attest to the imbalance in his rational faculties.

Lope's Rodrigo evinces the literary representation of the common notions about jealousy that Burton also records in his pseudo-scientific *Anatomy:* "Of all passions . . . love is most violent, and of those bitter potions which this love-melancholy affords, this bastard jealousy is the greatest." As in other cases of melancholy disorders studied in this book, I do not wish to suggest that Lope patterned his portrayals of the variations of love melancholia on specific ethico-medical works on melancholy. The notion bears repeating that what the artistic

51. Ibid., 59, 159.

authors and their medical counterparts articulate is not original in its basis but rather part of literary and medical traditions without temporal or national restrictions. Burton, in fact, cites a passage from Luis Vives's *De Anima* in the first paragraph of his own section on the symptoms of jealousy—further evidence of the interplay of ideas that well-traveled scholars like Vives helped to facilitate between Spain and her European neighbors. Burton writes:

> Jealousy, saith Vives, "begets unquietness in the mind, night and day: he hunts after every word he hears, every whisper, and amplifies it to himself (as all melancholy men do in other matters) with a most unjust calumny of others, he misinterprets everything is said or done, most apt to mistake or misconstrue," he pries into every corner, follows close, observes to a hair.[52]

Rodrigo fits such a pattern in Lope's play, but he is by no means the only murderous character deranged to such an extent by love and melancholic tendencies in Golden Age drama. The other important cases I will consider differ from his only in that they do not involve unmarried suitors but lawfully wedded men who nevertheless demonstrate the imbalances of melancholic jealousy.

With regard to such aberrations, Burton, like the majority of Renaissance scientists and doctors, considers love to be "a species of melancholy" and adds that heroical love is "a frequent cause of melancholy [that] deserves much rather to be called burning lust, than by such an honourable title." He continues: "It will not contain itself within the union of marriage, or apply to one object, but is a wandering, extravagant, a domineering, a boundless, an irrefragable, a destructive passion: sometimes this burning lust rageth after marriage, and then it is properly called Jealousy."[53] The sort of jealousy that Rodrigo displays in *El caballero de Olmedo* is dramatized within the bonds of marriage by Calderón's famous wife-murderers. In *El médico de su honra, A secreto agravio, secreta venganza,* and *El pintor de su deshonra,* Calderón expresses his age's mistrust of the overly contemplative individual by demonstrating the unhappy consequences of the obsessive ruminations of a melancholy mind in situations that center on problematical marriages and external threats to conjugal stability from other lovesick personages. The elements that Burton identifies as part of what was then popularly and scientifically accepted about the dangers of a marriage premised upon melancholy jealousy are evident in these three Calderonian honor dramas.[54] Although the Spanish playwright does not portray

52. For both Burton quotations in this paragraph, see *Anatomy of Melancholy,* 575.
53. Ibid., 450, 541.
54. See Soufas, "Calderón's Melancholy Wife-Murderers."

licentious men as his protagonists, they are all jealous once they fall in love and marry. The unscrupulous former lovers of their wives, however, are themselves victims of the illicit sexual appetite and the "destructive passion" of the heroical lover that the English scientist describes. Like Lope, Calderón portrays the secondary character in the role of the traditional spurned lover. His noble protagonists, however, demonstrate a propensity toward excessive thought undertaken in solitude that leads to behavior and attitudes that separate the individual from the proper social and intellectual system and its basis of communication and understanding. The playwright thus dramatizes the most negative aspects of love in these plays through the violence inherent in *amor hereos* as a pathological melancholy disorder.

In *A secreto agravio, secreta venganza,* Calderón depicts Don Lope de Almeida as an individual of naturally choleric temperament—a characteristic suggested by his preference for the life of a soldier, his active military exploits that predate the beginning of the play, and thus his association with Mars, the god of war and the planetary patron of the choleric. The purported expert on love melancholy, Ferrand, explains the accepted notion that this melancholic malady is brought on by "the Adustion of Choler, of the blood, or of the Naturall Melancholy."[55] Thus Calderón is in keeping with the general understanding of one of the variable causes of heroical love. Early in act 1, Don Lope speaks of his recent marriage and voices the hope that "Marte ceda / a amor la gloria" (Mars cedes the glory / to love).[56] Such a statement raises the question of one sort of violent nature succeeding another, since dangerous extremes of emotions and actions are associated with love. The negative quality of the implication strengthens as Lope and his *criado* (servant) discuss the new marriage, for it has been contracted in haste and does not seem to suit the nobleman. Manrique says to his master:

> ¿Y no miras que es error
> digno de que al mundo asombre
> que vaya a casarse un hombre
> con tanta prisa, señor?
>
> (And don't you see that it is an error
> worthy of startling the world
> that a man go to marry
> with such haste, master?)[57]

55. *Erotomania,* 63–66.
56. In *Obras completas,* ed. A. Valbuena Briones, 1:425.
57. Ibid., 426.

Like Cervantes, Calderón indicates his own rejection of Huartian determinism with regard to humoral types. Although Don Lope's humoral makeup is depicted as best suited for one sort of undertaking (i.e., military life) and not another (a married man, settled into a domestic routine), his return to soldiering at the end of the play is not portrayed as a triumph. A step taken after his commission of a vicious double murder, it leads him on a doomed campaign for the Spanish troops, as the seventeenth-century audience could recall. In canonical works, like this play, Spanish authors seem to refute consistently Huarte's notion of preference for humoral excesses and professional categorization. Certainly, as is made clear in *La vida es sueño* (Life is a dream), Calderón adheres to the need to know and understand oneself in order to triumph over biological and/or astrological inclinations.

Don Lope of *A secreto agravio, secreta venganza* eventually begins to show many symptoms of the suspicious and unstable nature of jealous melancholics. His initial frustrations seem more rooted in his retirement from active military duty, but his melancholy resentments soon focus on his wife Leonor and on circumstantial evidence of wrongdoing on her part. The faulty interpretation of sensory evidence is the central issue with regard to the murders Lope commits in the third act, for it reveals the unfavorable view Calderón takes of the highly active melancholic intellect of such a character. Much of Don Lope's contemplation of evidence occurs in private and when he does interact with others, his suspicious mind is further aggravated by remarks that do not always convey the message of dishonor that he believes he hears. Like Quijote, however, his imagination functions adequately in its capacity of conduit for sensory information, but his overly active intellect disrupts the balanced functioning of his faculties.

Another type of unsuitability for marriage is portrayed in *El pintor de su deshonra,* in which the protagonist, Don Juan Roca, is an elderly scholar of melancholic disposition who has dedicated his life to study and art. Only in the late years of his life has he acceded to the pressure of friends to marry in order to produce an heir for his considerable fortune. From the first scene, when his friend Don Luis describes him, the humoral make-up of the protagonist is clearly presented:

> Ya sé las dificultades
> que hubo en vuestra condición
> para esa plática, y que
> siempre que en ella os hablé,
> hallé vuestra inclinación
> muy contraria, habiendo sido

de vuestro divertimiento
lo postrero el casamiento;
pues en libros suspendido
gastabais noches y días;
y si, para entretener
tal vez fatigas de leer,
con vuestras melancolías
treguas tratábades, era
lo prolijo del pincel
su alivio, porque aun en él
parte el ingenio tuviera.

(I know the difficulties
that were involved in your condition
with regard to this subject, and that
whenever I spoke of it to you,
I found your inclination
very negative, marriage
having been for you
the least appealing pleasure;
since you spent nights and days
caught up in your books;
and if, perhaps to relieve
the fatigues of reading,
you made treaties
with your melancholy,
your relief was
your untiring paintbrush, because
your genius also took part in it.)[58]

Since Juan Roca is elderly, his association with melancholy is further emphasized because the medical tradition had for centuries associated melancholy
with the later stages of the human life cycle.[59] His new status as loving husband,
however, exaggerates this link because old persons are also said to be more
vulnerable to jealousy.[60] Echoing several contemporary accounts, Burton tells
us that old men "are cold and dry by nature. . . . Old age is a disease of itself,
loathsome, full of suspicion and fear."[61] Babb points out another factor with
significance for Juan Roca's case: "It is clear, then, that melancholy inclines men

58. In *Obras completas,* 1:868.
59. Babb, *Elizabethan Malady,* 11–12.
60. See also López de Villalobos, "Los problemas de Villalobos," in *Biblioteca de Autores
Españoles,* 36:420–22, for an example of the standard advice against older men marrying younger
women.
61. *Anatomy of Melancholy,* 568.

to jealousy. On the other hand, jealousy may cause melancholy."[62] Juan Roca is therefore caught in what will be a vicious cycle of characteristics that exacerbate each other.

Alan K. G. Paterson's scrutiny of the development of melancholy characterizations and imagery in *El pintor de su deshonra* leads him to conclusions different from my own. He recognizes a blend of dialectical elements in the presentation of the plot and *dramatis personae* that evince the absurdity and the turbulence of the dramatized situation. He does not, however, account for the disaster of the play's end in terms of the melancholy intellect that Calderón depicts as the source of error, imbalance, and disruption of the cosmic harmony. What Paterson contends is Calderón's projection of "a universe without providence [that] should not be taken to imply any crisis in the dramatist's faith" shifts emphasis away from the melancholy of Juan Roca. In spite of the depicted "inadequate or perverted individual judgement," Paterson contends that Roca is no villain.[63]

Roca's scholarly thought, nevertheless, precedes all that he does: not marrying in his earlier years, later taking a wife as an old man, and plotting the deaths of Serafina and Alvaro. He is an outstanding example of a character who embodies the transvaluation of melancholy. As a respected scholar, his dedication to his books has earned him the admiration of those who know him. His scholarship has isolated him, however, and his close friends and relations obviously disapprove of this sort of life. His intellectualization sets him apart, but once he marries, his interaction with others only leads to a disastrous resolution. He is never portrayed as anything but a melancholic, and through varying stages of emotional and physiological comfort and discomfort, he consistently fails to participate as a fully integrated member of society.

In *El médico de su honra,* Calderón portrays a worsening of the melancholia that the protagonist Gutierre displays through his suspicious nature and potential for violence. In the play's prehistory, his mistrust of a former fiancée, Leonor, has prompted his abrupt ending of their relationship. Seemingly able to love deeply, and indeed possessively, Gutierre subsequently marries Doña Mencía, and their marriage is the focus of the play's action. His melancholy tendency to think in solitude is particularly evident at the important midpoint of the play. Having found circumstantial evidence of a visit by a man to his wife, Gutierre delivers a long monologue prefigured by his desire for solitude in which to think about what he perceives to be a threat to his honor ("¡Ay,

62. Babb, *Elizabethan Malady,* 141; Burton, *Anatomy,* 575.
63. Alan K. G. Paterson, "The Comic and Tragic Melancholy of Juan Roca: A Study of Calderón's *El pintor de su deshonra,*" 259, 256.

honor!, mucho tenemos / que hablar a solas los dos" [Ah, honor! We have much / to discuss privately, we two]).[64] The thought process that Gutierre exhibits in his monologue is in keeping with what Burton considers to be the recognized mental symptom of deranged melancholy lovers whom Burton describes as:

> full of fear, anxiety, doubt, care, peevishness, suspicion . . . They are apt to mistake, amplify, too credulous sometimes, too full of hope and confidence, and then again very jealous, unapt to believe or entertain any good news . . . These doubts, anxieties, suspicions, are the least part of their torments; they break many times from passions to actions, speak fair, and flatter, now most obsequious and willing, by and by they are averse, wrangle, fight, swear, quarrel, laugh, weep. . . . So their actions and passions are intermixt, but of all other passions, Sorrow hath the greatest share; Love to many is bitterness itself.[65]

Gutierre does articulate these alternating thoughts and feelings. Speaking of his "agravios" (offenses) and "penas" (sorrows), he acknowledges his sorrow and desire to weep but quickly begins mentally to sort through the external evidence he has encountered in order to find a logical basis for a belief in his wife's innocence: "¿. . . no pudiera / no estar culpada Mencía?" (. . . couldn't / Mencia be blameless? [2.1589–90; 1640–41]). Seizing upon the notion that the knife left behind in his house by Prince Enrique is merely proof of a tryst with a household maid, Gutierre exclaims: " ¡O, cuánto me estimo haber / hallado esta sutileza!" (Oh, how much I appreciate having / hit upon this fine point! [2.1645–46]). Then this train of thought changes almost immediately:

> Y así cortemos discursos,
> pues todos juntos se cierran
> en que Mencía es quien es,
> y soy quien soy; no hay quien pueda
> borrar de tanto esplendor
> la hermosura y la pureza.
> Pero sí puede, mal digo;
> que al sol una nube negra,
> si no le mancha, le turba,
> si no le eclipsa, le hiela.
>
> (2.1647–56)

(And so let us end discussion,
since everything persists in that

---

64. Pedro Calderón de la Barca, *El médico de su honra*, ed. D. W. Cruickshank, 2.1401–2. Subsequent quotations (act and verse) are from this edition and are cited in the text.
65. *Anatomy of Melancholy*, 500–501.

Mencía is who she is,
And I am who I am; there is no one who can
erase the beauty and purity
from such splendor.
But yes someone could, damn it;
for a cloud blackens the sun,
disturbing it, if not staining it,
chilling it, if not eclipsing it.)

These last lines suggest the cold and darkness of melancholy as well. The metaphor of sickness and needed cure upon which Gutierre seizes indicates the pathological condition dramatized. Unfortunately, the unbalanced thought of the obsessive melancholic leads him to contrive a treatment for his honor that entails bleeding his wife to death. In *A secreto agravio, secreta venganza*, Calderón also depicts this sort of melancholy thinking as Don Lope contemplates his suspicions about the stranger he has seen lurking in the neighborhood and Leonor's easy acceptance of his plan to leave for military duty. Both men internalize their efforts to interpret the evidence before them, and prefer to think and to plot in secret, as is typical of villainous melancholics.

Though the husbands in the three honor dramas are the homicidal culprits who murder their wives, the men who make them suspicious in the first place are also developed as melancholy lovers. In each case, this character is a former lover of the woman in question, and he learns abruptly of her recent marriage. Don Luis in *A secreto agravio, secreta venganza*, Don Alvaro in *El pintor de su deshonra*, and Prince Enrique in *El médico de su honra* all behave and speak as unrequited melancholy lovers and carry out their plans for the "destructive passion" that Burton links to the heated emotions of love and lust which sometimes convert to jealousy after marriage, and "sometimes before . . . is called Heroical Melancholy."[66] These are the two manifestations of love melancholy that Calderón portrays, and their sufferers (the husbands and the lovers) are jointly responsible for destroying the women they love.

Calderón also carefully supports the melancholy characterizations in these dramas with melancholy imagery. Don Lope's adust melancholy with its so-called heated and cold properties is matched figuratively by the flames of the house fire and the shipwreck at sea that he uses to hide the deaths he inflicts on his wife Leonor and on Don Luis. Gutierre hires a barber to bleed Mencía to death in *El médico de su honra* (a standard remedy for many humoral distempers), but the wish he expresses more than once during the drama—"yo cubriré

66. Ibid., 451.

con tierra mi deshonra" (I will cover my dishonor with earth [2.2048])—calls to mind the natural element matched to melancholy. Roca, too, plunges into the sea in deranged and terrible melancholy desperation after Don Alvaro kidnaps the unconscious Leonor from her husband in the aftermath of a house fire that reflects the younger man's heated and lustful stage of love melancholy. In addition, as in *El médico de su honra,* in whose final scenes Mencía is locked in her quarters to await death by her Saturnine husband, in *El pintor de su deshonra* Leonor is also imprisoned. Held against her will by her melancholy lover Alvaro, she is murdered by her husband, who is himself locked behind a *reja* (iron bars) in a balcony enclosure.

Darkness also abounds in these three plays and is frequently the background for the secret plots or the misfortunes of the protagonists. Gutierre perhaps best expresses the melancholic preference for darkness and solitude and secret activity when, in act 2, he returns unannounced to his house to spy on Mencía:

> En el mudo silencio
> de la noche, que adoro y reverencio,
> por sombra aborrecida,
> como sepulcro de la humana vida,
> de secreto he venido.
>
> (2.1861-65)

> (In the mute silence
> of nighttime, which I adore and worship,
> through detested shadow,
> like the grave of human life,
> I come secretly.)

All three men likewise express the love melancholic's wish for death, though in each drama it is the wife who dies as the victim of the pathological melancholy that deranges her husband. Calderón's pessimistic opinion of the highly active and autonomous melancholy mind is apparent in these three plays, in which monstrous crimes are committed and in which no sign is given that the three protagonists recognize the true nature of their actions or come to understand themselves better. Each ends the play by facing a future that parallels his life before marriage. Lope returns to war and a more stereotypically appropriate outlet for his naturally choleric system. Gutierre is married by royal decree to Leonor, whom he already mistrusts. Juan Roca is clearly saddened at the close of *El pintor de su deshonra* and, left alone again without a wife or prospect of heirs and having killed two people, he asks to be killed: "Matadme todos" (Kill me, everyone). No one complies, and he leaves expressing his desire to be alone—"me quitaré de delante" (I will remove myself [3.1034]).[67] These men are all important members of their societies, but they do not behave as members of a community. Gutierre and Juan Roca adopt metaphorical roles that separate them from a proper identity and place within the whole of society. As is the case with the majority of melancholics in Golden Age literature, the contemplation and thought to which they are prone is depicted as deviant. Calderón shows his audience the terrible consequences of the deepening of the melancholia of three men whose love is perverted to violence because they think too much and do not maintain effective contact with a community outside themselves.

In the wife-murder plays, however, Calderón presents the outside community as also incapable of providing appropriate means for solving the protagonists' dilemmas. In El médico de su honra, for instance, Gutierre tries to appeal to the king for justice against the prince only to be disappointed by the monarch, who displays his own melancholia through hallucinations and suspicions.[68] In El pintor de su deshonra, the prince is likewise a defective agent of order and stability and behaves as a lovesick libertine whom Paterson identifies as a participant in "love's pantomime."[69] While carrying on his affair with Porcia behind her father's back, the prince also pines for Leonor in accordance with the typology of the lover's disease. It is significant that his love melancholy prompts him to commission the portrait of Leonor that brings her into the view of her dangerously obsessed melancholic husband. In A secreto agravio, secreta venganza, the advice Don Lope seeks from his friend Juan seems to be given under the influence of the melancholy the latter feels over his own failed love affair and from an act of violence associated with it. The king too provides statements that not only do not reassure Lope of his honorable status in the community but also deepen his uneasiness concerning his reputation and his suspicions.

Calderón's conservative point of view concerning melancholy is dramatized in the honor plays, which extend in dates of production from the 1630s to 1651; in the latter year he turned his attention primarily to the writing of autos (religious allegories) and to the composition of El pintor de su deshonra, which centers clearly on the quintessential figure of transvalued melancholy, the scholar. Though Calderón's is a generally serious treatment of the behavior and ruminations of such characters, it does include laughable elements, not unlike Lope's presentation. One clearly comical aspect of a melancholy disorder in the wife-murder dramas is presented through the the gracioso Coquín, who

67. Pintor, 3.1019; 3.1034.
68. See Teresa S. Soufas, "Beyond Justice and Cruelty."
69. Paterson, "Comic and Tragic Melancholy," 248.

jokingly complains about a fashionable affectation of another clinical melancholy syndrome called "hipocondría" and thought to be produced by the
flatulence of the trapped humors in a diseased melancholy system without the
proper purgative function of the spleen.[70] Coquín says to Mencía's maid
Jacinta:

> Metíme a ser discreto
> por mi mal, y hame dado
> tan grande hipocondría en este lado
> que me muero.
>
> (3.2418–21)

> (I became wise
> to my detriment, and I have been taken over
> by so great a hypochondria in this side
> that I am dying.)

To Jacinta's question "¿Y qué es hipocondría?" (And what is hypochondria?),
Coquín explains:

> Es una enfermedad que no la había
> habrá dos años, ni en el mundo era.
> Usóse poco ha, y de manera
> lo que se usa, amiga, no se excusa,
> que una dama, sabiendo que se usa,
> le dijo a su galán muy triste un día:
> "tráigame un poco used de hipocondría".
>
> (3.2422–28)

> (It is an illness that did not exist
> two years ago, nor was it known in the world.
> Recently it is in fashion, and therefore, because
> what is in fashion, my friend, cannot be ignored,
> a lady, knowing that it was in vogue,
> said very sadly to her suitor one day:
> "bring me a little hypochondria.")

With his claim that "Metíme a ser discreto," Coquín alludes to the vogue of
melancholy and those who feign its symptoms in order to be considered intelligent. His description, however, is of hypochondria, a disorder that often
receives separate attention in the contemporary medical texts on melancholy.

70. See Teresa S. Soufas, "Calderón's Joyless Jester: The Humanization of a Stock Character."

Among such Spanish treatises, for example, even Murillo's relatively late study is entitled *Aprobacion de ingenios, y curacion de hipochondricos, con observaciones, y remedios muy particulares* (Approval of wits, and cure of hypochondriacs, with observations, and very particular remedies), and other earlier treatises such as Velásquez's contain information about the disorder.[71] In Felix Platter's medical textbook, first published in 1602, there is a section dedicated to this sort of melancholia, and in it he, like other physicians writing on the symptoms, discusses the trapped wind that causes pain in the side.[72] Artistic representation of such a sufferer usually depicts his or her pressing a hand or arm to the left side of the body in discomfort, as Dürer's self-portrait and the figure of Hypochondriacus in the frontispiece to Burton's *Anatomy* demonstrate. Hypochondria in its modern sense connotes an imaginary illness or obsession with medical syndromes and treatments, but this is not the definition accepted from the time of Galen through the seventeenth century. There is, nevertheless, a measure of recognition of the obsessions of the melancholic and the transvalued appreciation of melancholia evident in some of the early seventeenth-century descriptions of hypochondriacal melancholy. Platter, for example, writes:

> These patients are convinced that they have various diseases, and some are true, others imaginary. This is especially true of men who are intelligent and delve into matters deeply, especially physicians that study the causes of diseases. They suppose they have diseases, and tire out the physicians by telling about them, some write and talk that every part of their body, internally and externally, was diseased when, however, they can eat, sleep and drink well. They also may persuade themselves that they have lost all their natural heat and have many imaginary diseases in their brain, stomach, lungs, liver, kidneys. . . . Others complain of some true diseases but in addition they imagine many others. This is what I saw happen to a certain nobleman who for forty years tortured himself almost continuously with this kind of thoughts and used many remedies and who, nonetheless, lived to an advanced age.[73]

This passage suggests the applicability of Coquín's comical statements to his master Gutierre, a highly intelligent but melancholy man who does not complain about the painful physical symptoms of hypochondriasis but does manifest its psychological aberrations. Delving deeply into the matters that concern him, he contemplates a metaphorical disease and becomes convinced of its reality.

71. See, for example, *Libro de la melancholia*, fol. 57v.
72. Felix Platter, Abdiah Cole, and Nicholas Culpeper, *A Golden Practice of Physick*, 15 and 28.
73. Ibid., 92–93.

The imagery of the wind, which is continually cited by Gutierre as a danger to the instruments of light and therefore to clear sight and understanding, to the health of his wife, and to his honor because of its power to carry rumors, is also highly suggestive of the hypochondria to which the play's clown refers. Another of the names used to identify this sort of melancholia is "the windy melancholly," as Platter notes.[74] Lemnius, among others, also describes it in this way, and Burton lists the numerous abdominal areas troubled by the flatulence from which vapors ascend to the brain, disrupting the apprehensive capabilities of the imagination and initiating reactions of fear, sorrow, discontent, and even vivid hallucinations.[75] During Calderón's play, furthermore, the *gracioso* himself becomes a saddened, wiser, and melancholy character. Coquín recognizes the mistaken interpretations made by his master, and what was once only his self-conscious and laughable pretense to melancholy intelligence finally manifests itself as real when he is the only character who, in the last scene, can tell the king the truth of what has happened to Mencía. As in the case of Alonso in *El caballero de Olmedo,* the melancholy that Coquín represents is first a comic element (his expressed sadness is comically exaggerated in act 2, 1221–34, for example) but one that becomes his psychological and physiological reality as he demonstrates in his speech to King Pedro as an "hombre de muchas veras" (man of much truth) decrying that laughter is an element out of place in that society.

In *El caballero de Olmedo* and the wife-murder plays, Lope and Calderón demonstrate that the melancholy mind is a threat to spiritual and social harmony. The most positive reaction to melancholy suggested in these works on love's aberrations is laughter at those who artificially cultivate its characteristics. Beyond that, the only appropriate response, the playwrights indicate, is to use the highly intelligent melancholy mind to reassert one's place in society and the epistemological order that recognizes the secular and religious hierarchy leading to God. Calderón's Coquín tries to reestablish order by appealing to the king, but the monarch fails him, too. Lope's Alonso reasserts his belief in the strength of the community by recalling to himself the rules of nobility that govern members of the aristocracy:

> Pero ya no puede ser
> que don Rodrigo me envidie,
> pues hoy la vida me debe;
> que esta deuda no permite
> que un caballero tan noble

74. Ibid., 32.
75. Respectively, *Touchstone of Complexions,* fol. 142v, and *Anatomy of Melancholy,* 351.

en ningún tiempo la olvide.
(3.2285–90)

(But now it cannot be
that Don Rodrigo envies me,
since today he owes me his life;
for this debt prohibits
so noble a gentleman
from ever forgetting it.)

Rodrigo, however, has not reaffirmed his own position within that social and communal context, and so Alonso's dependence on the aristocratic unity is unfounded. Like Calderón's wife-murderers, the melancholy Rodrigo remains isolated and thus separated both from others and from right thinking, and his plotting also results in the death of an innocent character.

Though Lope and Calderón allow us to laugh for brief periods at some aspect of the depicted melancholy—Coquín's *hipocondría* and Alonso's affectation—the transvalued status of the condition at issue in the plays requires a readjustment in that reaction. These two Golden Age dramatists examine the polarity of the evaluation of melancholy at the same time that they consider the ideological and intellectual underpinning of that evaluation. The secular mind that thinks too independently is shown to be faulty and dangerous, and the society that applauds or tolerates such intellectual activity is depicted as disorderly from the royal figure on down.

4

The Melancholy Malcontent (The Picaresque)

Algunos, por la mala costumbre de despreciarlo todo, contrajeron el hábito de disgustarse por cualquier cosa . . . Suplen la sabiduría con la displicencia, no dando aprobación a nada . . . Con este título [de censor] se halagan mucho, y ante los espectadores necios cobran fama de ingeniosos. *Luis Vives*

(Some, following the evil custom of despising everything, picked up the habit of being displeased about anything whatsoever. . . . They substitute discontentment for knowledge, giving approval to nothing. . . . With this title [of censor] they flatter themselves greatly and gain fame as ingenious before the foolish spectators.)

T he disruptiveness to society associated with melancholy figures in the *comedia* (drama) also provides a background for the development of the *pícaro,* another component of the period's response to the strength of the secular intellect and its range of activity and influence, which in this case, encompasses the tradition of the melancholy malcontent and its own special form of self-conscious participation in the vogue of melancholy. The widespread interest in melancholy prompts myriad poses by those aspiring to be recognized for their intellectual greatness, and, according to some theorists, this posturing can include the mannerisms of the melancholy lover as well as the pretentions of other disaffected complainers. The vociferous railers are known as malcontents, a melancholic type that is not among those subdivided by the doctors into clinical categories. Instead, as a social and literary phenomenon, the malcontent provides interesting evidence of the widespread popular fascination with melancholy and its transvalued status.

Much critical attention has been paid to the melancholy malcontents of the Elizabethan and Jacobean periods in England. Identified and represented as figures who, usually upon return from travels in Italy, raise a vituperative voice against many things, including the injustice of society's failure to recognize their superiority, the malcontents often aim their complaints against the general social and cultural corruption of which they are likely to be a part. Being frequently a villainous scoundrel, the malcontent is understood to be reduced

101

to crime because of hunger and vices adopted in foreign travels. Recognizing the Spanish *pícaro* as one European manifestation of malcontentedness within a literary tradition that flourished elsewhere in the last two decades of the 1500s not only provides another method for meaningful reading of a genre that has proven difficult to categorize but also helps to account for the overwhelming popularity of the picaresque novels outside of Spain in the sixteenth and seventeenth centuries.

The *pícaros* share with other literary figures numerous attributes of malcontentedness that encompass melancholy personality traits: the element of travel with its potential for corruption; a bright but perversely cunning mind; enough of a scholarly bent to lead them into occasional contact with universities and to motivate, in moments of *ocio,* the solitary act of writing an autobiographical account of adventures by means of a literary genre within which they exist as a self-conscious and affected source of laughter. The satiric quality of the picaresque novel is of further significance in establishing this literary form within the melancholic malcontent tradition, for as Alvin Kernan asserts, there is "a vague but tenacious link between the writing of satire and abnormal mental states variously identified as saturnine, malcontent, pensive, and finally as melancholic."[1]

In his study of the malcontent characters in John Marston's plays, Zera S. Fink asserts that

> as a literary figure, [the malcontent] traveler was the Italianated Englishman as developed in some respects, and modified in others, in the period between 1570–1590, the development and modification coming about because of the actual appearance in England in the late eighties of a type of traveler who in the life approximated the literary figure which resulted from him.[2]

In agreement with this assessment, Babb contends that the "disgruntled or seditious traveler . . . was the original melancholy malcontent" but, he adds, the term "malcontent" is even "extended to melancholy types only tenuously connected with the returned traveler."[3] This personality emerged from social context and flourished in literary portrayal in England as either an affected or a

---

1. *The Cankered Muse: Satire of the English Renaissance,* 113.
2. "Jaques and the Malcontent Traveler," 239. In this chapter my consideration of the context of melancholy malcontentedness as a component in the emergence of the picaresque in Spain will focus primarily on *Lazarillo de Tormes* and *Guzmán de Alfarache* as, respectively, the prototype and the most fully developed work in this Spanish literary tradition to which other later works were written in response. Thus, in order to avoid repetition, I have chosen to make only brief references to other books in this tradition.
3. *Elizabethan Malady,* 75.

genuine melancholic, and the inclination of such a figure to consider himself or herself victimized by society corresponds to the rhetoric of the Spanish *pícaro*'s narration.[4] Since revenge is likewise a primary motivating factor for marginalized and often villainous malcontents, the retribution the *pícaros* frequently seek because of their alleged victimization is appropriate to this portrayal.

Because the European malcontent frequently suffers poverty and hunger and gains a villainous reputation as well as fame for the vices and bad habits adopted in foreign countries, he or she is prone to serve as a tool-villain. In considering such figures in Elizabethan drama Babb suggests:

> A great man who needed an instrument for criminal service would be likely to look for just such a person. The malcontent is shrewd and ambitious, but frustrated, poverty-stricken, and embittered. One would suppose that he could be bribed, either with money or with promise of preferment, to perform the greatest iniquities. His bitterness and his melancholy have smothered all his scruples; his needs are urgent; he has little to lose and everything to gain.[5]

The typical structure of the well-known picaresque texts is premised on the protagonist's recounting of service to numerous masters who often depend on the rogue's penchant for dishonest activities and reinforce the notion of the all-pervasive quality of melancholy in its transvalued status as a condition to be feared or mistrusted as well as a medium for accomplishment.

Melancholy as a general condition of society is therefore an implied aspect in depictions of malcontentedness, since the malcontent protagonist reflects the society at whose margins he or she is forced to remain. In *Lazarillo de Tormes*, for example, numerous characters are represented as abusive of religious office: among them, the *ciego* (blindman) who in Tratado I does not recite conscientiously the prayers he is hired to intone; the hypocritical *sacerdote* (priest) of Tratado II; the swindling *buldero* (seller of indulgences) of Tratado V; and the adulterous *arcipreste* (archpriest) of Tratado VII. They are not unlike the malcontent characters engaged in simonical careers in plays by Marston who are considered by some to be particularly representative of this melancholic type. In addition, the poor *hidalgo* of Tratado III is not only a well-defined example of the Spanish literary satire of *honra* (inherited honor), but also displays the theatrics of dissatisfaction that link him to the malcontent type. Such a figure is

---

4. See the description of the melancholy malcontent by Theodore Spenser, "The Elizabethan Malcontent," in *J. Q. Adams Memorial Studies,* ed. J. G. McManaway et al., 529–31.

5. *Elizabethan Malady,* 85.

described, for instance, in the sixteenth century by Thomas Nashe in *Pierce Pennilesse:*

> All malcontent sits the greasie son of a Cloathier, & complaines (like a decaied Earle) of the ruin of ancient houses. . . . Sometimes (because Love commonly weares the liverey of Wit) hee will be an *Inamorato Poeta.* . . . Hee will despise the barbarisme of his own Countrey, & tel a whole Legend of lyes of his travailes unto "Constantinople."[6]

Lyons responds to Nashe's description, saying: "The kind of melancholy [condemned] is not only wilfully 'taken up' in such external manifestations as gait and countenance, but it is also childishly and petulantly self-regarding."[7] The squire in *Lazarillo de Tormes* is characterized in a similar way. He not only poses as a lover in the comical scene of his courtship of prostitutes, but his home and way of life emphasize the darkness, gloom, and sadness of melancholia that also purportedly instill fright in the young Lazarillo. Melancholy poverty pervades as well the whole episode of Lázaro's experience with this character. Lázaro is therefore merely the central figure in a work that depicts a whole range of malcontent/melancholy figures, in a narration controlled by the malcontent character himself, a fact that represents the circularity of mutual influence between society and its melancholic critic.

The two critical camps that polemicize over the ending of the second half of *Guzmán de Alfarache* disagree over Guzmán's conversion and the sincerity of his religious convictions. The depiction of the cardinal whom he serves is also an issue related to the world of religious office and its portrayal in this work, and likewise generates conflicting critical interpretations. The interpretations Joan Arias and Carroll B. Johnson offer demonstrate the hypocrisy and cruelty instead of the humility and charity of this church figure.[8] Arias says, for example: "For if such a man, a distinguished, well educated churchman, is chained to his own passions, hoarding sweets which he refuses to share, surrounding himself with luxury and using his servants cruelly for his own amusement, how much more can we expect from Guzmán?"[9] The villainous hypocrisy of the novel's protagonist himself is expressed more than once and even in his late admission of consistent self-serving tendencies: "Aunque fui malo, deseaba ser bueno, cuando no por gozar de aquel bien, a lo menos por no verme sugeto de

6. Thomas Nashe, *The Works of Thomas Nashe,* ed. Ronald B. McKerrow, 1:168–69.
7. Lyons, *Voices of Melancholy,* 21; see also Babb, *Elizabethan Malady,* 79.
8. Arias, *Guzmán de Alfarache: Unrepentant Narrator,* 55; and Johnson, *Inside Guzmán de Alfarache,* 80.
9. *Unrepentant Narrator,* 80.

algún grave mal" (Although I was bad, I wanted to be good, if not to enjoy that good, then at least so as not to find myself subject to some grave evil).[10] Soon after, in the same chapter, he resolves to take up holy orders. During his thought process, we are also reminded of his education to that point and his potential for further studies. Guzmán parodies the true melancholic scholar and his love of books and study, for his motivation is, as he admits, purely a practical one:

> Con esto me graduaré. Que podría ser tener talento para un púlpito y, siento de misa y buen predicador, tendré cierta la comida y, a todo faltar, meteréme fraile, donde la hallaré cierta . . . Bien veo que no me nace del corazón, ya conozco mi mala inclinación.

> (And so I will graduate. For I could have talent for the pulpit and, I am sure that by saying mass and being a good preacher, I will be sure to have food; and if all else fails, I will become a friar, by which I will certainly eat well. . . . It is obvious that mine is not a heartfelt conviction, for I know my evil inclination.)[11]

Though a tirade against such decisions and against such persons of that resolve in the clergy follows Guzmán's resolution to seek safety and comfort in the religious life, he nevertheless enters into the endeavor with practical and selfish motivations. But for his sudden falling in love—which, along with his studies and religious environment, is also suggestive of his link to melancholia—we are asked to believe that he would have completed his studies and taken orders. At this declared important juncture in his life, Guzmán is thus, like Lázaro, in contact with several major elements of melancholic depictions that he himself embodies.

The satirization by and of malcontent figures often, and not surprisingly, involves charges of religious heresy in England, where the satirists' accusations of melancholy malcontentedness could, depending on the point of view, be aimed at Catholics and Puritans alike.[12] Lyons, who also notes the association between the malcontent and "extremes of religious opinion,"[13] considers as part of this context a quotation from *The Metamorphosis of Ajax* (1596) by Sir John Harington. In it the author describes a dreamed episode during which he distinguishes between malcontented political disaffection based on religious affiliation and legitimate discontentedness.[14] Drawing a conclusion from this

10. Mateo Alemán, *Segunda parte de la vida de Guzmán de Alfarache: Atalaya de la vida humana*, ed. Benito Brancaforte, 361-62.
11. Ibid., 364.
12. Babb, *Elizabethan Malady*, 82.
13. Lyons, *Voices of Melancholy*, 18.
14. The passage referred to is from Sir John Harington, *A New Discourse on a Stale Subject Called The Metamorphosis of Ajax*, ed. Elizabeth Story Donno, 250-51.

passage that as well has implications for both the importance of purity of blood and a legitimate standing as a *cristiano nuevo* (newly converted Christian) in the picaresque genre, Lyons explains:

> a malcontent was defined not only by his own activities and attitudes, but also by the degree of rigour with which his society demanded conformity, and the extent to which self-serving individuals were willing to aggravate fears of dissent. The more exacting criteria of political obedience against which the malcontent's activities came to be measured now included religious conformity, and therefore a more deep-rooted attitude towards life than had hitherto been involved in political obedience.[15]

A distinctive element in *Guzmán de Alfarache,* then, is the spurious religious connection to the renegade Christian background of his, notably, Italian father. The abuse suffered by Guzmán in his attempts to make a show of honorable demeanor, if not rightfully to lay claim to it, are connected to his dishonorable origin and questionable religious background. He is never able to overcome these obstacles.

Familial shame and social ostracism because of contact with heretics such as Zaide in *Lazarillo de Tormes* or tainted blood and illicit practices as in the case of Buscón's mother ("Sospechábase en el pueblo que no era cristiana vieja" [It was suspected among the people that she was not of an all-Christian family])[16] are a typical ingredient in the canonical picaresque works and reinforce the association between melancholy and improper religious beliefs or activities. In general, the *pícaro*'s continual struggle to surpass his or her marginalization is yet further evidence of the prevalent Spanish Golden Age position with regard to the highly active secular intellect. The three aforementioned *pícaros,* whose literary undertakings are premised on a contemplative mental effort to convince others through their writing, never find an appropriate place in society and degenerate further, both morally and socially, because of deeds subsequent to the accident of a more or less humble birth. These deeds are scrutinized by means of the supposed process of autobiographical authorship that is, in the context of melancholy malcontentedness, as much message as it is medium because of its self-conscious quality.

English critics likewise attribute to certain malcontents a somewhat more sympathetic role as caustic philosopher who gives opinions forthrightly. Though often surly and satirical, "he has sufficient cause for his melancholy . . . having been disappointed, disillusioned, embittered. His case elicits sympathy, for his quarrel with the world is a just quarrel."[17] One need think only of

---

15. *Voices of Melancholy,* 18.
16. Francisco Quevedo, *La vida del Buscón llamado Don Pablos,* Domingo Ynduráin, ed., 83.
17. Babb, *Elizabethan Malady,* 92.

such obvious episodes in the picaresque novels as the reported delight of the crowd over Lazarillo's punishment at the hands of the blindman, the mistreatment of Guzmán de Alfarache when he is apprehended for crimes he has not committed on three occasions, or the saliva-covered Buscón at Alcalá in order to understand that the Spanish rogue frequently offers a self-portrayal as the embodiment of the justification for such feelings of persecution.

Barbara L. Ostwald also locates the malcontent clearly within the tradition of the figure of the cynic philosopher, which the Renaissance inherited from the classics and developed through confused legends and philosophy that blend the personality and the historical importance of Diogenes the Cynic with Diogenes Laertius, who wrote about him and many other philosophers. The composite Diogenes came to be thought of most commonly as "a corrector of manners and morals, a voice against the vices of the time, and thus a measure of them." Ostwald continues: "Since he was known for his scathing wit and personal oddities, he appeared in jest books and collections of witticisms. . . . his wit appeared largely in cruel vituperation and his oddities in flouting conventional decencies."[18] Alban K. Forcione, moreover, places Guzmán along with Cervantes's Licenciado Vidriera among the cynics of Spanish literature and calls attention to the sixteenth- and seventeenth-century association "of the Cynic and the picaresque railer." He likewise notes Boileau's desire to write a "vie de Diogène le Cynique" against a standard set by *Lazarillo de Tormes* and *Guzmán de Alfarache*.[19] Again the victimization that the young *pícaros* often endure and the general societal corruption they describe is pertinent to this context, though our source of information in the pseudo-autobiographical texts is ever to be questioned. Conversely, as Fink points out of the malcontent character: "He has lived a licentious life abroad and has picked up the characteristic vices of all nations. He is so corrupted that he sees even nature as tainted. . . . He rails at the abuses of the world when he is himself thoroughly polluted."[20]

The importance of travel to *pícaros* is obvious as they move through their course of adventures, and, in Guzmán de Alfarache's case, travel to Italy is a pivotal element in his development. In the last chapter of part 1, in fact, at the midpoint of his sojourn in Italy and after his dismissal from the cardinal's service, he remarks: "Entranse los vicios callando, son lima sorda, no se sienten hasta tener al hombre perdido. Son tan fáciles de recibir, cuanto dificultosos de dejar" (Vices enter quietly, they are a noiseless rasp, they are not felt until the man is lost. They are as easily received as they are difficult to

18. "Fool and Malcontent: The Dramatic Function of the Licensed Commentator in Elizabethan Drama," 81. See also Ronald Paulson, "The Fool-Knave Relation in Picaresque Satire."
19. Alban K. Forcione, *Cervantes and the Humanist Vision*, 293; 293 n. 133. See also 292 n. 32.
20. Fink, "Malcontent Traveler," 245.

leave behind).[21] The captain whom he serves during the journey to Italy does utilize him as well in the capacity of tool-villain for a series of swindles, the principle one involving the *platero* (silversmith) and the sculpture of the agnus dei. The captain's subsequent rejection of Guzmán, however, is indicative of the treatment the latter constantly endures. The officer himself seems almost to articulate the epistemological response of the Golden Age authors to their melancholy characters, for he fears Guzmán's cunning: "Hallábase bien con mis travesuras, temíase dellas y de mí. Con este rescoldo pasó hasta Génova, donde, habiendo desembarcado y teniendo de mi servicio poca necesidad, me dio cantonada" (He liked my pranks, but he feared them and me. With this doubt he journeyed to Genoa, where, having disembarked and not really needing my services, he abandoned me). Left, in melancholy fashion, with very little money ("Dióme algunas monedas de poco valor y unos reales españoles, todo miseria, con que me fui de con él" [He gave me some coins of little worth and some Spanish coins, a mere pittance, with which I took my leave of him]; 361), Guzmán strikes a pose of malcontentedness which he describes in the following terms as he enters Italy:

Iba la cabeza baja, considerando por la calle la fuerza de la virtud, que a ninguno dejó sin premio ni se escapó del vicio sin castigo y vituperio. Quisiera entonces decir a mi amo lo en que por él me había puesto, las necesidades que le había socorrido, de los trabajos que le había sacado y tan a mi costa todo; mas consideré que de lo mismo me hacía cargo, apartándome por ello de sí como a miembro cancerado. Viendo mi desgracia y creyendo hallar allí mi parentela, me dio por todo poco. Fuíme por la ciudad, tomando lengua, que ni entendía ni sabía, con deseo de conocer y ser conocido. (361)

(I went with head bowed, along the street thinking about the force of virtue, which left no one without reward nor, having escaped from vice, without punishment and vituperation. Then I wanted to tell my master what I had gone through because of him, the needs I had helped him with, the toils I had saved him from and all at my own expense; but I figured that he had made me responsible for them, separating me for that reason from himself as if I were a cancerous member. Seeing misfortune and believing that I would find my relatives there, I considered all to be of little consequence. I went through the city, acquiring the language, for I neither understood nor knew it, with a desire to become acquainted and to be known.)

Isolated linguistically and emotionally, a foreigner in a strange place, and feeling unappreciated, abused, and unknown, Guzmán begins the next chapter with one of his numerous digressions. This one is, significantly, on poverty and

21. Mateo Alemán, *Primera parte de Guzmán de Alfarache,* ed. Benito Brancaforte, 452–53. Subsequent references are to this edition and are cited in the text.

contains overtly stated malcontent sentiments such as "el discreto pobre viene a morir comido de necios" (the prudent poor man dies devoured by fools [366]).

The travel of the *pícaro,* like that of many malcontent characters of the Renaissance, is additionally important as a component of corruption with regard to negative intellectual development. With his or her cunning, such a figure contributes to the Renaissance fascination with variations of the pilgrimage of knowledge. Movement without moral motivation or growth is a target for condemnation in that period, and Forcione convincingly argues that Cervantes's mad Licenciado is one of the many figures whose depiction reveals the temptation of forbidden knowledge and the illicit nature of obsessive and idle curiosity.[22] The *pícaro,* especially one like Guzmán, likewise fits such a pattern; he leaves home in part because "[a]lentábame mucho el deseo de ver mundo" (the desire to see the world inspired me greatly [143]). From the novel's early pages, moreover, he is clearly identified as an idle character, "aprovechándose del ocioso de la galera" (taking advantage of the idle life of the galley ship [89]) and an "hijo del ocio" (child of idleness [90]).

Alemán, in fact, begins his work with prefatory material that ostensibly is for the benefit of the reader's comprehension but that, like so much of his and other picaresque narrations, doubles back upon itself. The fictional *pícaro* Guzmán is the vehicle of intellect through which the minds of reader and author participate in an examination, among other things, of the very thought process that they simultaneously engage in and question. Alemán declares to his reader: "En el discurso, podrás moralizar, según se te ofreciere; larga margen te queda. Lo que hallares no grave ni compuesto, eso es el ser de un pícaro, el sujeto deste libro" (In the treatise, you can moralize, as you may see fit; you have great leeway. Whatever you may find neither serious nor well composed, that is the being of a rogue, the subject of this book[87]). Guzmán and the other *pícaros* reveal their society's intuitive rejection of an intellectual system that values the "reasoning practice," for never being comfortably absorbed or reconciled at any level, these figures embody the unacceptable quality assigned the overly active melancholy mind. The sense of difference articulated through the thoughts of such a character emerges as a negative element that is nevertheless transvalued by virtue of the fact that as each text progresses, the distance between the *pícaro* and his neighbors is understood to diminish. Even though Guzmán, for example, openly acknowledges the hierarchies of society, in particular during the last episodes that relate his experience on the galley ship,[23] he nevertheless does not content himself, any more than his picaresque counterparts, with occupying

22. *Humanist Vision,* 233.
23. See Johnson, *Inside Guzmán,* 147–50.

his assigned place in that hierarchy. His is a self-conscious manipulative view of such a social and intellectual structure and yet he vainly tries to become part of it.

The emerging epistemological system that celebrates a "reasoning practice upon the world" is thus enacted by the *pícaro* and represented by his failures. The alternative reaffirmation of the "discursive exchange within the world," however, brings us to a view of society's disintegration because of its collective corruption. The malcontent posture—superior in its heightened awareness of its powers but devalued by society because of its minoritarian position— is developed in a text that is the object of its own discourse. As Anthony Zahareas, among others, points out: "Una novela picaresca es un autorretrato de doble perspectiva: recuerda *ahora* la historia pasada como narrador, habiéndola protagonizado *antes* como pícaro" (A picaresque novel is a self-portrait of double perspective: as narrator, it recalls past history *now,* having performed it *before* as rogue).[24] The *pícaro* is ever careful to blame his mischief on the influence of the world, a technique also self-consciously utilized by the English author Marston in his more sympathetic treatment of the melancholy satirist "as one whose imbalance is a reflection of the world's illness."[25] The *pícaro* capitalizes on such a characteristic and ultimately satirizes and subverts it for his own use in order to manipulate his reader.

What is intriguing is that even though malcontentedness may not be a separate topic of investigation by the doctors and scientists, in several cases the expository works on melancholy also demonstrate the same degree of contrivance in terms of melancholy serving as both the subject and the medium of expression. Lyons, for example, has shown that Burton's significant achievement is better understood when his reader recognizes the *Anatomy* "as a work of literature [that portrays] the melancholy mind in action, even while it is occupied with melancholy as a formal subject." She further contends that the "chief manifestation . . . of the malcontent spirit in the *Anatomy* is in the character of Burton himself as he projects it in his work."[26] Burton communicates to his reader by means of a mask, his self-portrait as "Democritus," a device "that will ensure freedom of speech, but which at the same time is meant to be seen as an extension and elaboration rather than a concealment of the personality beneath."[27] If this formal device is, as Lyons argues, "Burton's main

24. "El género picaresco y las autobiografías de criminales," in *La picaresca: orígenes, textos y estructuras,* ed. Manuel Criado de Val, 82.
25. Lyons, *Voices of Melancholy,* 67.
26. Ibid., 114, 120; see also Fish, *Self-Consuming Artifacts,* 303–52.
27. Lyons, *Voices of Melancholy,* 121; see Lawrence Babb, *Sanity in Bedlam,* 36–37.

debt to the dramatic malcontent literature," then the implications of such a narrative tactic are worthy of consideration in connection with the picaresque novel and its innovative place within the malcontent tradition. This is a fictional form, moreover, that relies for its articulation upon the protagonist's identity as a solitary author whose writing proceeds from self-conscious contemplation. The *pícaro,* nevertheless, seems to occupy a place between Burton's openly declared self-portraiture and Erasmus's Folly, who speaks her author's mind while he remains outside the circle of characters.[28]

The Spanish rogue, however, depends upon the whole body of preceding literary and scientific notions about melancholy. The fact that the picaresque novel and the expository works often share a discourse of malcontentedness is also indicative of the still blurred lines of distinction between diverse forms of literature, the lack of distance between the medical writer and the raconteur.[29] In addition, despite what Lyons claims as Burton's originality in his literary techniques, conceits, and the metaphorization of melancholy for its articulation, there is evidence in works such as Velásquez's *Libro de la melancholia* that some of Burton's Spanish predecessors had already fused process and product in their texts on melancholy. Furthermore, the self-conscious discourse of the malcontent in these works provides an intriguing link between the novel as an artistic literary form that portrays a melancholic type and the scientific literature that purports to explain melancholy. In his prefatory remarks, Velásquez adopts a malcontent pose with regard to the need to defend himself against the "murmuradores" (gossips) who are ever present in society and ready to attack a diligent but unappreciated scholar like himself: "Si los que han escripto benigno y discreto lector, uvieran tenido atencion, a las contradiciones que cada dia nacen de los malevolos animos y los detractores: nunca las ciencias ovieran llegado a la perfection y cumbre en que ahora estan" (If, kind and wise reader, those who have written, had paid attention, to the contradictions that are born every day from malicious minds and detractors: knowledge would never have reached the perfection and height in which it is now found).[30] Allusions to his efforts to reach "un buen puerto" (a good port) also cannot help but remind his reader of Lazarillo's goal and what seems to be an acknowledgment of shared framing devices between a then new form of fictional prose (that in the year of the publication of Velásquez's *Libro*—1585—was still a unique, though popular,

---

28. See Lyons, *Voices of Melancholy,* 121–22; George A. Shipley, "The Critic as Witness for the Prosecution: Resting the Case Against Lázaro de Tormes," in *Creation and Re-creation: Experiments in Literary Form in Early Modern Spain,* ed. Ramond E. Surtz and Nora Weinerth, 123.
29. See Lyons, *Voices of Melancholy,* 125.
30. *Libro de la melancholia,* fol. 8.

phenomenon) and the self-conscious non-fictional treatise. The picaresque genre is thus imbued with the malcontent spirit—itself a self-conscious medium for contemplation for the melancholic turned even further inward—which also often informs the medical texts on melancholy.

The imperfect separation between the author and the narrator/protagonist-subject matter in a text premised on and about malcontentedness is a device readily useful to an author in a controlled environment like Spain in the sixteenth and seventeenth centuries. Without invoking authorial intention, it is worth considering that the charges of being a *converso* (convert) were not taken lightly in post-Tridentine Spain, and the convergence in this regard of the two *conversos,* Alemán/author and Guzmán/literary creation, is surely no accident when the frame of the novel's text is a form of melancholy so clearly connected to those holding religious beliefs considered spurious by a collective society. The silence of Lázaro's unnamed author is, as Shipley argues, suggestive of the need to contend with the difference between "what the author is capable of saying (because he is a great artist) [but] deems necessary and urgent to say (because he is an anxious citizen) and . . . what the community in general and the powerful in particular will tolerate and reward."[31] If, as Ruth El Saffar contends, the apparently insane Licenciado Vidriera is Cervantes's surreptitious mouthpiece for societal criticism, then the possibility exists that the use of the then acceptable though recent convention of the malcontent figure was useful in the same way for Lazarillo's anonymous creator, and for Mateo Alemán, López de Ubeda, Quevedo, and other authors of picaresque works who could use their disreputable scoundrels as a buffer between themselves and the censorship to which they were ever vulnerable.[32]

In addition, Alemán's prologues anticipate Burton's, entitled "Democritus to the Reader," in which the English author makes use of numerous devices that his contemporaries Jonson and Marston incorporate into the satire of their dramas. These include not only the critical railing by the author, who also makes great show of defending himself against attackers, but also the melancholic self-effacement—all of which combine to produce a satiric position of aggressive and defensive rhetoric aimed at the reader.[33] Stanley Fish's reading of Burton's *Anatomy* leads him to a conclusion that has implications for Alemán's text as well: "To a great extent the preface (and finally the whole of the

31. "The Critic as Witness for the Prosecution," 122; see also Stephen Gilman, "The Death of *Lazarillo de Tormes,*" 151.
32. El Saffar, *Novel to Romance: A Study of Cervantes's "Novelas ejemplares",* 55. See also Fink, "Malcontent Traveler," 251, on a related idea.
33. Lyons, *Voices of Melancholy,* 117-18.

Anatomy) is a series of false promises which alternately discomfort the reader and lead him on."[34] This technique, traced by Lyons and Fish, produces the satirical about-faces in the narration of Burton's preface and leads, for example, from addresses to "Gentle Reader" through unfulfilled narrational assertions and on to subversion of declared discursive intention and open hostility directed to the reader in statements like: "If any man take exceptions, let him turn the buckle of his girdle, I care not. I owe thee [the reader] nothing, I look for no favour at thy hands, I am independent, I fear not." There are also declarations of total humility and finally concluding sentences that declare: "I presume of thy good favour and gracious acceptance [gentle reader]. Out of an assured hope and confidence therof, I will begin."[35]

Alemán accomplishes similar goals by means of his characters' and his own narrational inconsistencies. The two prefaces to part 1 are, respectively, addressed to the "enemigo vulgo" (common enemy) and the "discreto lector" (wise reader). To the first Alemán directs such questions as "¿Cuán mordaz, envidioso y avariento eres?" (How scathing, envious and greedy are you?); "¿Cuál atriaca miran tus ojos, que como basilisco no emponzoñes?" (How much like the fire-producing stone do your eyes look, that you poison like the basilisk?); "¿Qué inocencia no persigues?" (What innocence do you not persecute? [82]). His attitude is later one of abjection in the second prologue and he refers to his "rudo ingenio y cortos estudios" (crude wit and scant studies) yet also claims "mucho escogí de doctos varones y santos" (I selected much from the saintly and scholarly men). Guzmán does no less. A passage in part 1 exemplifies his ploy to undermine the reader's complacency, and, like the malcontent voice of Burton's *Anatomy,* the *pícaro* changes direction several times within the space of a few sentences. After one of his many digressions, Guzmán ostensibly presents his reader with a thought that is not his own, saying: "Aquí se acaba de apear un pensamiento" (Here a thought has just put foot to ground). Immediately he then declares, "Véndolo por mío . . . Dirélo, por haberme parecido digno de mejor padre" (Passing it off as mine . . . I will say it, for having seemed worthy of a better father), thereby accepting responsibility for the notions expressed. The reader, he implies, has the freedom to judge the worth of these words: "tú lo dispón y compón según te pareciere, enmendando las faltas" (dispose of it or compose it as you see fit, correcting the faults). The reader is thus an integral part of the communication process, and the *pícaro* then proceeds with proverbial sayings before humbling himself ("Ya sabes mis

34. *Self-Consuming Artifacts,* 304.
35. *Anatomy of Melancholy,* 77, 78.

flaquezas" [You already know my weaknesses]) as well as defending himself
("Quiero que sepas que con todas ellas nunca perdí día de rezar el rosario
entero, con otras devociones" [I want you to know that with everything, I never
missed a day praying the entire rosary, along with other devotions]; 271). There
follows an unanticipated attack against the very reader to whom he has just
deferred: "y aunque te oigo murmurar que es muy de ladrones y rufianes no
soltar [el rosario] de la mano, fingiéndose devotos de Nuestra Señora; piensa y
di lo que quisieres como se te antojare, que no quiero contigo acreditarme"
(and although I hear you mutter that it is typical of thieves and ruffians not to let
[the rosary] out of their hands, pretending to be devout to the Virgin; think and
then say what you wish as it pleases you, for I do not wish to justify myself with
you).[36] These rhetorical vacillations precede Burton's exaggerated satiric narrational posture by some twenty years.

The difficulty in defining the picaresque is an enduring critical problem, but
an examination of the attributes of malcontentedness within the canonical
works of this genre reveals an additional dimension to the responsive antag-
onism each articulates to its predecessors. *Guzmán de Alfarache* is often held as
the standard for the picaresque label and is replete with elements that also
reveal its paradigmatic quality within the corpus of literature on melancholy
and the tradition of malcontentedness. Significantly, early in the "Libro primero" (first book) of the novel's "Primera Parte" (first part), Guzmán recounts the
mythological replacement of the god Contento (Happiness) by Descontento
(Unhappiness) on earth because of humanity's inobedience and complete
absorption in worshipping the former. By decree of the neglected god Jupiter
and through the good offices of Mercury, Contento was brought back to heaven
and Descontento was "metido en su lugar y propias vestiduras, del modo que el
Contento estaba . . . con que los hombres quedaron gustosos y engañados,
creyendo haber salido con su intento, teniendo a su dios consigo. Y no fue lo
que pensaron" (put in his place and in his very clothes, in the same way that
Contento was . . . so men remained happy and deceived, believing that they
had gotten their way, having their god with them. And it was not as they
thought [189]). Guzmán insists, moreover, that "este yerro vive desde aquellos
pasados tiempos, llegando con el mismo engaño hasta el siglo presente" (this
error has existed since those past times, having come with the same deceit to this
very century).[37]

---

36. *Primera parte*, 271–72; see also Johnson's reading of this section, *Inside Guzmán*, 49–53,
and Arias, *Unrepentant Narrator*, 26–27.
37. *Primera parte*, 189. The frontispiece to the first edition of *La pícara Justina*, which pictures
numerous figures inside "La nave de la vida picaresca" (The ship of the picaresque life) sailing on

Several elements at work in this chapter of the novel draw Guzmán firmly into the circle of the malcontents. The most obvious is the term *descontento,* which, as Guzmán argues, is ever present on earth: "Ajeno vives de la verdad, si creyeras otra cosa o la imaginas" (You live far from the truth, if you believe or imagine any other thing [189]). In addition, the emphasis on the outward deceptive quality of Descontento's disguise ("Donde creíste que el contento estaba, no fue más del vestido y el descontento en él" [Where you believed happiness was, it was nothing more than the clothing inside of which was unhappiness]; 190) is in keeping with the tradition of the dichotomy of outer and inner qualities of the malcontent figure as a participant in the vogue of melancholy. This is a component that Ostwald insists in her exposition of the malcontent is a literary type with great value as an agent of satire because of the dual nature of his or her representation—the "important split between a public pose of honest simplicity or righteous indignation and a private bent toward arrogance, sensationalism, and prurience."[38] Recent critical assessments of what was once taken by modern scholars to be Lazarillo's innocence and Christian charity in the episode of his service to the impoverished squire have demonstrated that the description of the child's offerings of food "stresses the meanness of the interaction, not the giving," for he needlessly delays sharing with the squire the food he has begged. Lazarillo's provisional skills in Toledo are moreover based on his ability to play the role of sickliness or piety in order to beg the bread and meat of which he eats the larger portion before bringing home the remaining scraps to dole out to his *amo* (master).[39]

In the latter half of the chapter in which Guzmán digresses on Contento and Descontento, it is not surprising to find in his words and portrayal evidence of

---

the "Río del olvido" (River of forgetfulness) (the latter recalling the notion about problems with the memorative faculty in a melancholic brain), also interprets Guzman's character as belonging to the tradition of melancholy and melancholy malcontentedness. The ship is steered, for instance, by Tiempo with his Saturnian overtones as a version of Kronos/Chronos (Lyons, *Voices of Melancholy,* 4). His oar bears the inscription "llevolos sin sentir" (I carry them without their feeling it) thus reinforcing the elements of time's relentless passage toward old age and death. Indeed, he rows the ship toward the "Puerto de la Muerte" (Port of Death), where the mirror of "Desengaño" is exhibited. Guzmán himself is present in the vessel and labeled "Pobre y contento" (Poor and content,) a reference which, of course, is mockingly deceptive if the observer knows anything of Guzmán's desire to overcome his penury, declared in moments of economic distress throughout the novel. He is, after all, ultimately sentenced to the galley for stealing from his last employer. The label satirizes the standard association between poverty and melancholy and thus is strongly suggestive of Guzmán's pronouncements about the falseness of an exterior appearance of "contento" which, he explains in his digression, is really earthly Descontento.

38. "Fool and Malcontent," 86.

39. "The Critic as Witness for the Prosecution," 113; Alan Deyermond, *Lazarillo de Tormes: A Critical Guide,* 69; see also L. J. Woodward, "Author-Reader Relationship in the *Lazarillo de Tormes*," and Frank Durand, "The Author and Lázaro: Levels of Comic Meaning."

just such metatheatrical behavior. Claiming on the one hand, "Hice como muchacho simple, sin entendimiento ni gobierno" (I pretended to be an innocent boy, without understanding or control [191]) in seeming acknowledgment of the affectation of his public pose, he recounts one of the moments when he is unjustly accused of a crime. Though innocent of the theft of some jewelry, he and a muleteer are verbally and physically abused by the authorities who want to recover the goods and punish the criminals. The "public pose" of "righteous indignation" is struck with justification, but Guzmán also reveals his less sympathetic private self when he describes, in terms that emphasize the outer and inner effects of the experience upon him, his delight over the harsher punishment meted out to his companion: "Y aunque mucho me dolía, mucho me alegraba entre mí, porque daban al compañero más y más recio al doble" (And although it pained me greatly, I was privately very glad, because they gave my companion doubly harsh treatment [192–93]).

For Guzmán, the inner/outer discrepancy initially seems to emphasize a somewhat different message, for he insists on the vanity of worldly pleasure compared with the eternal pleasure of life after death ("¿Ves ya cómo en la tierra no hay contento y que está el verdadero en el cielo?" [Do you see how on earth there is no happiness and that true happiness is in heaven?]; 190). His railing is in keeping with the philosophizing and moralizing tendencies of the malcontent in the role as cynic, and this tone of malcontent complaining is doubly important. While we are warned about the disappointments lurking for all humans behind the surface appearance of the world, we receive this caveat from a literary figure who throughout his narration affirms his own reliance upon the art of engaño (illusion) and his belief in role-playing, dressing for a part, and a whole list of deceptions based on clothing, disguise, and/or visual illusions. Guzmán, though, assumes his role as cynic moralizer just as he does any other part, and his theatrics enhance his association with Diogenes and his philosophical school. Forcione explains, in fact, that the Cynics "are obsessed with the vision of life in civilization as theatrical performance, in which the authentic being of the actor is consumed by his role, and they would constantly remind the ignorant that they are in fact possessed, indeed enslaved, by what they desire to possess, be it honor, success, wealth, material goods, or pleasure."[40]

Lázaro's disgust with the "negra honra" (damned honor) that motivates the penniless but affected hidalgo rings true in such a characterization, but the pícaro exposes society's foibles while trying always to become part of the collective through a willingness to adopt whatever corruptions necessary to

40. *Humanist Vision*, 247.

attain that end. Lázaro eventually ends his account with the seventh installment that articulates his own concerns with wealth, material goods, success, and social position—all parodied in the *menage à trois* with which he contents himself. Though Forcione likewise considers Guzmán to be the most outstanding "Cynic of Spanish literature,"[41] he judges him to be repentant, a quality unsupported by the figure's unreliable and contradictory claims and his highly materialistic interest in even his most so-called spiritual undertaking, his preparation to take holy orders. Like Lázaro and the *pícaros* in general, Guzmán transvalues the Cynics' railings, insistence on simplicity, and demasking abilities by adopting that pose as a mask itself, and he goes so far as to perform overtly as the court buffoon for the French ambassador.[42] Ulrich Wicks calls attention to the histrionics typical of the *pícaro:* "The *pícaro* is a Protean figure who can not only serve many masters but play different roles . . . metamorphoses and changing of roles are part of the *pícaro*'s survival kit—as the world is in flux, so he can change roles to face it. Picaresque life is a constant change of masks on the world-as-stage."[43]

Further underscoring the changeability of the *pícaro*'s life is a pervasive melancholic symbolism that involves the *pícaro*'s direct contact with the sea. The subtitle of Guzmán's pseudo-autobiography, *Atalaya de la vida humana* (Watchtower of human life), alludes to a watchtower from which a caller "denuncia a gritos lo que pasa en aquellos alrededores" (announces shouting what happens in those environs).[44] The word *atalaya* also names the edifice well-known to seafarers, a pillar built to delineate the edge of land and useful for the individual in the water, whether skillful navigator or victim of shipwreck. Guzmán moreover begins his narration with a sentence that includes the following address to the reader: "El deseo que tenía—curioso lector—de contarte mi vida, me daba tanta priesa para engolfarte en ella" (The desire that I had—curious reader—to tell you my life, urged me to plunge you into it [99]). The word "engolfar" carries with it more than one meaning, as the *Diccionario de Autoridades* reveals. The primary definition is: "Entrar la náo, embarcacion o baxél mui adentro del mar, apartandose tanto de las costas y de la tierra, que no se divise, y solo se vea de ordinario agua y cielo" (The ship, craft or vessel

41. Ibid., 248.
42. "The Critic as Witness for the Prosecution," iii.
43. "The Nature of Picaresque Narrative: A Modal Approach," 245-47; see also Hortensia Morell, "La deformación picaresca del mundo ideal en 'Ozmín y Daraja' del *Guzmán de Alfarache*," 116-17; Bruce Wardropper, "The Implications of Hypocrisy in the *Lazarillo de Tormes*," in *Studies in Honor of Everett W. Hesse,* ed. William C. McCrary and José A. Madrigal, 179-80; Ostward, "Fool and Malcontent," 13.
44. Carroll B. Johnson, "Mateo Alemán y sus fuentes literarias."

goes far out to sea, separating itself such a distance from the coasts and from land, so that it is not even seen, and ordinarily one sees only water and sky). This meaning is further clarified by means of a quotation from chapter 4 of Antonio de Guevara's *Arte de marear:* "La navegacion de la galera es algo segura quando costéa, mas quando 'engolfa' es mui peligrosa" (The navigation of a galley is somewhat safe when it sails along the coast, but when it "loses sight of land" it is very dangerous).[45] This connotation communicates the literal risk of venturing out to sea a great distance from shore as well as an inherent reference to the figurative danger Saturn's influence poses to melancholics.

A secondary meaning of *engolfar* is its usage as a reflexive verb that carries with it an obvious connection to melancholy contemplation and the mental games and literary undertaking of the *pícaro*'s autobiographical project: "Vale tambien por translacion dexarse llevar de la imaginacion, pensamiento y afectos, abstrahiendose y elevandose: como les acontece a los Santos en sus fervorosas meditaciones y Oracion: y tambien a los que se embeben y transportan en algun discurso, leccion o estúdio" (It also means metaphorically to let oneself be carried away by imagination, thought and emotions, being lost in thought and going into a rapture: as happens to the Saints in their fervent meditations and Prayer: and also to those who become engrossed and carried away with some treatise, lesson or study). It is not difficult to make the connection to melancholic secular and religious thinkers whose scholarship and thought can be detrimental.

Guzmán effectively affirms his own place in the sea, both figuratively and literally, for he is a malcontent prisoner on a galley ship during the entire narration of the novel. Even at the end of part 2, though liberated from his chains, he is still at sea and waiting indefinitely until he will be again on land (earth, of course, is also Saturn's element). The desire expressed in the novel's first sentence to "engolfarte" carries both a sarcastic accusation toward the reader, who by implication belongs with Guzmán on the sea with all its melancholy ramifications, and the irony that surrounds Guzmán and the judgments made by one on melancholy Saturn's domain. Literally at sea, he is figuratively unable to disassociate himself from what he rails against. Johnson's considerations of Guzmán's efforts to absolve "his own individual evil conduct by absorbing it into the collective" reiterate Maurice Molho's observation that Guzmán "a une âme, identique à toutes" (has a soul identical to all).[46] Such comments, however, reveal that Guzmán/narrator has been successful in communicating the

45. *Diccionario de Autoridades,* 471.
46. Johnson, *Inside Guzmán,* 14; Mohlo, *Les Romans picaresques espagnols,* lvii.

all-pervasive quality of melancholy that Burton propounds some twenty years later and that motivates the extensive amount of study of melancholy during the same period when so many picaresque novels were written.

In spite of the confidence Guzmán inspires in a number of Hispanists with regard to his final recantation of evil deeds and his profession of religious convictions and intent to mend his ways, other readers, including myself, question just how much one can believe of what Guzmán claims, either in the recitation of adventures, the accounts of society's abuse of him, or in the passages in which he professes his moral *desengaño*.[47] Johnson's assessment of the lack of difference between the ethical outlook of Guzmán as narrator and protagonist of the pseudo-autobiography leads to the conclusion that the "hypothesis—that Guzmán after the conversion is fundamentally different from Guzmán before the conversion—is untenable and must therefore be abandoned."[48] Such a judgment is even more defensible within the context of melancholy malcontentedness, for the self-conscious melancholy mind of the galley slave is the ostensible source of all we read, and what he describes is the series of exploits of a cunning malcontent villain.

That it is the older Guzmán who judges the motivations and actions of his younger self is significant but does not alter the lack of sincerity in his "final conversion." Describing himself as a self-serving student who pursued his holy vocation for purely practical reasons, so too Guzmán the galley slave with full hindsight of life claims to recant his sins, but reveals himself to be consistent in his untrustworthiness. In the final pages we learn of his mistreatment by other jealous galley slaves when he enjoys the easier conditions and the confidence of the captain and officials on board. He is so utterly alone and outside any organized level of society that even on the galley he is set further apart from his fellow prisoners, a fact he understands and laments after his severe punishment: "Y el mayor dolor, que sentí en aquel desastre, no tanto era el dolor que padecía ni ver el falso testimonio que se me levantaba; sino que juzgasen todos que de aquel castigo era merecedor y no se dolían de mí" (And the greatest distress that I felt in that disaster, was not so much the pain that I suffered nor seeing the false testimony that was raised against me; but rather that they all thought that that punishment was deserved and they did not feel sorry for me).[49] That he strives to keep his favored position is understandable in view of the prisoners' circumstances on the prison ship, but he expresses his strategy to do so in terms that reiterate his deceitful, contemplative, self-service: "mi cuidado era sólo atender

47. See Arias, *Unrepentant Narrator,* 4–9 for a discussion of the opposing views on this issue.
48. *Inside Guzmán,* 45.
49. *Segunda parte,* 474. Subsequent page references are cited in the text.

al servicio de mi amo, por serle agradable, pareciéndome que podría ser por él o por otro, con mi buen servicio, alcanzar algún tiempo libertad" (my concern was only to attend to my master, to be agreeable to him, for it seemed to me that it could be through him or through another, with my good service, that I could obtain my liberty some time [467]). When implicated by the other slaves in the earlier theft of his master's goods, Guzmán is further isolated from even those ranks of "society" which he could rightfully call his own.

Completely outside all facets of society, his alienation is more thoroughgoing than that of even the seditious, traitorous individual who plots to overthrow the established system, for Guzmán plots and successfully betrays the mutiny planned by the other criminally bent galley slaves. He reasons:

> hice mi consideración, y como siempre tuve propósito firme de no hacer cosa infame ni mala por ningún útil que della me pudiese resultar si les faltara en aquello, temiéndose de mí no los descubriese, me levantarían algún falso testimonio para salvarse a sí, diciendo que yo, por salir de tanta miseria, los tenía incitados a ellos. (478)

> (I thought about it, and as always I resolved firmly not to do anything terrible or bad in exchange for any benefit to myself, for if they failed in anything, then fearing that through me they would be discovered, they would concoct false charges against me in order to save themselves, saying that I, so as to escape from such misery, had incited them.)

Eventually set free from his chains and seemingly awaiting liberation from the ship after his act of informing, Guzmán nevertheless remains at the conclusion of the novel indefinitely aboard the vessel at sea, where he has written the text we read. Understood within the context of the *pícaro*'s melancholy malcontent-edness, the first sentence of the novel that declares Guzmán's desire to "engolfar" his audience serves as the first clue in a series of many with regard to that frame of reference that the last chapter completes. To draw the reader, and thus all of society, into the melancholy realm from which he practices his license to criticize, Guzmán does not set out to right the wrongs he witnesses and criticizes as was the wont of numerous literary malcontents and licensed com-mentators of then contemporary England. Instead, he seems to aim merely to assert his own rightful place within the society of his fellows by diminishing the moral and social distance between himself and them, or vice versa. In the process, he uses his mental acuity in a self-conscious way to present a text that will accomplish those ends by manipulating its readers into accepting his judg-ments. After all, like the literary audiences willing to listen to the entertaining outcast malcontents on stage, the sixteenth- and seventeenth-century readership of the picaresque works could with ease listen to or read the words of the criminal misfit who himself tells ridiculing stories at his own expense.

Though in general the literary malcontent evolved from a playacting mimic of melancholia to a figure more thoroughly imbued with melancholic antisocial and even criminal tendencies, that figure continued to maintain an affected quality in literary depiction. The *pícaro,* however, does not seem to fall victim to the shallow conventional quality that scholars identify in the English stage malcontent who displays at worst "adherence to a codified role" that reveals "very little of the man behind the role" or at best the "interaction between man and mask [which] finally becomes more important than the precise nature of either."[50] The *pícaro* is a more fully developed figure whose contradictions and ambiguities of portrayal never fully overshadow the qualities that make such a character a tantalizing and complex aspect of the dialectical tension over the power of the secular mind.

Even the social and political elements that Spencer connects to the appearance of malcontent characters in England and the general expressions there of dissatisfaction with humanity's condition in the late sixteenth century were not unlike those same phenomena in Spain. Among the problems mentioned are the campaign against Spain and its Armada (the verso of Spain's disaster) that culminated in a military victory but without economic benefit, and "the whole miserable mass of distress, crime and vagabondage that crowded the gallows, prisons, streets and highways of the time."[51] Harry Sieber likewise discusses important issues in the socio-historical context of the picaresque novel, including vagrancy, organized begging, increased crime, growing poverty, and unstable social conditions. He concludes:

> The emphasis of the picaresque on poverty, delinquency, "upward mobility" (self-improvement of the *pícaro*), travel as an escape from despair, social satire of a system unresponsive to the needs and desires of a growing active community of "have-nots," all reflect the socio-historical contexts. . . . The "literature of roguery" has always been of interest to literate society but it reached the proportion of an international obsession precisely at the end of the sixteenth century.[52]

The social elements Sieber lists are the same ones included in the socio-historical and literary contexts of the malcontent, and the period of time referred to is, of course, the precise period when the texts on melancholy were published in

50. Ostwald, "Fool and Malcontent," 13.
51. Spencer, "The Elizabethan Malcontent," 534.
52. Harry Sieber, *Language and Society in "La vida de Lazarillo de Tormes,"* 9.

many nations and when the picaresque novel flourished at home in Spain and in translations in numerous European languages.

The international obsession with this figure thus coincides with the extensive literary use and interest in melancholy in general. As is the case in England, no single malcontent type can be held up as standard in Spain's literature of the period, for present in the various portrayals are such factors as travel to Italy, exposure to neoplatonic views on melancholy, the desire for recognition of genuine or pretended intelligence and importance, debauchery through exposure to vice, needs imposed by hunger, isolation from society's mainstream, and bitter pronouncements against the ills and abuses of contemporary society through satirical means, often with the ironic overtones of self-censure. Above all, whether a feigned or a bona fide melancholic, the *pícaro* as a manifestation of the malcontent is presented with identifiable trappings and symbolism of the humoral condition. Thus a *pícaro* like Guzmán who participates in the literary and cultural phenomenon of melancholy malcontentedness likewise shares many of the above melancholic traits with his more narrowly conventional English and Continental counterparts.[53]

The *pícaro* and his or her text can and should be categorized as a more fully human treatment of the malcontent melancholic, coeval with the depictions of the figure elsewhere in Europe that have come to be thought of as conventional. There are many points of reference between the *pícaro* and other manifestations of the malcontent whose popularity as a literary figure in the late sixteenth and early seventeenth centuries can help explain why the picaresque novel also found such an enthusiastic audience outside of Spain. In general, the *pícaro* is a poser and appreciates him- or herself more than society does. This figure's wit is a weapon in the battle for social and economic betterment, but whatever success is attained is short-lived or nonexistent in spite of efforts to end his or her marginalization and ascend the social hierarchy to a station more suited to self-perceived worth and talent. Society, as the *pícaro*/narrator presents it, does not accept his claims of superiority, and so society and the narrator become mutual targets of complaints and scorn in a dialectical tension that proceeds as a discourse from the mind of the malcontent pseudo-autobiographer and affirms the transvaluation of melancholy. The brilliance of the *pícaros* is often acknowledged, and often feared, by those whom they serve (for example, the unscrupulous priest in Tratado II of *Lazarillo de Tormes* or the captain in part 2, book 2, chapter 10 of *Guzmán de Alfarache*), but always it must be remembered that what is presented in the text is a product of the intellectual

53. See Babb, *Elizabethan Malady*, 73–101, and Lyons, *Voices of Melancholy*, 17–20.

activity of a self-serving mind that manipulates the reader. The undertaking is entirely a mental one.

It is an undertaking imbued with overtones of melancholy, and the scholarly effort to write an account of one's life is in itself a component of the melancholy framework incorporated into the Spanish picaresque tradition. The text produced nevertheless is one that reveals the suspect nature of the narrator/protagonist along with the suspicious nature of the whole of society. Guzmán wishes to *engolfar* his reader, and indeed, in a sense all the manipulative *pícaros* do ensnare their audiences in their circle of malcontentedness, for the transvaluation accomplished with regard to the *pícaro*'s melancholy wit and criminality brings about a redefinition of the values and the worth of a society that may victimize or promote such a figure. The ostensible trajectory of the *pícaros* is to show their superiority and the appropriateness of a higher station in life. What such characters accomplish by means of a malcontented discourse is to dissolve the distance between themselves and others but in such a way that the rest of society is judged to be no better than the scoundrel of questionable background. This vision, too, is in keeping with the articulation of malcontentedness, for Burton's proclamation—"all the world is mad, that is melancholy"—is found in his own malcontent text.[54]

I suggest, therefore, that the depiction of what was known elsewhere in Europe, particularly in England, as a malcontent figure is more fully developed in the portrayal of the cerebral *pícaro*. Babb, for instance, insists:

> The various specimens of the primary malcontent type do not, of course, agree with one another in every detail, and one detects subspecies within the species. But the main features are clear enough: surly preoccupation, taciturnity, and unsociability; folded arms and hat pulled low; negligent disorder in dress; sense of superiority; tendency to rail enviously at an unappreciative world; inclination toward treachery and sedition.[55]

A survey of the Elizabethan portrayal of the malcontent indeed reveals for the Hispanist the context of melancholy that supersedes national boundaries to include numerous characters, among them the *pícaro*. Thus, it is not surprising to find that Nathaniel Field's verse pronouncements about the perversion of the malcontent's mental acuity brings to mind the Spanish rogue:

> Wit's a disease that fit employment wants;
> Therefore we see those happiest in best parts,

54. *Anatomy*, 202; see Babb, *Elizabethan Malady*, 37.
55. *Elizabethan Malady*, 83.

And fortunes under-born unto their merits,
Grow to a sullen envy, hate, and scorn
Of their superiors; and at last, like winds,
Break forth into rebellious civil wars
Or private treasons: none so apt for these
As melancholy wits, fetter'd with need.[56]

56. "A Woman is a Weathercock," in *A Select Collection of Old English Plays,* ed. Robert
Dodsley and W. Carew Hazlitt, 11:63.

5

The Melancholy Debate
The *Conceptista* / *Culteranista* Controversy (Góngora)

> Audaz mi pensamiento
> el cenit escaló . . .
> > *Luis de Góngora*
>
> (My audacious thought
> reached the zenith . . .)

The polemical tension generated between the poetic schools now known as *conceptismo* and *culteranismo* lies at the heart of the Renaissance intellectual currents that reshaped and re-evaluated medieval ideas and issues while also transforming the very mode of thinking and knowing. Melancholic personae and humoral symbolism in Spanish Golden Age poetry represent a further dialectical means of articulating the separation from the medieval social and intellectual order that is not only scrutinized in sixteenth- and seventeenth-century poetics but also informs aesthetic expression in Siglo de Oro Spain just as in other European nations. Whereas in the drama and prose of the period, the humoral melancholics think excessively and cease to function as part of the religious, social, and political whole, the association of melancholy with the brilliant and contemplative mind of the poet also provides an important but little studied dimension to Siglo de Oro poetics. Spanish poets like Lope de Vega and Quevedo, who value the traditional *concepto* (conceit) and its system of extended comparisons, are offended by what I will argue is the darker, more self-consciously melancholic, introspective, and disjointed discourse of Góngora. His poetry reveals a thought process that openly celebrates a departure from the more medieval conceptualization and, in fact, demonstrates his recognition of the efficacy of privileging the intellect.

The hypertrophic melancholy *entendimiento* is Góngora's self-proclaimed badge of distinction, which he actively proclaims in his poetics and his artistic expression. It is what sets him apart from his seventeenth-century detractors who, clinging to their efforts to reaffirm the older epistemology that is clearly in a state of transition in Europe, do laud Góngora as a great artist but rebuke him as an intellectual renegade, as a non-Christian, and as a poet who raises a non-Spanish voice. This debate should thus be understood as a paradigm of the crisis of the Renaissance epistemological model. Beyond the formalistic concerns of *conceptista* and *culterano* poetry are the important intellectual, social, and political issues of Spanish and European Renaissance culture that suggest the centrality of a solitary Góngora who approvingly portrays melancholy protagonists with a language and poetic structure completely new to Spain.

The *concepto* as it was understood in the Siglo de Oro is defined by Gracián as "un acto del entendimiento, que exprime la correspondencia que se halla entre los objetos" (an act of the intellect, that wrings out the correspondence that is found between objects).[1] Unlike some of the literary theorists of Golden Age Spain (for example, Luis Carballo), Gracián does not echo Huarte's stress on the connection between a creative imaginative faculty and poetic composition; rather, Gracián reiterates the classical notion of the faculties and the intellect's foremost role of interpreting information from the imaginative conduit of sensory information while depending on the storehouse of memory. Huarte's notions about the more active capabilities of the imagination, on the other hand, provide an important example of the transition and evolution in epistemology that was taking place in Europe. As Bundy argues, the classical and medieval theories of the imagination provide evidence that during those periods the imaginative faculty is understood and described as, at best, an instrument of the intellect but not a creative faculty.[2] The terms *imaginatio* and *phantasia,* which by the Middle Ages had become almost synonymous, likewise in that period did not imply an inventive capacity; and even in certain contexts where *phantasia* suggests greater creative freedom, it is also made clear that reliance on this faculty is likely to lead to errors in judgment. These theories of creativity insist on the connection between the imagination and sensory information, although mystic expositions about the imagination—deriving ultimately from the *Timaeus*—posit the power of both angels and demons to influence humans through the imaginative faculty. Bundy traces the evolution of the synthesis of the mystical and empirical views of the imagination through Bonaventure, Jerome, Cassiodorus, Maimonides, and Aquinas, contending that, in particular, the belief in diabolical influences upon the imagination "was to constitute one of the most persistent beliefs of the late Middle Ages and of the Renaissance."[3] The demonic influence thought to transform the religious

1. Baltasar Gracián, *Agudeza y arte de ingenio,* ed. Evaristo Correa Calderón, 1:55.
2. See Bundy, "The Theory of Imagination," 159, 163–64, 257–80.
3. Ibid., 267.

ascetic into a religious melancholic is evidence of such explanations, as Tirso's depiction of Paulo demonstrates. There was thus a general fear and mistrust of the imagination in its most non-sensitive capacity, yet that capacity itself maintained the imagination as a passive channel submitting to a source outside itself for sensory information.

In Spain, Huarte's own explanation of the *concepto* in the *Examen* reveals his ambivalence toward the roles of the intellect and the imagination. At one point, claiming a productive value for the intellect, he says:

> Pero hablando con los filósofos naturales, ellos bien saben que el entendimiento es potencia generativa y que se empreña y pare, y que tiene hijos y nietos, y una partera . . . que le ayude a parir. Porque de la manera que en la primera generación el animal o planta da ser real y sustantífico a su hijo, no lo tiniendo antes de la generación, así el entendimiento tiene virtud y fuerzas naturales de producir y parir dentro de sí un hijo, al cual llaman los filósofos naturales noticia o concepto, que es *verbum mentis.*

> (But speaking with the natural philosophers, they know well that the intellect is a generative faculty and that it becomes pregnant and gives birth, and that it has children and grandchildren and a midwife . . . that helps it give birth. Because just as in the act of engendering, the animal or plant gives real and substantive being to its young, which is without it before birth, thus the intellect has virtue and natural forces for producing and bearing within itself a child, something the natural philosophers call knowledge or thought, which is *verbum mentis.*)[4]

The generative act, however, is described in terms of procreation, which necessitates participation of another agent for conception. Huarte thus reveals his own underlying ambivalence with regard to the epistemological change he proposes concerning the powers of invention. Perhaps more importantly, however, he reveals himself as a thinker of the transitional period of the late sixteenth century, one sensitive to the European intellectual currents that were heralding the emerging hegemony of the secular mind and the bourgeois individual. Though Huarte associates mental and artistic creativity with the imagination ("Esto de fingir fábulas y comparaciones cierto es que se hace con la imaginativa, porque es figura y dice buena correspondencia y similitud" [This business about inventing stories and comparisons certainly is done with the imaginative faculty, because it is an image and speaks of good correspondence and similarity]), here too his explanation is in terms of a generative process. It presupposes a partner or cooperating agent, and he asserts that from the imagination "nacen todas las artes y ciencias que consisten en figura, corresponden-

4. Huarte de San Juan, *Examen de ingenios,* 426–27.

cia, armonía y proporción" (are born all the arts and sciences that consist of image, correspondence, harmony, and proportion), first among which is poetry.[5]

As Malcolm Read notes, Gracián and Huarte differ in their explanations of poetic creativity and thus the basis of the *concepto,* though "both literary writer and scientist saw the universe as a metaphorical poem, made up of conceits, which, they believed, must be deciphered and understood, if man is to understand fully the nature of God's creation." As already noted, Huarte's somewhat unorthodox suggestions concerning the creative powers of the human mind posit an autonomy to the mental activity and a rejection of many of the tenets of Platonic and Aristotelian notions about knowledge because "neither [classical view] allowed for the role of human creativity."[6] Huarte's biological determinism, however, also undermines the freedom implied in his ideas about the power of the intellect, and he reveals his underlying vacillation regarding his own pronouncements.[7] Whereas he asserts the primacy of the third kind of wit his system accounts for—"unos ingenios tan perfectos que no han menester maestros que los enseñan" (wits so perfect that they do not need teachers to instruct them)—his insistence on the natural inclinations and somatic basis to learning and abilities "showed this freedom to be, if not illusory, at least of a severely circumscribed kind."[8]

The independent creativity of the poetic mind is an important issue in Renaissance/Baroque poetics and the attention given to the creative powers of the mind is a corollary to the emerging hegemony of the *cogito.* The position on this issue taken by canonical authors is of critical interest. Scholars have singled out Lope, for example, as a Spanish proponent of the inventive capabilities of the imagination. Though Lope does indeed seem to prize the imagination, identifying his *comedias* as "imaginaciones" and proclaiming in the dedication to *El valor de las mujeres* (The value of women) that, "[f]undó la imaginativa la esencial parte del poeta, la oficina de sus conceptos y pensamientos" (the imagination established the essence of the poet, the office of his ideas and thoughts), he also clearly transvalues this faculty's powers.[9] By 1631—late in his life—when he wrote *El castigo sin venganza* (Punishment without vengeance) Lope regards the imagination as a negative faculty: "una manera del alma / que

5. Ibid., 194, 164.
6. Read, *Juan Huarte de San Juan,* 109, 62; on Platonic and Aristotelian notions, see 105.
7. Ibid., 67.
8. Huarte, *Examen de ingenios,* 130–31; Read, *Juan Huarte de San Juan,* 67.
9. See Bruce W. Wardropper, "La imaginación en el metateatro calderoniano," in *Studia Hispanica in Honorem R. Lapesa,* ed. Eugenio de Bustos, et al., 2:623. Lope is quoted in John Dagenais, "The Imaginative Faculty," 323.

más engaña que informa" (a manner of the soul / that deceives more than it informs).[10]

The Golden Age poets and literary theorists are far from univocal in their pronouncements about the value of imaginative creativity, but the polemics surrounding Góngora's *culterano* works provide a key to understanding what was for that period a central epistemological problem for the more conservative poets who admire Góngora at the same time they attack him. As in the other cases of the Renaissance transvaluation of the melancholy mind, Góngora's intellectual autonomy parallels his religious and social isolation—or marginality—which provides his literary adversaries much polemical ammunition. Through the character César in *La Dorotea,* for example, Lope asserts his appreciation of "el nombre *culto*" (the term *culto*) contending that "no puede haber etimología que mejor le venga que la limpieza y el despejo de la sentencia libre de la oscuridad" (there is no etymology that suits it more than the purity and fluency of the sentence free of obscurity). César complains, however, "que no es ornamento de la oración la confusión de los términos mal colocados, y la bárbara frase traída de los cabellos con metáfora sobre metáfora" (that the confusion of badly placed terms and the rough statement dragged by the hair with metaphor upon metaphor is not an ornamentation of speech). For Lope, the complication of the metaphors is negative precisely because of the unnaturalness of its conceptual basis, and César's companion Ludovico elaborates: "Viciosa es la oración en buena lógica, que se saca por términos oscuros e impropios, y que más oscurece que declara la naturaleza de la cosa definida" (In good logic any sentence is vicious, that is produced through obscure and improper terms, and that confuses more than explains the nature of the thing defined).[11]

The poetics that Lope admires remains premised on traditional epistemology. He understands invention not in the modern sense but rather reaffirms the more traditional mimetic notion of image production via the imagination as the faculty that processes sensory information with its own potential to recombine images to be presented to the *entendimiento* for interpretation. Again through César, Lope affirms that "la invención es la parte principal, si no el todo, e invención e imitación sean también una misma cosa" (invention is the principal part, if not everything, and invention and imitation are also the same

10. Lope de Vega Carpío, "El castigo sin venganza," in *Lope de Vega: Obras escogidas,* ed. Federico Carlos Sainz de Robles, 1:943; see Alan S. Trueblood, *Experience and Artistic Expression in Lope de Vega,* 625.
11. *La Dorotea,* ed. Edwin S. Morby, 159.

thing).[12] This is not the epistemological system in which Góngora participates. David Foster and Virginia Foster remark, in fact, that "one must acknowledge the degree to which Góngora turned away from the standard concept of imitation to develop a whole new style of poetic reality rooted in the concept of the poem as object, as the genesis of substantive art."[13]

More than one critic, nevertheless, claims to identify Lope's affirmation of the poet's creative imagination and thus his ideological link with what is considered to be Huarte's more modern stance on this point.[14] At best, such an affirmation on Lope's part is uneasy and ambiguous, and the first sonnet of his collection *Rimas humanas* (1602) contains material that evinces a conservative attitude toward the creative powers of the poet's mind. The first quatrain reads as follows:

> Versos de amor, conceptos esparcidos,
> engendrados del alma en mis cuidados;
> partos de mis sentidos abrasados,
> con más dolor que libertad nacidos.

> (Amorous verses, scattered conceits,
> begotten of my soul in my worries;
> products of my burning senses,
> born with more pain than freedom.)[15]

Characterizing his poetry as his offspring thus alludes to a secondary agent outside the poet that has contributed to the composition—the engendering—of the creations. Such a process reflects the ambiguity of Huarte's description of the intellect. The references to the emotional disruption that accompanies the poetic production suggests furthermore the pain and the mental imbalance that afflict the love melancholic and the studious thinker, as well as the numerous melancholy imbalances that, from ancient times, were thought to interfere with the proper functioning of the imagination and sensory perception. The high degree of emotional pain, specifically, supersedes the poet's liberty in this undertaking: "con más dolor que libertad nacidos." According to Lope, then, the imaginative process is not an act of autonomous creation but rather one of joint production just as in the case of divinely inspired poetry; it is, as well, a

12. Ibid., 157.
13. *Luis de Góngora*, 25.
14. See, for example, Wardropper, "La imaginación," and Daniel L. Heiple, "Lope's 'Arte Poética,'" in *Renaissance and Golden Age Essays in Honor of D. W. McPheeters,* ed. Bruno M. Damiani, 106–19.
15. In *Obras poéticas,* ed. José Manuel Blecua, 1:23.

consequence of unhappiness in love. Lope characterizes as dangerous precisely this link between the passions and the imagination in a ballad from *La Dorotea:*

> ¡O gustos de amor traidores,
> sueños ligeros y vanos,
> gozados siempre pequeños,
> y grandes imaginados!

> (Oh traitorous pleasures of love,
> vain and rapid dreams,
> always small when enjoyed,
> and great when imagined!)[16]

As Trueblood points out, this song, though published in such a late work as *La Dorotea,* is probably one of Lope's earliest, and its message matches that about the deceptive quality of the imagination's information referred to in *El castigo sin venganza.*[17] Lope's understanding of the imagination appears to be consistent in this regard.

While Lope acknowledges in "Versos de amor" the potential for intellectual autonomy, he still embraces the classical system of thinking and adheres to the positive notion of the traditional interdependence of the faculties and their interpretative function. In the first tercet of the sonnet, he includes mythological references that elucidate his devaluing of the autonomous thinker outside the familiar epistemological model:

> pues que le hurtáis el laberinto a Creta,
> a Dédalo los altos pensamientos,
> la furia al mar, las llamas al abismo.

> (since you steal from Crete the labyrinth,
> from Dedalus the lofty thoughts,
> the fury from the sea, the flames from hell.)[18]

In addition to the allusions to Saturn's sea and the prison-like confusion of the labyrinth, this verse also refers to the famous inventor Daedalus. One of his creations is, of course, the maze itself, with its negative connotations of confinement and disorientation, here depicted as paralleling the verses produced by the daringly creative poetic intellect. It is Daedalus's other invention, however, that

16. Ibid., 203.
17. *Experience and Artistic Expression,* 625, 943.
18. *Obras poéticas,* 23.

is more evocative of Lope's appraisal of the notion of independent poetic creativity: the wings with which Icarus soared too close to the sun were constructed—invented—by his progenitor. With them, the boy attempted what was not proper for a mortal being, and fell to his death. The father, whose "altos pensamientos" (high thoughts) were the basis of his offspring's disaster, is thus depicted in terms of the mistake to which Lope himself feels vulnerable if he follows the growing European praise for the independent, secular mind. The implied disaster in his case would be an intellectual and literary one, affecting his "versos" as the creations of his "altos pensamientos." The reference to hellfire suggests the image of the fall, not only of Icarus but of the poet through the failure of a parallel poetic endeavor. There is also the implied reference to the pride of the Fall of Humanity itself if the system of right thinking is abandoned, portrayed by Dante as a losing of the good of the intellect.[19]

A far more radical break with the classical system is evinced in Góngora's poetic theory, and an examination of the references to various muses in the *Polifemo* and the *Soledad I* is essential in a consideration of his poetics and his divergence from both the traditional mimetic process and the Platonic notion of poetic inspiration. The recognition of Melancholy as a muse is bound up with the connection between great poetic and artistic minds and a melancholic system. It is as well of interest for Renaissance mythographers whose reinterpretations of mythological material have implications for the transvaluation of melancholy in the poetics of that period and for Góngora's theory of the source of poetic images. In a recent study of "L'Allegro" and "Il Penseroso," Stella P. Revard considers the influence of the Renaissance myth books on Milton. As she argues, Milton follows the authority of the mythographers of his

19. See *Inferno*, 46; Isabel G. MacCaffrey (*Spencer's Allegory: The Anatomy of Imagination*) addresses the efforts of Renaissance poets to grapple with such notions. With regard to Sidney and his theoretical *Apologie for Poetry*, she explains: "Sidney speaks of alternative worlds and the power of the poet to create *ex nihilo* in terms that may strike us as very modern. And, in fact, the audacity of such a position was acknowledged and deplored by writers in the following century, who saw that the poetic imagination was to be feared not simply because it dealt with licentious subjects and sensuous images, but because it presumptuously, even blasphemously, preferred its own creations to the divine handiwork" (20). In his *Apologie*, Sidney also considers how the poet "lifted up with the vigour of his own invention, doth grow in effect into another nature, in making things either better than Nature bringeth forth or, quite anew forms such things as never were in Nature" (20–21). Sidney, too, however connects this creative power with the Fall: "Neither let it be deemed too saucy a comparison to balance the highest point of man's wit with the efficacy of Nature; but rather give right honour to the heavenly Maker of that maker, who having made man to His own likeness, set him beyond and over all the works of that second nature: which in nothing he showeth so much as in Poetry, when with the force of a divine breath he bringeth things forth far surpassing her doings, with no small argument to the incredulous of that first accursed fall of Adam: since our erected wit maketh us know what perfection is, and yet our infected will keepeth us from reaching unto it." (In MacCaffrey, *Spencer's Allegory*, 21). See also MacCaffrey's discussion of this passage (21).

age rather than the ancient poets in establishing the identity of the muses responsible for inspiring the tone of each of his two poems. Tracing the patronage of poetic contemplation to the divine figure that the Renaissance understood as Melancholy, Revard explains that the muses—Melancholy and her sisters—belong "to the line of Saturn. . . . Begotten by Saturn's father, Uranos (Coelus), they are closely linked to the heavens and to science and contemplation, over which Saturn presides."[20] In addition, though this genealogy is common to all the muses, Urania is the one who reigns over the eighth heaven and is known as the heavenly muse. The Renaissance mythographer Natalis Comes posits such a connection as does Goefredius Linocerius.[21] Gyraldus describes the muses as born "sub Saturno," and the Spanish mythographer Juan Pérez de Moya lists the following heritage among those possible for the muses: "Minermo dice ser las Musas hijas de Celo y mas antiguas que Iúpiter" (Minermo reports the Muses to be daughters of Heaven and older than Jupiter).[22] He likewise lists Urania as "ánima del cielo estrellado o firmamento" (spirit of the starry sky or firmament), and Polimnia as belonging to "los orbes o cielos de Saturno" (spheres or heavens of Saturn) and dominating those individuals who are "saturninos . . . por ser de temperamento frío y seco, [y] les promete mucha memoria de cosas pasadas e inclinarse a diversos estudios, según diversos aspectos de planetas" (Saturnine . . . because of a cold and dry temperament, [and] she promises them great memory for past things and inclination to various studies, according to the varied aspects of the planets).[23]

The correspondence of the muses with the mental faculties is generally recognized by the Renaissance mythographers. According to Revard: "Several mythographers note the ancient theory, which they usually attribute to Aratus or Cicero, that the muses as qualities of mind were at first three: *mneme* (mind or memory), *melete* (exercise or meditation), and *aoede* (song); or four: *mneme, melete, aoede,* and *thelxiope* (charm)."[24] Such notions are incorporated into Pérez de Moya's discussion "De Musas," and Linocerius and Gyraldus likewise address these issues.[25] Gyraldus contends, for example, that the muses are products of Jove, who is connected to understanding (*to noktikon*), and Mnemosyne, whose realm is memory (*to mnemonikon*).[26] Linocerius credits

20. "'L'Allegro' and 'Il Penseroso': Classical Tradition and Renaissance Mythography," 343.

21. Natalis Comes, *Mythologiae, sive explicationum fabularum. Libri decem,* 506; Geofredius Linocerius, *Mythologiae Musarum libellus,* 1102.

22. Lilius Gregorius Gyraldus, *De deis gentium varia et multiplex historia,* 356. *Philosophia secreta,* ed. Eduardo Gómez de Baquero, 2:94.

23. *Philosophia secreta,* 96.

24. "Renaissance Mythography," 349.

25. "De Musas," in *Philosophia secreta,* 2:94–98.

26. *De deis gentium,* 358.

Jupiter with being the parent of all things, and explains that in his capacity of cognition the mythological deity generated the muses from memory. Linocerius further explains that as the contemplators of the eternal evidence conceived of by the intellect, the muses ponder and, through the senses and external information, come to know hidden and celestial things. Their very name, he asserts, connotes inquiry.[27] Because they are the companions of philosophers, the muses foment solitary and meditative work during the nighttime hours.[28] In the Renaissance the muses are understood as "patronesses not only of poetry but of science and philosophy,"[29] and indeed Pérez de Moya notes that "les atribuían tener fuerza y sabiduría en cosas de música y poesía y en toda ciencia" (they were said to have strength and wisdom in musical topics and poetry and all science).[30]

Góngora is specifically associated with the muses and even figuratively fused with Saturn in a poem by his friend Hortensio Félix Paravicino y Arteaga. The poem, replete with melancholy imagery, proclaims Góngora: "Hijo de Córdoba grande / padre mayor de las musas" (son of great Cordoba / main father of the muses).[31] This description, written by someone in sympathy with Góngora's poetics, is striking in that it acknowledges the relationship between the muse and the contemplative, melancholy poet that informs the *Polifemo* and the *Soledad I*. In Paravicino's tribute, Góngora is considered the source of the muses' very existence, that is, the tables are turned and poetry finds its source in the poet himself whose progeny—both his written poems and his daughters/ muses—become vehicles for the repetition and communication of his poetic creation.

Paravicino merely reiterates here what Góngora articulates in his two famous *culto* works, beginning with their initial lines. In the first strophe of the *Polifemo*, Góngora addresses the Count of Niebla, to whom he dedicates and ostensibly directs his retelling of a myth of metamorphosis. The muse Thalia is identified by the narrative voice as simply a source of information, "Estas que me dictó, rimas sonoras / culta sí, aunque bucólica Talía" (These sonorous rhymes that the elegant though bucolic Thalia told me).[32] The muse does not inspire the composition, she only recounts or dictates it to the narrator, who

27. *Mythologiae Musarum*, 1080; see also Ambrosius Calepinus, *Dictionarium*, 2:52.
28. Lucius Annæus Cornutus, *Natura deorum gentilium commentarius*, 63–64; see also Revard, "Renaissance Mythography," 343.
29. Revard, "Renaissance Mythography," 343.
30. *Philosophia secreta*, 2:96.
31. In Ana Martínez Arancón, ed., *La batalla en torno a Góngora*, 284.
32. In *Obras completas,* ed. Juan Millé y Giménez and Isabel Millé y Giménez, vv. 1–2. All poetry and prose quotations are taken from this volume and cited, respectively, by verse or page number in the text.

receives it and then becomes its secondary vehicle of repetition. As such, the narrator partially parallels the Count, who will serve as audience / receiver of its new retelling and will thus become a counterpart for the muse Thalia, who received it from its original composer. The poem's reception is part of the mimetic process and bound up with the imaginative faculty's function as receptor of sensory information but not with creative composition. This latter activity for Góngora is solely aligned with the *entendimiento*. In his "Carta en respuesta" (Letter in reply), he makes his clearest theoretical statements, and devotes much attention to the importance of the *entendimiento*, saying at one point: "demás que, como el fin de el entendimiento es hacer presa en verdades . . . en tanto quedará más deleitado, cuando obligándole a la especulación por la obscuridad de la obra, fuera hallando debajo de las sombras de la obscuridad asimilaciones a su concepto" (besides which, as the goal of the intellect is to seize the truth . . . until it is more delighted, when obliging it to speculate due to the obscurity of the work, it would go finding assimilations to its conceit beneath the shadows of obscurity [897]).

In the third strophe of the *Polifemo*, the last of the dedicatory section, the narrator declares:

> Alterna con las Musas hoy el gusto,
> que si la mía puede ofrecer tanto
> clarín—y de la Fama no segundo—,
> tu nombre oirán los términos del mundo.
> (21-24)

(Alternate today the Muses with your pleasure, for if my muse is able to offer such a great trumpet—not a second to Fame's—the ends of the earth will hear your name.)

Góngora transcends the mythological and the poetic conventions, for not only does the human poet triumph by going beyond the traditional dependence on the inspiration of the ancient divinities, but he refers to the muses within contexts that run counter to their institutionalized sphere of influence. Thalia is the muse whose realm of inspiration includes comedy and yet Góngora makes of her the vehicle of repetition of a poem of heroical love that ends in violence and the destruction of love's union. Similarly, his reference to Euterpe in the dedicatory section of the *Soledad I* functions to transcend the myth of her influence over tragedy, for this composition is the story of a wedding, the quintessential ingredient for a work with a happy ending in Golden Age Spain. The *Soledad II* does not even make reference to such a mythical figure, thus implying Góngora's declaration of total independence from the external inspirational forces.[33] This treatment marks a sophistication in thought and a natural evolutionary passage in Renaissance/Baroque humanism, for the human element is transcendent in the complicated interchange between the pagan deities and the free will of the Christian humanist. While the Catholic writers do not dare to usurp God's place, they do create successful characters and personae who show how to triumph over external forces, often developed in mythological or astrological terms, that incline or subvert the Christian away from right thinking and action. Calderón's Segismundo wins just such a victory. The difference between a Calderón and a Góngora, however, is the former's stress on the Christian God as the transcendent and immanent element, whereas the latter celebrates to a higher degree the human component in the equation.

As Góngora makes clear in the early strophes of the *Polifemo,* the muses as well as human taste and enjoyment ("gusto") facilitate and perpetuate the reception of the poem, which enhances the fame of the Count and the poet. Góngora forges a connection between all participants of the experience of his poem, a composition whose origin is internal, not external, and thus is conceived of neither in mimetic terms nor within the tradition of divine inspiration. This source is articulated from within the poem itself, for Polifemo is the mighty poet *faber* whose song-within-song is the only section presented in quotation marks as words directly attributable to their composer. Polifemo's active role as author of his love poem is enhanced through Góngora's consistent characterization of the muses as simply the medium of its repetition. As Polifemo begins to sing, the poetic voice of the contextual description calls on the muses to repeat and not to inspire the giant's poem: "referidlo, Piéredes, os ruego" (recount it, Muses, I beg you [360]). The song-poem comes from the gigantic poet whose proportions are monstrous though impressive and who parallels Góngora himself through his difference, his melancholia, and the solitary contemplation in which he writes his poetry.

There is an origin for the poem we know as the *Polifemo* and this origin, according to the narrative voice, lies beyond the muse. The muse is not primary but rather corresponds, in Góngora's poetics, to the imagination as a secondary

33. Góngora's treatment here is beyond the rejection of the pagan invocation and the scrupulous distinctions between proper and improper references to them in sixteenth- and seventeenth-century Spanish literature. See Green's discussion of this issue in *Spain and the Western Tradition,* 3:190–202. This transcendent stance is a significant step in the use of mythological material—beyond the mere parodic transformation of myth to which Góngora contributed his well-known "Hero y Leandro" and "Píramo y Tisbe." See Marcia Welles, *Arachne's Tapestry: The Transformation of Myth in Seventeenth-Century Spain,* for a comprehensive study of the parodic transformation of myth in Golden Age literature.

faculty of repetition, not as the source of information to be interpreted. He thus reverses the flow of poetic production from the traditional imaginative/mimetic one to one which depends on internal invention that springs from the intellect. He enhances and calls attention to this reversal by reversing the location of poet and poetic subject, for Polifemo emerges from within the poetic composition as its source. Melancholia is the disposition of the poetic intelligence; the melancholic's preference for solitude and tendency for contemplation are conditions that facilitate the creative act. Melancholy the muse is a vehicle for relaying the poetic creation which is, according to Góngora, a product of the poet's *entendimiento*.

Góngora's rupture with the classical mimetic notion of poetry was a growing tendency in the Baroque period, in general, but one of which he serves as a most accomplished and self-conscious practitioner. Foster and Foster explain Góngora's poetic process: "No more is the poet compelled to impress his audience with imitation and recreation, but rather the new aesthetic was to startle with extravagance, to bring a new horizon of poetic reality."[34] John R. Beverly contends furthermore that "[w]hat is evident is that the debate over the *Soledades* in the literary circles of the Court of Philip III quickly escalated beyond questions of literary taste and decorum. The suggestion of the heretical status of Góngora's new manner . . . was more a charge that [his] way of doing poetry departed from the canons of the prevailing poetics."[35] This new "way of doing poetry" is easily understood in terms of the epistemological difference between Góngora and those who were part of the same historical and artistic moment but who were not willing to endorse a poetics that shook the very structure of thought itself. As the Fosters conclude, Góngora's art "broke the bonds of harmony, verisimilitude, credibility and natural reality, bringing forth out of chaos a new totally creative patterning of relationships, a new Nature individually interpreted, and supposedly far superior in its complexity to the trite, mimetic *loci amoeni* of the previous age."[36]

A comparison of seventeenth-century theorists' statements with Góngora's declarations in the "Carta en respuesta" (in which he promotes the activity of the *entendimiento* as the basis for writing and reading his poetry) is very revealing of the great difference of opinion regarding the reading and interpretation of poetry. Luis Alfonso de Carballo writes in his *Cisne de Apolo* (Apollo's swan; 1602) about the process of interpreting poetic images and

34. *Luis de Góngora*, 25.
35. John R. Beverley, *Aspects of Góngora's "Soledades"*, 11.
36. *Luis de Góngora*, 25.

metaphors but, unlike Góngora, reveals his basic reliance on the classical theory of the mental faculties:

> Y essotro que tu llamas falsamente sentido literal, que quieres que se conciba inmediatamente de las palabras, no se concibe con obra del entendimiento, que sería vano el que tal concibiesse, antes es fantasía de la imaginativa, con que se imagina y fantasea aquella fiction, como q[ue] Cupido es ciego, lo qual es obra de la imaginativa differente cosa del ente[n]dimiento, no conviene ser el amor ciego, como la imaginativa lo fantasea, antes passando adelante concibe lo q[ue] el auctor quiso significar.

> (And this other that you incorrectly call literal sense, that you wish to be understood immediately through the words, is not understood by means of any effort of the intellect, since it would be a vain effort for it to understand such things; instead it is a fantasy of the imaginative faculty, with which that fiction is imagined and fantasized, such as that Cupid is blind, which saying is a product of the imagination, something different from the intellect, not meaning that love is really blind, as the imagination fantasizes it, but rather proceeding forward understands what the author wanted to mean.)[37]

Although, as Read explains, Carballo "attempts to carve out a role for the understanding in literary activity," he still values the imagination as the origin of poetry and follows closely the deterministic doctrines of Huarte.[38] The role he describes for the intellect, however, is not an innovation, for the images that the imagination forms pass "adelante," as he explains, to be interpreted and compared by the *entendimiento* in terms of "lo que el auctor quiso significar." Alonso López Pinciano, also aligned with Huarte in critical opinion, puts great emphasis on the imagination in poetic endeavor. Pinciano writes of the imagination: "El instrumento desta facultad pide calor con sequedad, compañeros del furor, a cuya causa es un sentido muy co[n]veniente para la poética" (The functioning of this faculty demands heat with dryness, the mates of frenzy, for which reason it is a very appropriate sense for poetry). His explanation of the imagination, however, is also derived from the medieval notion of a sensorially based system of contact with the external world: "Digo, pues, en suma, que el sentido interior y principal recibe las especies y imágines de los sentidos exteriores . . . mediante las quales conoce las cosas de afuera y las discierne y juzga" (Thus, I say, in summation, that the interior and principal sense receives the visions and images from the exterior senses . . . by means of which it knows the outer things and discerns and judges them).[39] Sanford Shepard likewise com-

37. *Cisne de Apolo,* ed. A. Porqueras Mayo, 1:100.
38. *Juan Huarte de San Juan,* 108.
39. *Philosophia antigua poética,* ed. Alfredo Carballo, 1:48–49, 64.

ments upon such notions of Pinciano: "Para Pinciano . . . [l]a imaginación encuentra su origen natural en la percepción de los sentidos. Ella, si no la mente, es una *tabula rasa* en la que escriben los sentidos. Una nueva disposición de los materiales del mundo perceptible produce las fantasías de la mente" (For Pinciano . . . the imagination finds its natural origin in the perception of the senses. It, if not the mind, is a *tabula rasa* on which the senses write. A new ordering of the physical properties of the perceptible world produces the fantasies of the mind).[40] And indeed, Pinciano claims:

> No atie[n]de la imaginación a las especies verdaderas, mas finge otras nuevas, y acerca dellas obra de mil maneras: unas veces, las finge simples; otras, las compone; ya finge especies de montes q[ue] nu[n]ca fueron; ya de las especies del mo[n]te y de las del oro, haze un mo[n]te de oro; ya del oro haze un coloso, y ya un animal q[ue] ten[n]ga cabeça de ho[m]bre, cuello de cavallo, cuerpo de ave y cola de pece . . . porque abraça las especies passadas, presentes y aun futuras.

> (The imagination does not pay attention to true images, but invents other new ones, and around them it works in a thousand ways: at times, it creates simple ones; at others, it puts them together; here it invents images of mountains that never were; there from the ideas of mountains and those of gold, it makes a mountain of gold; then it makes from the gold a colossus, and now an animal with the head of a man, neck of a horse, body of a bird and tail of a fish . . . because it incorporates the past, present and even future images.)[41]

Like the medieval notion of fantasy and imagination, Pinciano's explanation attributes to these faculties the ability to combine and distort images. This is not, however, imaginative invention in the modern sense, and indeed his definition of literature, and poetry in particular, emphasizes the element of imitation by means of language: "Assí que poesía no es otra cosa que arte que enseña a imitar con la lengua o lenguaje" (And so poetry is nothing but the art that shows how to imitate with the spoken or written language).[42]

Presented as a product of the poetic intellect that is not dependent on anything but its own inventive abilities, Gongora's *Polifemo* is basically a recounting of the consequences of heroical love, and Polifemo is a lovesick poet/ shepherd associated with the sites and behavior patterns conducive to melancholia. Living in a cave, he inhabits one of the places associated with Saturn, and one that Góngora describes in terms of its connection with melancholy:

40. *El Pinciano y las teorías literarias del Siglo de Oro,* 33.
41. *Philosophia antigua poética,* 1:48–49.
42. Ibid., 1:195; see Shepard, *El Pinciano,* 46–57.

> De este, pues, formidable de la tierra
> bostezo, el melancólico vacío
> a Polifemo, horror de aquella sierra,
> bárbara choza es, albergue umbrío.
>
> (vv. 41–44)

(The melancholy space of this formidable yawn of the earth is a crude hut, a dark shelter for Polyphemus, the horror of that mountain.)

Within two strophes, Polifemo is himself described as "adusto hijo de este Pirineo" (grim son of these Pyrenees [v. 62]). Like the Calderonian wife-murderers Don Gutierre and Don Juan Roca, he destroys through jealousy because he loves so obsessively.

The scenes and episodes described by Góngora alternate between descriptions of water/sea images and land, thus suggesting the Saturnine imagery. Góngora's poetic persona also narrates the unrequited love of the sea gods Glauco and Palemo, from whom "[h]uye la ninfa bella" (the beautiful nymph flees [v. 129]). The land-dwelling men who likewise love Galatea without hope of her reciprocal affection eventually neglect their duties—as love melancholics do:

> Arde la juventud, y los arados
> peinan las tierras que surcaron antes,
> mal conducidos, cuando no arrastrados,
> de tardos buyes cual su dueño errantes;
> sin pastor que los silbe, los ganados
> los grujidos ignoran resonantes
> de las hondas, si en vez del pastor pobre
> el Céfiro no silba, o cruje el robre.
>
> (vv. 161–68)

(Youth burns, and ploughshares that before ploughed now comb the earth, badly guided, when not dragged, by slow oxen as errant as their owners; without a shepherd to call them with a whistle, the flocks forget the resonant creakings of the slings, unless the west wind whistles instead of the poor shepherd, or the oak creaks.)

Such disorder causes the poem's narrator to beseech: "¡Revoca, Amor, los silbos, o a su dueño / el silencio del can siga, y el sueño!" (Revoke, oh Love, the whistles, or let the dog's silence follow his master, as well as his sleep [vv. 176–77]).

Galatea's beloved Acis is likewise a being associated with water and land: "gloria del mar, honor de su ribera" (glory of the sea, honor of its shore [196]), and his ultimate fate is his transformation into a river after being buried by the rock and earth thrown on him by the enraged Saturnine giant. Foster and Foster note of Polifemo, Galatea, and Acis that "all three are sea elements which have come upon land, so to speak." They contend that these creatures are out of place and consider this a parallel of the conflict between art and nature that the poem represents: "Góngora's composition is an imposition upon Nature."[43] The figures and their relation to melancholy and Saturn, however, make their association with land and sea a convention within the representation of melancholy.

The love song of Polifemo is a composition that proceeds from his own *amor eroico* and inspires the melancholy emotion of fear in Galatea as it expresses the giant's unrequited love in melancholy terms. At one point, for instance, Polifemo tells of his enactment of Saturn's role as patron of shipwrecked sailors at a time in the past when he saved the life of such a victim:

> "Segunda tabla, a un Ginovés mi gruta
> de su persona fue, de su hacienda:
> la una reparada, la otra enjuta.
> Relación de el naufragio hizo horrenda."
>
> (vv. 449–52)

("My grotto was a second plank to a Genoese for his body and his possessions: the one rested and the other dried out. He told a horrendous tale of the shipwreck.")

As son of either Neptune or Jupiter, Polifemo's heritage is traceable directly to Saturn through the confused genealogies of the ancient deities provided by the Renaissance mythographers. Pérez de Moya records, among several descriptions of Jupiter, that he was "hijo de Saturno y de Opis . . . Fue este Júpiter el más famoso y que más nombre tuvo en el mundo" (son of Saturn and Opis. . . . This Jupiter was the most famous and the one with the most fame in all the world).[44] Of Neptune, he notes: "Neptuno, dios del mar, fue hijo de Saturno y Opis, y hermano de Júpiter" (Neptune, god of the sea, was son of Saturn and Opis, and brother of Jupiter). This same mythographer lists as well the family history of the Cyclopses, explaining: "fueron hijos de Neptuno, y según Hesíodo, de Celo y de la Tierra" (they were children of Neptune, and according to Hesiod, of Heaven and Earth)—and therefore members of the same genealogy as Saturn and the muse Melancholy. Pérez de Moya goes on to a description of Polifemo as one of the Cyclopses, saying: "estos dijeron ser ciento, y el

---

43. *Luis de Góngora*, 109.
44. *Philosophia secreta*, 1:69.

principal era Polifemo" (these were said to number one hundred, and the foremost one was Polyphemus).[45] The lines cited above from the *Polifemo* thus reiterate the giant's traditional link with Saturn and immediately precede the strophes that tell of the jealous rage of the giant and his heroical love, which worsens to the point of violence in the solitary and idle existence traditionally linked with such a characterization.

The *Soledad I* is a reaffirmation or reiteration of the issues raised in the *Polifemo* as well as a continuation of the development of melancholy symbolism. The protagonist is also a suffering melancholic and a victim of a shipwreck, reminiscent of the related elements in the *Polifemo*. The greed and obsessive drive toward an ultimately self-destructive goal that the old *serrano* (highlander) laments in his tirade against seafaring and the voyage that has claimed the life of his son is yet another reference to the negativity of Saturn's association with both shipwrecks and the type of behavior and thought that leads other literary melancholics to destruction. The *serrano,* however, both decries and admires the riches that lure the adventurers and conquerors out to sea toward foreign shores where they will raid and destroy in order to claim.[46] In so doing, he transvalues such enterprises as well as the two poles of melancholia involved in his recitation, for as a contemplative, bitter elderly person—a traditional melancholic type—he recounts and seems to step briefly and empathetically into the role of the unscrupulous, even villainous, conqueror whose acts are prefaced upon covetous thoughts that lead to destruction.

The old *serrano*'s tale ends with lines that summarize his own pain:

> quédese, amigo, en tan inciertos mares,
>   donde con mi hacienda
> del alma se quedó la mejor prenda,
> cuya memoria es buitre de pesares.
>   (vv. 499–502)

(let it remain, friend, in such uncertain seas, where along with my property the best jewel of my soul remained, whose memory is vulture of my sorrows.)

The obsessive, hardened memory that is a hindrance to Don Quijote here also diverts another of its victims from productive interaction with the community.

45. Ibid., 1:102; 2:166; 2:266.

46. Mary Gaylord Randel, "Metaphor and Fable in Góngora's *Soledad primera*," 100–107. Greed and miserliness are also characteristics traditionally associated with Saturn, and in *Saturn and Melancholy* Kilbansky et al. include in the artistic representations provided "Saturn counting money" (fig. 43) and "The Melancholic as a miser" (fig. 73), among others in which a money bag serves as part of the imagery of Saturn and/or melancholy.

The allusion to Prometheus's suffering conjures up the famous story of pride that leads to a downfall and connotes extreme sadness. Pérez de Moya explains that some versions of the Prometheus story report that "por pena deste hurto [del fuego] enviaron a la tierra los dioses, enflaquecimientos, tristezas, enfermedades y mujeres" (as punishment for this theft [of fire] the gods sent to earth weaknesses, sadness, illnesses and women).[47] The sadness and infirmity of lovesickness combine the same ingredients as does this version of the myth and its traditional (and mysoginistic) list of ills visited upon earth, and indeed heroical love is the affliction that the young *náufrago* (shipwreck victim) suffers.

The next stanza of the *Soledad I,* in fact, begins with descriptions of the extreme sadness of the old man and makes clear the equal strength of the youth's lovesick distress. Like his disruptive poetic language, however, Góngora's poetic narrative is not premised on the ongoing interpretive process, for the young man's ability to match the old man's sad tale is never demonstrated: "Consolalle pudiera el peregrino / con las de su edad corta historias largas" (The pilgrim could have consoled him / with long tales of his short life [vv. 507–8]). At this point the wedding preparations and initial festivities interrupt the potential telling of the tale. Within a few stanzas, the youth is once again unable to repress his sadness when the young bride reminds him of his love. For a second time he cannot interact effectively in order to share his personal thoughts with a community outside himself: "el joven, al instante arrebatado / a la que, naufragante y desterrado, / le condenó a su olvido" (the youth, shipwrecked and exiled, in that moment deeply moved by her resemblance to the one who condemned him to her forgetfulness [vv. 734–36]). His overly dry memory retains the image with which he is obsessed, and he cannot proceed to new interpretative connections. The pensive sadness of heroical love typically turns to despair and is described in the context of love melancholy:

> Este pues Sol que a olvido le condena,
> cenizas hizo las que su memoria
> negras plumas vistió, que infelizmente
> sordo engendran gusano, cuyo diente,
> minador antes lento de su gloria,
> inmortal arador fue de su pena.
>
> (vv. 737–42)

(This Sun, then, that condemns him to oblivion, made ashes of the black feathers

47. *Philosophia secreta,* 2:189.

that his memory wears and that unhappily engender a deaf worm, whose tooth was formerly a slow miner of his bliss, immortal ploughshare of his pain.)

Even the light of celebration from the rockets lit in the tower of the temple is a negative element from the point of view of the old man:

> Los fuegos pues el joven solemniza,
> mientras el viejo tanta acusa tea
> al de las bodas dios, no alguna sea
> de nocturno Faetón carroza ardiente,
>   y miserablemente
> campo amanezca estéril de ceniza
> la que anocheció aldea.
>
> (vv. 752–58)

(Thus the youth celebrates the fires, while the old man denounces the torch to the wedding god, for fear that it might be a nocturnal fiery chariot of Phaeton, and that which closed the night as a village might awaken miserably as a sterile field of ashes.)

Like the systemic dregs of adust melancholy left behind by the burning of an overly hot passion, the external scene is in danger of being left a landscape of sterile ashes to parallel the disastrous consequences of Phaeton's chariot ride and the cold, dark ashes of memory that unsettle the *peregrino*.

These strophes precede the description of the wedding scene, itself announced by the musical invocation to Himeneo, the deity of weddings, who in some mythological accounts is said to be the son of Urania; a superstitious appeal to Himeneo is traditional to prevent his jealous reprisal against a bride and groom. Though considered inventor of the wedding ceremony, he is nevertheless reported to have been killed during one such celebration when a house collapsed on him, and "fue por esto tomado en costumbre que todos los que se casasen le hiciesen sacrificios, por aplacar su saña, para que no les hiciese mal" (for this reason it became a custom that all those who were to marry made sacrifices to him, to appease his fury, so that he would not do them harm). Pérez de Moya continues this account and explains that people "creían que éste, estando entre las ánimas infernales, le pesaría que bodas hiciesen los otros ni que tomasen gozo en aquello en que a elle costó la vida; y porque deste enojo no les hiciese mal, honrábanle como supersticioso" (believed that this figure, being among the infernal souls, would be distressed that others had weddings or took delight in that which had cost him his life; and so that he would not do them wrong because of this anger, they honored him superstitiously).[48]

48. On Himeneo and Urania, see ibid., 1:269; 270; 270–71.

The songs to Himeneo interrupt the *joven*'s (youth's) painful memory of his own lover and he is left, suspended melancholically with the discomfort of his memories and his hurtful thoughts, which are nevertheless eased by the traditional musical remedy for melancholia. He, like Himeneo, is placated temporarily with the song and thus, like the mollified but potentially jealous deity, he and his unspoken threat to the happiness of the celebration disappear from the poem. The contests and games as part of the wedding festivities, moreover, entail on the one hand the competition for prizes that parallels the thirst for adventure and booty that the old *serrano* has earlier bemoaned, and on the other prefigure the "batallas de amor" (battles of love) of the wedding night.

The imagery of such works as the *Polifemo* and the *Soledad I* offers merely the formal evidence of the ideological implications of the melancholy mind that are inherent in Góngora's *culterano* poetry. The polemical attacks between him and his detractors go beyond aesthetic and linguistic differences. Separating the two poetic camps is also an epistemological orientation based both on the value, or lack thereof, placed upon the various mental faculties and on the dialectical transvaluation of the melancholy mind. Góngora chooses conventional topics and familiar literary material through which to assert his affirmation of the emerging intellectual order that places a high valuation upon the creative and autonomous mind. Such a mind, prized by Góngora but scorned by those who mistrust the new potential for thought, is characterized in both negative and positive senses as melancholically contemplative.

Francisco Cascales's harsh criticism of Góngora's *Polifemo* clearly enunciates the various levels of attack aimed at Góngora by the conservatives. The uneasiness over *culteranismo* as well as the epistemological concerns articulated in theoretical pieces by Cascales and others are similar to those raised in Lope's sonnet "Versos de amor." In his *Cartas filológicas* (1634), Cascales denounces the darkness ("obscuridad") of Góngora's *culterano* poetry, asserting at one point: "Entrando, pues, en este crítico laberinto, pregunto si la obscuridad es virtud o vicio. Cualquiera responderá con Tulio y con Quintiliano y con los demás maestros de la elocuencia, absolutamente que es vicio" (Entering thus in this critical labyrinth, I ask whether the darkness is virtue or vice. Anyone will respond with Cicero and with Quintilian and with the rest of the masters of eloquence, that absolutely it is vice).[49] Darkness carries with it, besides the notion of linguistic confusion, strong suggestions about the melancholy figure. Choosing to express disapproval of Góngora's poetry by means of this term (as do theoreticians like Pedro de Valencia in his "Carta escrita a don Luis de

---

49. *Cartas filológicas*, ed. Justo García Soriano, 1:178-79.

Góngora en censura de sus poesías" [Letter written to Don Luis de Góngora in reproach of his poetry] and Juan de Jáuregui in his "Antídoto contra la pestilente poesía de las *Soledades*" [Antidote against the pestilent poetry of the *Soledades*]), several of his critics also declare their implied stance within the polemical understanding of melancholia.[50]

Elaborating his disapproval of "los que afectan la obscuridad" (those who affect obscurity), among whom he numbers Góngora, Cascales complains of the "palabras trastornadas con catacreses y metáforas licensiosas, que cuando fueran tropos muy legítimos, por ser tan continuos y seguidos, unos tras otros, habían de engendrar obscuridad, intrincamiento y embarazo" (words confused with catacreses and licentious metaphors, which though they might have been very legitimate tropes, must engender obscurity, impenetrability, and obstruction for being so continuous and unbroken, one after the other). It is precisely the rupture of the continuous and connective quality of poetic correspondence ("tan continuos y seguidos") that Cascales rails most against. The poet's intellectual effort to attain this sort of disruptive composition lies at the heart of the problem, since Góngora's mind, the source of the poetry, has no connection to other legitimate sources:

> Que si yo no la entendiera por los secretos de naturaleza, por las fábulas, por las historias, por las propriedades de plantas, animales y piedras, por los usos y ritos de varias naciones que toca, cruzara las manos y me diera por rendido, y confesara que aquella obscuridad nacía de mi ignorancia, y no de culpa suya, habiéndolo dicho dilucida y claramente como debe.

> (For if I did not understand it through the secrets of nature, through the fables, through the stories, through the properties of plants, animals and stones, through the rites of different nations that it touches, I would fold my hands and admit defeat, and confess that that obscurity was born of my ignorance, and not from its own fault, having articulated it neatly and clearly as it should.)[51]

Góngora's attackers also echo the ancient tenets about metaphor found in the writings of Aristotle, Cicero, Quintilian, and in the anonymous *Rhetorica ad Herenium,* all of which stress in one manner or another the proper and clear use of both literary and figurative language for explanation and interpretation of nature and the world. A passage in the *Rhetorica* argues:

> Metaphor occurs when a word applying to one thing is transferred to another,

50. De Valencia, in *La batalla en torno a Góngora,* 5; de Jáuregui, ibid., 161.
51. *Cartas filológicas,* 1:180-81.

because the similarity seems to justify the transference. . . . They say that a metaphor ought to be restrained so as to be a transition with good reason to a kindred thing, and not seem an indiscriminate, reckless, and precipitate leap to an unlike thing.[52]

Terence Hawkes points out that although metaphor was appreciated by the classical theoreticians as "pre-eminent amongst the tropes," it was nevertheless held to be before all else a poetic device of language and not part of ordinary speech "and subsequently . . . one of the slightly suspect devices available to the stylist only for special ornamental 'effects.'"[53] The medieval notion of metaphor derives from the classical ones, but emphasizes its mediating value in the interpretive act undertaken to understand God's meaning.

During the Renaissance, the function of metaphor still adheres to the medieval principles, but from the theoretical standpoint of the sixteenth-century English poets, metaphor is not a medium for communicating authentic sensuous experiences but rather for articulating belief in an underlying order beneath the surface of nature. Basing his arguments upon Rosamund Tuve's discussion of the function of metaphor, Hawkes stresses that the poet thus "is concerned with values and meanings that are not private and personal but generally accepted and believed." Hawkes reinforces this argument, contending:

In a sense, the metaphor had a didactic role and was concerned to manifest truths, ideas and values that carried public assent. Its function was to reinforce an established view of the world, certainly not to challenge or question that view by means of a particular "local" or "singular" insight. . . . The poet's metaphor draws attention, not to his own powers, but to God's who wrote the "book" he is interpreting. The relationships that the metaphor establishes are created in the first place by God; the poet merely discovers them.[54]

Góngora's use of metaphor therefore violates this standard, according to the tenets of his opponents, who seek to reaffirm the older mode of thinking based on a predisposition to discover analogical similarities among things as well as the human being's place within creation. Góngora prizes his mind as the primary source of poetic images and does not reinforce their public and communal quality. His metaphors instead draw attention to his own mental powers by virtue of a particular "local or singular insight," and his melancholic stance of

52. Terence Hawkes, *Metaphor,* 13–14.
53. Ibid., 15.
54. Ibid., 18, 20.

isolation and uniqueness entails the darkness attributed to it, but in a favorable sense.

Góngora does not make language the medium of mere imitation readily decipherable by the traditional act of making imagistic comparisons via the faculties—the process that Gracián's definition of the *concepto* continues to recognize. Góngora's verses are an intellectual impediment to the reader's re-creation of the image of a described landscape or figure. The poet has performed an act of the understanding—a "reasoning practice upon the world"—to disrupt and restructure the scenes he writes about. Since his is no imitative process in the traditional Renaissance sense, Góngora's readers must follow him—his "pasos" (steps) and "versos," as he explains in the first strophe of the *Soledad*—and undertake their own "reasoning practice" as well. Though he makes claims in the "Carta en respuesta" about "lo misterioso" (the mysteriousness [896]) hidden below the superficial level of his *poesía culta,* he does not practice Horatian didacticism but promotes the mental experience as its own goal and reward.

Góngora offers his readers a description that proceeds from his own intellect and that is disrupted, re-formed, and shaped according to his own intellectual efforts via a mode of expression that breaks existing conventions of reading and interpreting. Góngora's reader must fill in the gaps left when words are suppressed; for example, definite articles are, in Góngora's own words, "[excusados] donde no necesarios" ([superfluous] where not necessary [896]). Hindering direct or easy communication through intellectual "obscuridad" is, of course, most fully developed in the *Polifemo* and the *Soledad I.* The protagonists in both works cannot or do not communicate effectively through verbal means: Polifemo sings, but Galatea will not listen sympathetically; the *peregrino* never tells his tale. The only semblance of overt moral message in these works is articulated in the old *serrano*'s tirade against seafaring, a speech made too late to benefit his son or the *peregrino* and as well seemingly out of place in the pastoral context in which it is delivered. There is no internal audience in the poems that will allow the words to function as a medium for ethical behavior. Within each work, the emphasis is squarely upon the reception of the words by the listener and his or her personal, internal response to them.

The poetry that both the *conceptistas* and Góngora and his supporters value is intellectual in nature, of course, and requires mental effort for comprehension. Góngora's verses, however, do not offer a medium for the affirmation of a series of progressive *conceptos* that build upon each other and then enhance the communal understanding at the center of the conceit. Such an experience of interconnections is precisely the direct effect, for example, in Quevedo's "Afectos varios de su corazón fluctuando en las ondas de los cabellos de Lisi" (Varied feelings of his heart floating in the waves of Lisi's hair), which proclaims the golden beauty of the beloved woman's hair and its likeness to such objects and elements as gold, light, fire, and waves reflecting the sun's brightness. There is, in spite of the difficulty of some of the allusions, a forward movement of terms and language that make up the metaphors so that by the end of the poem, a unity is created around the expression of desire's frustration. Góngora's descriptions, on the other hand, comprise a difficulty that arises not only from the linguistic disjunctures he creates, but also from the absence of a communally recognizable message and ongoing series of connections.

Dámaso Alonso has, for instance, elucidated the suspension of the reader's mental movement through the Gongorine metaphors as a rupture of the natural order of the syntactical elements. Referring to lines 45–47 of the *Polifemo* (" . . . donde encierra / cuanto las cumbres ásperas cabrío / de los montes esconde" [. . . where he confines / all the goats that cover the rugged peaks / of the mountains]), Alonso assigns the order ABCDE to the normal order of the words as follows: A = donde encierra cuanto; B = cabrío; C = esconde; D = las cumbres ásperas; E = de los montes. He demonstrates that "los versos de Góngora nos dan ADBEC" (Góngora's lines give us ADBEC), which interrupts the expected progress from A to B, B to C, and D to E.[55] The difficulty of such lines requires the reader to retrace his or her own steps in reading, in search of the logical and syntactical sense of the expression. In the process, the reader retraces Góngora's steps ("pasos") of composition and linguistic restructuring in order to understand the metaphor so presented. The process elicits the active use of the intellect that Góngora himself acknowledges as the privileged faculty in his poetics:

> y la obscuridad y estilo entrincado . . . da causa a que vacilando el entendimiento en fuerza de discurso trabajándole . . . alcance lo que así en la letura superficial de [los] versos no pudo entender; luego hase de confesar que tiene utilidad avivar el ingenio, y eso nació de la obscuridad del poeta. (896)

> (and the obscurity and intricate style . . . causes the intellect, vacillating while working away with the force of its reasoning power, . . . to find that which in the superficial reading of the verses it was unable to understand; then it has to confess that it is useful to stimulate the wit, and that was born from the obscurity of the poet.)

Cascales's disagreement with Góngora's special syntax is evinced in another

---

55. Dámaso Alonso, *Poesía española*, 337–40.

of his *Cartas,* in which he further attacks Góngora's *culterano* works and their difficulty. Of the formal difference between the native Spanish syntax and the Latinate forms preferred by Góngora, Cascales writes: "Siendo, pues, cierto que la lengua latina y castellana corren por diferentes caminos, quererlas don Luis llevar por una misma madre es violentar a la naturaleza y engendrar monstruosidades" (Thus being true that the Latin language and Castilian take different paths, Don Luis's wanting to bear them in the same mother is to violate nature and engender monstrosities).[56] His reference to monstrosity likewise suggests sterility. A particularly telling passage in this document is that in which Cascales demonstrates his own negative evaluation of melancholia's association with poetry and derides Góngora's new style of poetry: "En fin, todo esto es un humor grueso que se le ha subido a la cabeza al autor de este ateismo y a sus sectarios que, como humor, se ha de evaporar y resolver poco a poco en nada" (In short, all this is a thick humor that has risen to the head of the author of this atheism and to that of his followers which, like a humor, has to evaporate and turn little by little into nothing).[57]

Góngora as a poet is, like other poets of the period, literally associated with melancholia, but his poetic and intellectual unorthodoxy is consigned by his attackers to the negative realm of pathological melancholy. His deviation from the norm is also couched in religious and political terms—the same context of deviance present in other literary genres in depictions of melancholics. Through his poetics, Góngora is a renegade from his age, his country, and the true religion, according to Cascales, who reiterates his opposition to the Góngorine intellectual willfulness to obfuscate ("afectar la obscuridad, eso se vitupera" [affect obscurity, that is condemned]) in the following terms: "¡Oh diabólico poema! Pues ¿qué ha pretendido nuestro poeta? Yo lo diré; destruir la poesía" (Oh diabolical poem! Well, what has our poet tried to do? I will say it; destroy poetry). Góngora is in effect accused of being a heretic and a non-patriotic renegade outside the boundaries of artistic, religious, and national propriety:

> Mas un perpetuo modo de hablar obscuro . . . nos lleve por aquellos soterranos, y nos diga qué países y qué gentes son aquéllas, y qué moneda es la que allí corre, que como ni tiene cruz, ni colunas de Hércules, ni castillos, ni leones, no la conocemos.

> (But a perpetually dark way of speaking . . . carries us to those burial places, and tells us what countries and what peoples are those, and what money it is that is used there, for since it has neither cross, nor columns of Hercules, nor castles, nor lions, we do not know it.)[58]

56. *Cartas filológicas,* 1:214.
57. Ibid., 1:219.
58. Ibid., 221, 220, 188–89.

These items listed by Cascales are, of course, found on the "escudo de España" (shield of Spain) as Justo García Soriano points out, and are as well the "(tipos) con que se acuñaba nuestra moneda" (the sort with which our money was minted).[59] Góngora's abandonment of traditional poetic forms and discourse is thus tantamount to his abandonment of Spain.

Though not comprising a manifesto, Góngora's *culterano* works were, in effect, received as such. Whereas Cervantes, Lope, and later Calderón, reject the melancholic's potential for independent secular thought and separation from the medieval epistemology, Góngora never does reject melancholy or portray a repentant failed melancholy figure. His *culterano* poetry affirms, both through process and product, the thinking and hyperactive mentality of the melancholic poet. The underpinning found in Milton's debt to the melancholic muse in *Il Penseroso* is not counterbalanced in Góngora's works by a tribute to the inspiration behind such a work as *L'Allegro*. Thalia and Euterpe figure in his poetic references, but they have no power to influence. It is the melancholic poet and not the melancholic or mirthful muse who produces and controls the poetic discourse. Góngora is not simply artistically but also ideologically at odds with the more conservative minds of his age.

By Góngora's own admission, his poetry is difficult for average or uneducated readers: "honra me ha causado hacerme escuro a los ignorantes, que esa [es] la distinción de los hombres doctos, hablar de manera que a ellos les parezca griego" (it has honored me to be obscure to the ignorant, for that is the distinction of the educated men, to speak in such a way that it seems to them to be Greek [896–97]). This desire to make of the thought process demanded of composer and reader of the poetry an end and not a means to further interpretation marks the major difference between Góngora and his contemporaries. It shows him to be the Spanish poetic intellect most in tune with certain intellectual currents flowing in the rest of Europe while so many of the other great Spanish minds were resisting such an impulse. In his *Discurso poético*, Jáuregui registers his displeasure with Góngora's *poesía culta* on just such grounds with regard to the relationship between the poet and the reader of a poem, a relationship that had for centuries offered an experience to communicate and share important truths:

En esta parte concedo que están hoy los ingenios de España muy alentados y que debe el que escribe alargarse a bizarrías superiores, porque muchos, no siendo poetas, no se espantan ya de los versos ni rehusan leerlos con el temor y sumisión que otro tiempo. Antes hay muchos animosos que previenen advertencia y deseo, no pidiendo a las Musas la facilidad y llaneza que los incapaces pretenden, sino maravillas y extremos.

59. In Cascales, *Cartas*, 189 n. 3.

(In this matter I concede that today the wits of Spain are very haughty and that he who writes ought to go to great lengths, because many, not being poets, are not startled now by verses nor do they refuse to read them with fear and submission of other times. Rather there are many spirited ones who forestall warning and desire, not asking of the Muses the ease and clearness that the incapable seek, but rather wonders and extremes.)[60]

Andrée Collard considers these statements to be the negation of distance between *culterano* poet and reader of the *culto* poem. She explains:

En realidad, Góngora inventa un nuevo género poético en que la "utilidad" desaparece frente al arte descriptivo, vehículo de una visión del mundo bien personal. Reúne rasgos de la poesía tradicional épica, lírica y dramática quitándoles su antigua función. Idealiza la sustancia poética hasta un punto de desrealización última, y derriba de esta manera la vieja noción del poeta-profeta sustituyéndola con la del poeta-artífice que se ha hecho a sí mismo a fuerza de ingenio y erudición.

(In reality, Góngora invents a new poetic genre in which "utility" disappears before the descriptive art, the vehicle of a quite personal world. He reunites elements of traditional epic, lyric, and dramatic poetry and takes away their former function. He idealizes the poetic essence to the ultimate point of destruction, and brings down in this way the old notion of poet-prophet, replacing it with that of poet-inventor who has made himself by force of wit and erudition.)[61]

The inspiration and composition of the poem come from within the poet and not, as in the classical notion of divinely inspired poetry, from an external source.

The successful reader of Gongorine *poesía culta,* then, does not approach such works as an affirmation of the hermeneutic process inherent in the classical and medieval epistemology. Góngora indeed begins with familiar tales—the myth of Polifemo and Galatea or the often treated pastoral format of the *Soledad I*—and makes of them an intellectual exercise that violates the older mode of thinking by prizing above all else, and as an end, the thought necessary to write and to read his *culto* poems. The lack of the external inspiration behind the production and the reception of such poetry—which its critics lament at the same time as its supporters insist on disassociating the poet from the traditional role of prophet—mean that both camps characterize *poesía culta* as empty, though for different reasons and in different terms. Cascales complains that it leads to "nada" (nothing [1:219]), as do other theoreticians of that

60. In Andrée Collard, *Nueva poesía: conceptismo, culteranismo en la crítica española,* 101-2.
61. Ibid., 102.

period, while one of Góngora's proponents, Francisco de Medrano, admiringly writes in his *Apologético* of the poetry's "perfiles de donaire" (profiles of cleverness) and describes it as "vana, hueca, vacía y sin corazón de misterio alguno" (vain, hollow, empty and without any heart of mystery).[62] In his "Carta en respuesta," Góngora defines what in his poetic system is the transcendent element. The experience of reading and understanding "dark" poetry takes place within the mind and is possible because the *culto* poet makes a unified undertaking of revealing and creating. He is simultaneously the poet *faber* and the poet *vates*. Asking, "¿han sido útiles al mundo las poesías y aun las profecías (que vates se llama el profeta como el poeta)?" (have the poetry and even the prophecies been useful to the world [for the prophet as well as the poet is called seer]?), he answers: "Sería error negarlo" (It would be an error to deny it [896]). His explanation, however, privileges the mental effort to contend with the darkness of the poetry in order that it "alcance lo que así en la letura superficial de sus versos no pudo entender" (find that which in a superficial reading of the verses it was unable to understand [896]).

In response to such notions, the opponents of Gongorine poems make parallel attacks on *culterano* works for their lack of moral content, which prevents them from teaching a moral lesson. Cristóbal Suárez de Figueroa charges that "sobre todo, sin la claridad no puede la poesía mostrar su grandeza; porque donde no hay claridad, no hay luz de entendimiento, y donde faltan estos dos medios no se puede conocer ni entender cosa" (especially, without clarity poetry cannot show its greatness; because where there is no clarity, there is no light of intellect, and where these two means are lacking one cannot know nor understand anything).[63] He claims further that the *culto* poet is, in his opinion, a person "peligrosa mucho, porque sólo comunica sus versos, no para desengaño, sino para ostentación, y assí se debe huir con todo cuydado" (who is very dangerous, because he only communicates his verses, not in order to reveal the truth, but rather to show off, and thus one ought to flee [from him] with great care).[64] Even Gracián, in spite of his admiration of Góngora, complains of the poems' lack of moral content:

Si en este culto plectro cordobés hubiera correspondido la moral enseñanza a la heroica composición, los asuntos graves a la cultura de su estilo, la materia a la bizarría del verso, a la sutileza de sus conceptos, no digo yo de marfil, pero de un finísimo diamante merecía formarse su concha.

62. See ibid., 102–3.
63. *El passagero*, 101.
64. Ibid., 89–90.

(If in this refined Cordoban plectrum the moral teaching had corresponded to the heroic composition, the serious matters to the cultured style, the material to the dashing verse, to the delicacy of its conceits, I say that its shell would be worthy of being formed not of marble but of the finest diamond.)[65]

Valencia likewise complains in his "Carta" to Góngora that the author of the *Soledades* and the *Polifemo* "huye también de las virtudes y de las musas y de las Gracias que tiene propias y se desemeja y escurece de propósito" (flees also from the virtues and from the muses and from the Graces which are his own, and he disfigures and darkens himself on purpose).[66] From this point of view, the internal, mental source primary to Góngora's poetic production is suspicious and unorthodox because it violates what has been valued heretofore.

The negative or positive value of the intellectual experience of reading and writing *poesía culta* therefore hinges on the evaluation of the emerging *cogito* that the melancholic embodies in Golden Age literature. Góngora is praised by certain admirers like Jerónimo de Villegas (in a dedicatory section of the 1659 edition of Góngora's *Obras*) for producing poetry "para que el Ingenio, no solamente se emplee en leer, sino en contemplar" (so that the Wit, is not only used in reading, but in contemplating). More often, however, he is attacked for "la oscuridad . . . que derivaba de la concepción artística misma [y] era irremediable, perniciosa y ociosa" (the darkness . . . that derived from the very artistic conception [and] was incurable, pernicious and pointless).[67] Contemplation as a productive undertaking or as a pastime of the idle is the polemical center of the transvaluation of melancholy and, as in the fictional and dramatic portrayals of melancholia, informs the two theoretical poles concerning the value of the melancholic mind for poetry.

The melancholy contemplation of the poet that Ficino re-emphasizes is openly appreciated in Góngora's poetics. His difficult poetic discourse is not in language that approximates oral communication. Though most lyric poetry is not, it nevertheless does bear more syntactical and terminological similarity to the original language from which it is articulated than does Góngora's. Further, it is to be read in solitude, thereby celebrating and insisting upon one of the primary attributes of melancholy. Góngora's cerebral approach to poetry calls attention to a substantial epistemological shift: from a system of correspondence to one of difference. Reworking the familiar themes, traditions, and *topoi* in both the *Polifemo* and the *Soledad I* within a formal and ideological context

65. *El Criticón*, ed. Santos Alonso, 363.
66. In Martínez, *La batalla en torno a Góngora*, 4.
67. In Collard, *Nueva poesía*, 108.

of melancholy, Góngora brings to the foreground the very act and art of poetic composition on his own terms. By means of his obfuscating discourse, he insists on altering very familiar material in such a way that demands his reader's effort to understand, to recognize, and ultimately to acknowledge the difference between earlier versions or models and his own through affirmation of the validity of his different and very personal presentation. Underlying Góngora's affirmation of independent thought and difference, however, is a sinister potential for destruction.

Like Ficino, who revels in the brilliance of his melancholy mind while recognizing the concomitant threat of pain and incapacitating sadness, Góngora weaves into his *poesía culta* the burden of his melancholy conceptualization. Thus *Polifemo* is the story of a monster whose one-eyed countenance marks both his separateness and the singular vision that make of him an unrequited melancholy lover, living and singing of his passion in solitude. The destructive power of the melancholic is represented in his act of violence against Acis, which results in a metamorphosis similar to, but ultimately different from, the Ovidian original.[68] Ovid's tale, narrated by the nymph herself, ends with Acis's conversion to a river from whose waters a recognizable anthropomorphic river god appears. Góngora emphasizes only the change to a new watery form, the form in which Acis is greeted mournfully by Galatea's mother Doris: "que con llanto pío, / yerno le saludó, le aclamó río" (who with merciful tears / greeted him as son-in-law, hailed him as river [vv. 503-4]). It is specifically the verbal act of acclaiming Acis a river that interests Góngora, whose *culto* poems celebrate the fashioning of a new reality out of words. His is not the mimetic art of traditional poetry, for he presents a familiar narrative or situational *topos* that, by means of an intellectual effort, the reader must mentally reconstruct in order to understand. Góngora's art is thus a combination of destructive and constructive efforts, and it both depends upon and calls attention to those extremes inherent in the dialectical nature of melancholy.

Crafted from language that does not articulate the communally recognizable metaphysical connections that such a great *conceptista* poem as Quevedo's "Afectos varios" articulates, Góngora's poems must be understood at the level of writing and not of speech. Fernando Lázaro Carreter considers the ideological difference, for example, between Quevedo's use of language and Góngora's in terms of the former's general comprehensibility as a vehicle of shared expression: "Quevedo, pues, frente a Góngora, se encierra deliberadamente en el español de su tiempo y se reduce las posibilidades de expresión a los elementos

---

68. See R. V. Young, "Versions of Galatea: Renaissance and Baroque Imitation," in *Renaissance Papers 1984,* ed. Dale B. J. Randall and Joseph A. Porter, 57-68.

que el caudal idiomático vigente le suministra" (Thus Quevedo contrasted with Góngora, closes himself up deliberately in the Spanish of his time and reduces the possibilities of expression to the elements that the prevailing linguistic flow provides him). Lázaro Carreter likewise considers the difference in the technique and articulation of metaphor in both poets. Looking at "A un hombre de gran nariz" (To a man with a big nose) as paradigmatic of Quevedo's poetic conceptualization ("[t]oda la obra de Quevedo está como en clave en este soneto" [all Quevedo's work is concentrated in this sonnet]), he explains the poem as a series of independent lines: "cada verso es una unidad esticomítica, independiente de la que le precede o le sigue" (each line is a stichomythic unity, independent of the one that precedes it or follows it)—with the exception of lines 13 and 14. Thus, in each metric unit, "el poeta instala un objeto distinto . . . que hace entrar en relación con el objeto central, mediante una identidad metafórica. El poema adopta así una estructura radial; cada verso es un radio que nos conduce al lugar común de todas las metáforas, es decir, en este caso, a la nariz" (the poet installs a different object . . . that he makes enter in relation to the central object, by means of a metaphoric identity. The poem thus adopts a radial structure; each line is a radius that leads us to the common location of all the metaphors, that is to say, in this case, to the nose).[69] Such poetry extends its process of connection beyond its final lines and affirms the system of connections to which it leads. Góngora's *poesía culta* requires the reader to keep his or her intellectual gaze fixed on the confines of its strophes. Like Polifemo's single eye, the mind is the single source of light for composition and interpretation of these works.

Góngora's poetic language is an invented medium that seeks to establish its own self-referential universe in defiance of the macrocosmic frame of reference. In this sense his poetic language is universal but not in the sense of a communally understood form of communication by untrained readers. It is necessary to enter into the universe of Góngora's poetic system while simultaneously exiting from the generally accepted macrocosmic order. Those who are unwilling to do so simply cannot understand the *culto* poems. Such works remain for them just language: words without meaning or message. Góngora suggests his self-conscious awareness of the monstrosity of such literature by means of the monster Polifemo, whose song-poem is not received in the way he intends. The consequence is disastrous for Acis, who is decimated by the gigantic poet, defeated by one whose poetry he would not or could not hear properly. Acis himself is, in effect, converted into linguistic components, as the last lines of the

69. *Estilo barroco y personalidad creadora*, 32–33.

Polifemo attest ("yerno le saludó, le aclamó río [v. 504]). The implication is clear in the reader's case. If the poem continues to be taken as merely words, the reader is defeated. The failure is his or hers and not Góngora's, for the melancholy, monstrous, and obsessed universe of the poem presents itself for understanding and acceptance, like Polifemo. The reader/receiver must make the effort to supplement the poetic discourse with his/her own mental activity to understand it; the *Polifemo* vividly depicts the negative consequences of a failure to do so.

It is thus possible to say that Góngora's imagination, being not merely a conduit of sensory material, is instead self-consciously superseded by his intellect. He demands no less a feat of his successful readers, who must, like the poet, value highly an "intellectual practice upon the world" that Góngora achieves, rather than a "discursive exchange within the world" that Lope, Quevedo, and others affirm. While the conservative minds of his age do not approve of such an orientation, the self-referential thought necessary to bring forth light from the apparent darkness of such works as the *Polifemo* and the *Soledad I* is precisely what Góngora, at the vanguard of the new European thinking, proclaims and celebrates. The one-eyed Polifemo is an appropriate protagonist for such a proposition. The writing and reading of Gongorine *poesía culta* are necessarily individual and personal accomplishments. Singular, solitary contemplation is demanded for such undertakings.

This intellectual process is effectively recreated in allegorical terms in the *Soledad I*. The reader, like the shipwrecked youth, is submerged in darkness at the beginning. It is only by the effort of meeting the challenge of that darkness—the sea or the difficult language which parallels it—that one finds a light. The youth finally makes his way to shore and sees a light that brings him to a source of explanation and interpretation of the reality in which he finds himself. The reader's experience is a counterpart to this undertaking, for through the act of reading further, the poem's language becomes more familiar and the context of its subject matter becomes more understandable. As the youth proceeds, moreover, he comes closer to a fusion with the poem's narrator. His role changes from described protagonist to observer of the action, and thus becoming the medium of vision for the physical, sensual world of the poem. As a character, he eventually vanishes at the point when the poem/song-within-the-poem to Himeneo is presented. The youth, who has been the subject of the earlier third-person narration and has overtly been portrayed as the listener/receptor of the *serrano*'s words and the chorus's song, serves in all capacities as the facilitator of the descriptions of the teeming natural world Góngora depicts. As both subject and seer of the abundant elements described, the youth enacts as well the role that the reader of Góngora's poetry must undertake, for he contemplates the world of the poem, but always as a solitary *peregrino* who offers nothing but his contemplation to the endeavor; it is significant that he never tells his own story. That the youthful personage disappears or is melded with the narrator completes as well his fusion with the reader, who must also occupy the only spot for effective understanding and contemplation of the work: the position of its creator, who demands that the enlightened reader/receiver of his *culto* verses depend on an actively functioning intellect.

The *peregrino* eventually disappears into the melancholy universe of the *Soledades*. By the end of the *Soledad II*, he is drifting aimlessly in a boat near the shore and representing the traditional melancholy figure as well as the lack of direction that Góngora himself indicates is also his own in the very structure of the seemingly unfinished composition.[70] Willing and self-conscious presence in the poetic universe of *poesía culta* seems to be its only end and reward, and perhaps the sterility of its monstrousness is thus suggested after all. The *peregrino* and the final poem that contains him lead in no definitive direction nor does anything new begin. An indefinite continuation of the same intellectual contemplation, once undertaken, leads only to its own continuation—the sentence or the reward of the melancholic mind.

The *Polifemo* is in effect a companion piece to the *Soledad I* in their articulation of the melancholic process of poetic composition and the experience of reading a poem. The *Polifemo* comprises a description of the setting and the circumstances surrounding the monstrous poet *fabro* who offers his love song to one who will not receive it. His melancholic characterization is cast in far more negative terms than the melancholia underlying the *Soledad I*, for it leads to violence. Polifemo is a monster, and as such is as unique as Góngora is to his detractors, who in grudging admiration, proclaim him and his poetry to be inimitable. In this sense Góngora discounts the notions articulated by Huarte and Lope with regard to engendering his creations with the aid of a partner outside himself. Like the natural monster whose uniqueness is perpetual because it cannot procreate like other beings, Góngora has no need of a partner. Because he rejects the ongoing discursive exchange of the older thought system, the notion of monstrosity is not connotative of a negative sterility but rather of the self-sufficiency of the autonomous, secular mind. The monstrous persona of his poem is a parallel of the *culto* poet, for in the excess of his size, his strength, his adjudged ugliness, and his domination over the setting, he remains

70. Beverly, *Aspects of Góngora's "Soledades,"* 103.

isolated in a contemplative stance. His melancholic energy leads not to any active participation with his milieu but to the composition of a song that unsettles those surroundings, just as Góngora's system of composition fashions the described reality to suit his purposes and in the process jars the literary circles of which he is considered a discordant part.

Though the *Soledad I* is premised on a base that constantly threatens violence through the untamable elements and processes of nature and the destructive impulses against the natural world that motivate human beings to action, the poem nevertheless celebrates the communication by a poet to a single reader in the act of the experience of the poem. The highly stylized world of nature emerges descriptively through the reading of the *Soledad I,* and to understand the description, Góngora's reader must also see and reconstruct the articulated images that emerge not by means of a recourse to the sensual world but instead by means of an intellectual process that recognizes the active power of the intellect. The poem's protagonist is the *peregrino* and the structure of the work is a verbal peregrination from chaotic darkness to recognition and understanding. This process is accomplished because of an intellectual effort made to reconstruct an image from disjointed and highly stylized linguistic elements and thus further exemplifies Góngora's reversal of the process of cognition that had depended on sensory information delivered up to the intellect by the imagination. Góngora composes *culto* verses that value not only the solitude and uniqueness of the poet but that of the reader too, for these works negate the oral tradition and its implied community, requiring instead the reception of written language that is to be deciphered in solitude by an individual reader. The muse dictated the verses of the two works, an activity that implies their written record. Góngora's *peregrino* enacts the experience of receiving information and facilitates this same level of activity for the reader.

It is appropriate, therefore, to conclude with a consideration of the context of melancholy within which Paravicino articulates poetically his admiration of Góngora and within which Cascales also expresses his displeasure concerning the studious mind in his letter "Contra las letras y todo género de artes y ciencias. Prueba de ingenio" (Against letters and all type of arts and sciences. Test of wit). In this epistle, Cascales begins with an apology for having failed to honor a social invitation the previous day. His self-defense relies on his friend's understanding of the debilitating effects of study upon the invited guest, for he explains: "No cumplí mi palabra, olvidado de mí mismo; porque sumergí tanto en la lección de algunos humanistas, que me robaron totalmente la memoria, pervertieron el juicio y casi me despojaron del sentido común" (I did not keep my word, having forgotten myself; because I was so deeply absorbed in the

reading of some humanists, that they robbed me totally of memory, they perverted my reason and almost divested me of common sense). This is a classic
description of the detrimental and drying effects of the studious melancholic
condition, seemingly induced in this instance by the mental endeavors that
Cascales, in hindsight, proclaims "malas ocupaciones, que cuestan tan caro al
cuerpo y al alma" (evil occupations, that cost the body and soul so dearly).
Extending the analogy between "letras" and their supposed dire consequences,
Cascales exclaims: "¡Oh letras! ¡Oh infierno! ¡Oh carnicería! ¡Oh muerte de los
sentidos humanos!" (Oh letters! Oh inferno! Oh carnage! Oh death of the
human senses!) thereby reiterating many of the manifestations of melancholia
already outlined in this study. Not only is the image of blackness and despair a
part of his description of the written figures, but he likewise associates the
destructive nature of these manifestations with the flames of hellfire as well as
the bloody violence they can provoke: "o seáis rojas, o seáis negras; que de esta
manera sois todos. Por lo rojo sois sangrientas, sois homicidas; por lo negro
sois símbolo de la tristeza, del luto, del trabajo, de la desdicha" (be you red, or
be you black; for you are all of this sort. Due to the red you are bloody, you are
murderers; due to the black you are symbolic of sadness, of mourning, of toil,
of misery).[71] The traditional link between melancholy and study is here assailed
as a detriment to productive living and as a hindrance to communication.

In his own poem written upon Góngora's death, Paravicino, on the other
hand, applauds this very connection as the basis of the *culto* poet's greatness.[72]
The *romance* is entirely steeped in images of darkness and night, beginning
with its title—"Romance, describiendo la noche y el día, dirigido a don Luis de
Góngora" (Ballad, describing the night and the day, addressed to Don Luis de
Góngora)—that alludes to the two poles associated with Saturn as the patron of
cold, dark places and the former ruler of the Age of Gold. As the poem begins,
night is overtaking the daylight: "cuando la luz, con las sombras / más obedece,
que lucha" (when the light, obeys rather than / fights with the shadows). Words
that evoke Góngora's own melancholy imagery in *Polifemo* and *Soledad I* also
appear throughout: "lánguidos bostezos" (languid yawns), "horror," "funestas
aves" (ill-fated birds), "muerte fecunda" (prolific death), among others. Paravicino situates within this section on darkness a four-line section that seems to
summarize Góngora's acknowledged system of poetics: "Moderna copia del
caos, / en cuya nada dibuja / más fantasmas el cuidado / que el sueño imágine
junta" (Modern copy of chaos, / in whose nothingness care / draws more

71. *Cartas filológicas*, 1:81.
72. In Martínez, *La batalla en torno a Góngora*, 281-84.

phantoms / than sleep imagines). By means of terms like "nada" and "caos" that Góngora's detractors use against him, Paravicino praises the power of the poet to create images from nothing as he leads into the section that describes the light's return, but only after the intensifying of the darkness: "Nuevo horror condensa el aire, / . . . / eternidades la noche / a sus abismos vincula" (A new horror condenses the air, / . . . / the night binds eternities / to its depths). Light does break forth (as Góngora indicates is possible through proper reading of his poetry), for ". . . alegres sospechas tiñen / una y otra nube oscura" (. . . happy suspicions tinge / this and that dark cloud) and "Resurrección es del día" (it is the resurrection of the day).

The sound of the sun's footsteps ("Del sol se sienten los pasos" [One hears the steps of the sun]) reminds Paravicino's reader of the process undertaken in the *Soledad I* of following the *peregrino*'s footsteps and the poet's verses through the figurative and literal darkness to the light of meaning. The scene alleged to be illuminated is one of abundant beauty, described in a section of lines that terminates with the words: "fragrante aborto tributan" (they pay respect to the fragrant abortion). The term "aborto" is central to Parvacino's implications, for the usual notion of *aborto* as "mal parto" (miscarriage) that the *Diccionario de Autoridades* lists as its primary definition suggests the notion of unproductiveness that Góngora's monster and monstrous poetic universe communicate.[73] The *Diccionario* also includes a second definition: "Se toma freqüentemente por cosa prodigiosa, sucesso extraordinario, y portento raro" (It is also frequently understood as a marvelous thing, an extraordinary event, a rare portent), certainly a meaning applicable to Góngora and his works by someone like Paravicino, who admires the *Polifemo* and the *Soledad I*. This definition, moreover, is exemplified in the *Diccionario* by the following passage from the *Empressas políticas* of Diego de Saavedra: "Si causa delectacion el ver un cuerpo monstruoso, quanto mayor será oir los prodigiosos abortos de la naturaleza, sus obras, y sus secretos ordinarios" (If seeing a monstrous body causes enjoyment, how much more enjoyable is it to hear of the wonderful marvels of nature, its word, and its ordinary secrets). The connection between monstrosity, admiration, and the prodigious revelation of secrets is an inherent one in Góngora's *culto* works, but the final definition associated with *aborto* is the most suggestive for Paravicino's context. The *Diccionario* lists the phrase "Es un aborto" (It is an *aborto*) with the explanation: "Phrase que se usa para exagerar el entendimiento, o habilidad de algun mozo, o niño, que es mayor de lo que al parecer permite su edad" (an expression that is used to exaggerate the

---

73. *Diccionario de autoridades*, 1:17.

intellect, or the ability of a youth, or a little boy, that is greater than his age would indicate). Certainly, it is the exaggerated use of the intellect that produces Góngora's poems, his *abortos* to which Paravicino alludes.

The *romance* continues with references to the sun as the eye of heaven and as the light of revelation and *desengaño* for our misperceptions: "Ya el ojo del cielo dora / cuanto los nuestros azulan" (Now the eye of heaven gilds / all that ours color blue). Soon Paravicino makes overt references to the *Polifemo* and the *Soledades* and refers as well to Góngora as "A quien el jayán de Ulises, / . . . / debe más luz que a su frente" (To whom the great strongman of Ulysses, / . . . / owes more light than to his forehead), again a reference to Polyphemus and to the intellectual light that Góngora's poetry emits. The play of light and darkness carries through the rest of the poem's remaining lines with the implication of honor, fame, and reputation that Góngora deserves in his capacity as "padre mayor de las musas" (principal father of the muses), that is, Saturn himself.

Conclusion

The melancholy characters examined in this study provide evidence of the usefulness of their collective type to various Golden Age authors who generally reject the strength and autonomy of the secular intellect which melancholics embody and which, in all cases but Góngora's poetry, is depicted as subversive to the proper analogical patterns of thought. Yet if the analogical system is the underlying structure that is affirmed when hypertrophic intellects are seen to fail, then these failures raise as many questions as are answered, for their very portrayal defies the notion of order that the medieval patterns of conceptualization afford. Whereas Cervantes, Tirso, Lope, Calderón, and the authors of the picaresque present disapproving portraits of their various melancholic characters and show them to be unsuccessful in their intellectual separation from the community, these writers also portray the larger society itself as fragmented and flawed. When figures like Quijote or one of the wife-murderers do reintegrate into the larger community at the end of their respective experiences, the societies are ready to ratify the madman or the murderer merely in order to postpone further madness or violence—a short-term solution and not a true restoration of order. The melancholy disorders that the protagonists display are thus not remedied, and the suggestion of such a foreboding permanence implies the seriousness of the threat to the older epistemological system that the melancholic mind represents.

Similarly, in works such as Tirso's play about *acedia* or Lope's dramatization of the death of the Knight from Olmedo, melancholy thought is the agent by which Christian principles are undermined. The monk despairs of salvation because he thinks rather than believes, and Alonso's true love for Inés, which ought to lead them to the altar, is unrealized because he plays too long at voguish melancholy and is ultimately killed because of his rival's pathological jealousy. Yet in Alonso's case, he meets with admiration from the general society. His very affectation, after all, is akin to the posture that also affords the *pícaro* a means to manipulate those who come into contact with such self-serving theatrics.

Melancholy, despite all the negative connotations it represents for Spanish Golden Age authors, however, is undeniably linked to the production of works of art and literature. In 1638, for example, Francisco Pacheco allegorically describes the art of painting in his *El arte de la pintura* (The art of painting, not published until 1649): "Tiene cabellos negros, crespos y sueltos, por los continos revueltos y vagos pensamientos de la imitación de l'arte de la naturaleza y

163

de la imaginación, en todos los efetos visibles; causa eficaz de muncha melancolía, que engendra adustión, como dicen los médicos" (It has black, curly, and unbound hair, due to the continuous disorder and vague thoughts about the imitation of nature's art and that of the imagination, in all the visible effects; effective cause of much melancholia, that engenders heat, as the doctors say).[1] Though similar to Góngora's melancholic expressions and descriptions of melancholy, Pacheco's definition still does not accord the inventive freedom to the melancholic that the author of the *Soledades* promotes. The artist continues to accept the mental activity that he describes as the basis for finding correspondences ("no es otra cosa el debuxo . . . que una aparente expresión y declaración del concepto que se tiene en el ánimo, y de aquello que se ha imaginado en la mente y fabricado en la idea" [the drawing is nothing else . . . than an apparent expression and declaration of the thought held in the soul, and of that which one has imagined in the mind and fashioned in the thought]).[2] The contemplative melancholy brain is the transvalued means of realizing that process.

The self-contemplation that the hypertrophic intellect undertakes is an important medium of the *desengaño* that underlies so much of the literature of seventeenth-century Spain, but the separation from a community that it also brings about for the isolated thinker is depicted literarily as detrimental to social harmony. In the prefatory pages of Acosta's treatise on a solitary life is found his counsel: "Pues melancolía no os faltará, que allende la vuestra natural, la divina scriptura llama triste al que vive solo y sin compañía" (Well, you will not lack melancholy, for besides your natural melancholy, divine scripture labels sad the one who lives alone and without company).[3] Therefore, the more widespread melancholy is perceived to be, the more threatened is the collective and cohesive fabric of society. Burton's perception of melancholy as a universal malady ("thou shalt soon perceive that all the world is mad, that it is melancholy")[4] is meaningful in this context and reflects what his Spanish medical contemporaries also record. Writing during the reign of Philip III, Pérez de Herrera describes the four humors and their corresponding temperaments and characteristics. About melancholy he says: "No hai hombre que se escape de alguna melancolia, ni pueda estar sin ella" (There is no man who escapes some sort of melancholy, nor is able to be without it).[5]

1. Francisco Pacheco, *El arte de la pintura*, ed. F. J. Sánchez Cantón, 1:99.
2. Ibid., 1:272–73; see also 261–62.
3. Acosta, *Tratado*, n. p.
4. *Anatomy of Melancholy*, 28.
5. *Proverbios morales y consejos christianos*, 281.

Not only is humanity in general vulnerable to melancholy, but it becomes an almost limitless disorder that encompasses numerous physical and mental imbalances. Jackson notes that "[i]n earlier centuries, clearly a wider range of conditions was included within those boundaries than has been the case since the early nineteenth century"; Alberto Escudero Ortuño likewise asserts that "[e]l concepto de melancolía era tan extenso, que en el se comprendieron casi todos los trastornos psíquicos" ([t]he concept of melancholy was so extensive, that within it are included almost all the psychic disorders).[6] This perceived breadth of melancholy's influence is a measure of the recognition of the growing hegemony of a more modern system of thought. Even the clinical debate concerning the humor's effect on the mental faculties reflects the progressively stronger link accorded between the highly active intellect and melancholia. By the eighteenth century, the general categorization of melancholia as partial insanity parallels a "trend toward the view that the primary damage, albeit circumscribed, [is] to the intellect."[7] Having been portrayed throughout the sixteenth and seventeenth centuries as a brilliance that cannot be trusted, the melancholy intellect in Golden Age literature represents the dangers of thinking gone wrong. As a transvalued concept, melancholy comes to be understood and depicted as the characteristic of mental superiority and insanity, as the curse of the isolated individual and the most unavoidable and common trait of human life, and as the means to new knowledge that inspires optimistic fascination as well as anxiety. In her consideration of such issues Dorothy Koenigsberger contends that their basis, which rests in part on the link during the Renaissance between melancholy and genius, is to be found in the simultaneous doubt about and attraction to a belief in the efficacy of the human being.[8] Pérez de Herrera's verse "Enigma" describes melancholy in a way that seems to summarize this dialectical tension: "Triste soi, y pensativa, / . . . / y sin mi no hallo quien viva" (I am sad, and pensive, / . . . / and without me I find no one alive).[9]

6. Jackson, *Melancholia and Depression*, 399; Alberto Escudero Ortuño, *El concepto de la melancolía en el siglo XVII (Un comentario a las obras de Robert Burton y Alfonso de Santa Cruz)*, 98.

7. Jackson, *Melancholia and Depression*, 400.

8. Koenigsberger, *Renaissance Man and Creative Thinking: A History of Concepts of Harmony 1400–1700*, 166.

9. *Proverbios morales y consejos cristianos*, 280.

Bibliography

Acosta, Cristóbal. *Tratado en contra y pro de la vida solitaria.* Venice, 1592.

Agheana, Ion T. *The Situational Drama of Tirso de Molina.* New York: Plaza Mayor, 1972.

Aguilar, Juan Bautista. *Teatro de los dioses de la gentilidad.* Valencia, 1688.

Albarracín Teulón, Agustín. *La medicina en el teatro de Lope de Vega.* Madrid: Consejo Superior de Investigaciones Científicas, 1954.

Alemán, Mateo. *Primera parte de Guzmán de Alfarache.* Edited by Benito Brancaforte. Madrid: Cátedra, 1984.

———. *Segunda parte de la vida de Guzmán de Alfarache: Atalaya de la vida humana.* Edited by Benito Brancaforte. Madrid, 1984.

Alighieri, Dante. *The Divine Comedy: Inferno.* Edited by John D. Sinclair. New York: Oxford University Press, 1975.

Allen, John J. *Don Quixote: Hero or Fool? A Study in Narrative Technique.* Gainesville: University of Florida Press, 1969.

———. *Don Quixote: Hero or Fool? (Part Two).* Gainesville: University of Florida Press, 1979.

Alonso, Dámaso, ed. *Poesía de la Edad Media y poesía de tipo tradicional.* Buenos Aires: Lozada, 1942.

———. *Poesía española.* Madrid: Gredos, 1971.

Aquinas, Thomas. *Summa Theologica. Basic Writings of St. Thomas Aquinas.* 2 vols. Edited by Anton C. Pegis. New York: Random, 1945.

Arias, Joan. *Guzmán de Alfarache: Unrepentant Narrator.* London: Tamesis, 1977.

Arias de la Canal, Fredo. "La locura de Cervantes." *Norte: Revista Hispano Americano* 266 (1975): 49–57.

Avalle-Arce, Juan B. "Cervantes, Grisóstomo, Marcela, and Suicide." *PMLA* 89 (1974): 1115–16.

———. *Don Quijote como forma de vida.* Valencia: Fundación Juan March y Editorial Castalia, 1976.

———. "Don Quijote, o la vida como obra de arte." *Cuadernos Hispanoamericanos* 242 (1970): 247–80.

———. *Nuevos deslindes cervantinos.* Barcelona: Ariel, 1975.

Avalle-Arce, Juan B., and E. C. Riley, eds. *Suma cervantina.* London: Tamesis, 1973.

Babb, Lawrence. *Sanity in Bedlam.* East Lansing: Michigan State University Press, 1959.

———. *The Elizabethan Malady.* East Lansing: Michigan State College Press, 1951.

Bastianutti, Diego L. "*El caballero de Olmedo*: sólo un ejercicio triste del alma." *Hispanófila* 2 (1973): 25–38.

Bataillon, Marcel. "*La Célestine" selon Fernando de Rojas.* Paris: Didier, 1961.

———. *Novedad y fecundidad del "Lazarillo de Tormes".* Salamanca: Anaya, 1968.

Beardsley, Theodore S. *Hispano-Classical Translations Printed Between 1482–1699.* Pittsburgh: Duquesne University Press, 1970.

Beverley, John R. *Aspects of Góngora's "Soledades".* Amsterdam: John Benjamins, 1980.

Bleznick, Donald W. "La teoría de los humores en los tratados políticos del Siglo de Oro." *Hispanófila* 5 (1959): 1–9.

167

Boorde, Andrew. *The Breviarie of Helthe*. London, 1547.

Bradbury, Gail. "Tragedy and Tragicomedy in the Theatre of Lope de Vega." *Bulletin of Hispanic Studies* 58 (1981): 103–11.

Brancaforte, Benito. "La tragedia de *El caballero de Olmedo*." *Cuadernos Hispano-americanos* 286 (1974): 93–106.

———. *Guzmán de Alfarache: ¿conversión o proceso de degradación?* Madison: The Hispanic Society, 1980.

Bravo de Sobremonte, Gaspar. *Resolutionum, & Consultationum Medicarum*. Lyon, 1671.

Bright, Timothy. *A Treatise of Melancholie. Containing the Causes Thereof, & Reasons of the Strange Effects It Worketh in Our Minds and Bodies: with the Physicke Cure, and Spirituall Consolation for Such as Have Thereto Adioyned an Afflicted Conscience*. London, 1586.

Bundy, Murray W. "The Theory of Imagination in Classical and Mediaeval Thought." *University of Illinois Studies in Language and Literature* 12 (1927): 7–289.

Burke, James. "The *Estrella de Sevilla* and the Tradition of Saturnine Melancholy." *Bulletin of Hispanic Studies* 51 (1974): 137–56.

Burton, Robert. *The Anatomy of Melancholy*. Philadelphia: J. W. Moore, 1852.

Calderón de la Barca, Pedro. "A secreto agravio, secreta venganza." In *Obras completas*, edited by A. Valbuena Briones, 1:421–53. Madrid: Aguilar, 1966.

———. "Darlo todo y no dar nada." In *Obras completas*, edited by A. Valbuena Briones, 1:1019–67. Madrid: Aguilar, 1966.

———. "El mágico prodigioso." In *Obras completas*, edited by A. Valbuena Briones, 1:603–42. Madrid: Aguilar, 1966.

———. *El médico de su honra*. Edited by D. W. Cruickshank. Madrid: Castalia, 1981.

———. "El pintor de su deshonra." In *Obras completas*, edited by A. Valbuena Briones, 1:865–903. Madrid: Aguilar, 1966.

———. "El príncipe constante." In *Obras completas*, edited by A. Valbuena Briones, 1:245–78. Madrid: Aguilar, 1966.

Calepinus, Ambrosius. *Dictionarium*. 2 vols. Venice, 1593.

Carballo, Luis Alfonse de. *Cisne de Apolo*. 2 vols. Edited by A. Porqueras Mayo. Madrid: Consejo Superior de Investigaciones Científicas, 1958.

Casa, Frank P. "Crime and Responsibility in *El médico de su honra*." In *Homenaje a William L. Fichter: Estudios sobre el teatro antiguo español y otros ensayos*, edited by David Kossoff and José Amor y Vázquez, 127–37. Madrid: Castalia, 1971.

Casalduero, Joaquín. *Sentido y forma del 'Quijote'*. Madrid: Insula, 1966.

Cascales, Francisco. *Cartas filológicas*. 3 vols. Edited by Justo García Soriano. Madrid: Clásicos Castellanos, 1930.

———. *Tablas poéticas*. Edited by Benito Brancaforte. Madrid: Espasa-Calpe, 1975.

Cascardi, Anthony J. "Cervantes and Descartes on the Dream Argument." *Cervantes* 4 (1984): 109–22.

Castro, Américo. *El pensamiento de Cervantes*. Madrid: Noguer, 1972.

Cervantes Saavedra, Miguel de. *Don Quijote de la Mancha*. Edited by Martín de Riquer. Barcelona: Editorial Juventud, 1966.

Charron, Pierre. *Of Wisdome*. Translated by Samson Lennard. London, 1640.

Chaucer, Geoffrey. "The Parson's Tale." In *The Canterbury Tales*, edited by A. C. Cawley, 530–607. London: Dent, 1958.

Close, Anthony. "Don Quijote's Sophistry and Wisdom." *Bulletin of Hispanic Studies* 55 (1978): 103-14.

———. *The Romantic Approach to "Don Quijote."* New York: Cambridge University Press, 1977.

Collard, Andrée. *Nueva poesía: conceptismo, culteranismo en la crítica española.* Madrid: Castalia, 1967.

Comes, Natalis. *Mythologiae, sive explicationum fabularum. Libri decem.* Venice, 1581.

Cornutus, Lucius Annaeus. *Natura deorum gentilium commentarius.* Venice, 1505.

Cortés, Jerónimo. *Lunario nuevo perpetuo y general y pronostica de los tiempos universales.* Madrid, 1598.

Costa, Richard H. "Intimations of *Don Quijote* in Sidney's *Defense of Poesy.*" *Ball State University Forum* 11 (1971): 60-63.

Covarrubias y Horozco, Sebastián de. *Tesoro de la lengua castellana y española.* Madrid: Turner, 1977.

Criado de Val, Manuel, ed. *La Picaresca. Orígenes, textos y estructuras.* Madrid: Fundación Universitaria Española, 1979.

Cros, Edmond. "Contribution à l'étude de la formation discursive au Siècle d'Or: Le Cas de *Don Quichotte.*" *Imprévue* 2 (1983): 21-33.

———. *Mateo Alemán: Introducción a su vida y su obra.* Salamanca: Anaya, 1971.

———. *Protée et le gueux. Recherches sur les origines et la nature du récit picaresque dans Guzmán de Alfarache.* Paris: Didier, 1967.

Cruickshank, Donald W. "Calderón's King Pedro: Just or Unjust?" *Gesammelte Aufsatze zur Kulturgeschichte Spaniens* 25 (1970): 113-32.

Dagenais, John. "The Imaginative Faculty and Artistic Creation in Lope." In *Lope de Vega y los orígenes del teatro español: Actas del I Congreso Internacional Sobre Lope de Vega,* edited by Manuel Criado de Val, 321-26. Madrid: EDI-6, 1981.

Dariot, Claude. *A Briefe and Most Easie Introduction to the Astrologicall Judgement of the Starres.* Translated by F. W. London: 1598.

Darst, David H. *The Comic Art of Tirso de Molina.* Madrid: Castalia, 1974.

———. "Lope's Strategy for Tragedy in *El caballero de Olmedo.*" *Crítica Hispánica* 6 (1984): 11-17.

———. "The Thematic Design of *El condenado por desconfiado.*" *Kentucky Romance Quarterly* 21 (1974): 483-94.

Davie-Peyre, Yvonne. "Deux exemples du mal d'amour dit 'héroïque' chez Cervantes: Du langage médical à la transcription rhétorique." *Bulletin de l'Association Guillaume Budé* 4 (1982): 383-404.

Daza Chacon, Dionisio. *Practica y teorica de cirugia en romance y en latin.* Valencia, 1673.

de Armas, Frederic A. "*La Celestina:* An Example of Love Melancholy." *Romanic Review* 66 (1975): 288-95.

———. "The Saturn Factor: Examples of Astrological Imagery in Lope de Vega's Works." In *Studies in Honor of Everett W. Hesse,* edited by William C. McCrary and José A. Madrigal, 63-80. Lincoln, Neb.: Society of Spanish and Spanish-American Studies, 1981.

Deyermond, Alan. *Lazarillo de Tormes: A Critical Guide.* London: Grant and Cutler, 1975.

Díaz, Francisco. *Tratado nuevamente impresso, de todas las enfermedades de los*

Riñones, Vexiga, y Carnosidades de la verga, y Urina, dividido en tres libros. Madrid, 1588.

Díaz Migoyo, Gonzalo. *Estructura de la novela. Anatomía del "Buscón".* Madrid: Fundamentos, 1978.

Diccionario de autoridades. 3 vols. Madrid: Gredos, 1979.

Diethelm, Oskar. *Medical Dissertations of Psychiatric Interest: Printed before 1750.* Basel: S. Karger, 1971.

DiSanto, Elsa Leonor. "Análisis sobre los discursos sobre la Edad dorada y las armas y las letras." In *Cervantes: su obra y su mundo: Actas del I Congreso internacional sobre Cervantes,* edited by Manuel Criado de Val, 799–807. Madrid: EDI-6, 1981.

Du Laurens, André. *A Discourse of the Preservation of the Sight: of Melancholike diseases; of Rheumes, and of Old Age.* Translated by Richard Surphlet. London: Shakespeare Association, 1938.

Dunn, Peter N. "Problems of a Model for the Picaresque and the Case of Quevedo's *Buscón." Bulletin of Hispanic Studies* 59 (1982): 95–105.

Durán, Manuel. "Erasmo y Cervantes: Fervor, ironía, ambigüedad." In *Cervantes: su obra y su mundo: Actas del I Congreso internacional sobre Cervantes,* edited by Manuel Criado de Val, 969–73. Madrid: EDI-6, 1981.

Durand, Frank. "The Author and Lázaro: Levels of Comic Meaning." *Bulletin of Hispanic Studies* 45 (1968): 89–101.

El Saffar, Ruth. "Cervantes and the Imagination." *Cervantes* 6 (1986): 81–90.

———. *Novel to Romance: A Study of Cervantes's "Novelas ejemplares".* Baltimore: The Johns Hopkins University Press, 1974.

Elyot, Sir Thomas. *The Castel of Helth.* New York: Scholars' Facsimiles Reprints, 1937.

Entrambasaguas, Joaquín de. *Estudios y ensayos sobre Góngora y el Barroco.* Madrid: Editora Nacional, 1975.

Escudero Ortuño, Alberto. *El concepto de la melancolía en el siglo XVII (Un comentario a las obras de Robert Burton y Alfonso de Santa Cruz).* Huesca: Imprenta Provisional, 1950.

Evans, Peter W. "Alonso's Cowardice: Ambiguities of Perspective in *El caballero de Olmedo." Modern Language Review* 78 (1983): 68–78.

Farinelli, Arturo. "Dos excéntricos: Cristóbal de Villalón. El Dr. Juan Huarte." *Revista de filología española* 24 (1936): 53–103.

Ferrand, Jacques. *Erotomania or a Treatise Discoursing of the Essence, Causes, Symptomes, Prognosticks, and Cures of Love, or Erotique Melancholy.* Translated by Edmund Chilmead. Oxford, 1640.

Ferrater Mora, J. "The World of Calderón." *Hispanic Review* 52 (1984): 1–17.

Fichter, W. L. "Color symbolism in Lope de Vega." *Romanic Review* 18 (1927): 220–31.

Ficino, Marsilio. *The Book of Life.* Translated by Charles Boer. Irving, Tex.: Spring Publications, 1980.

Field, Nathaniel. "A Woman is a Weathercock." In *A Select Collection of Old English Plays,* edited by Robert Dodsley and W. Carew Hazlitt, vol. 11. London, 1875.

Fink, Zera. "Jaques and the Malcontent Traveler." *Philological Quarterly* 14 (1935): 237–52.

Fish, Stanley E. *Self-Consuming Artifacts: The Experience of Seventeenth-Century Literature.* Berkeley: University of California Press, 1974.

Flores, R. M. "Sancho's Fabrications: A Mirror of the Development of His Imagination." *Hispanic Review* 38 (1970): 174–82.

Forcione, Alban K. *Cervantes and the Humanist Vision*. Princeton: Princeton University Press, 1982.

———. *Cervantes, Aristotle and the 'Persiles'*. Princeton: Princeton University Press, 1970.

Foresto, Pedro. *Observationum et Curationum Medicinalium sive Medicinae Theoricae & Practicae*. Frankfort, 1611.

Foster, David W., and Virginia R. Foster. *Luis de Góngora*. New York: Twayne, 1973.

Fothergill-Payne, Louise. "*El caballero de Olmedo* y la razón de diferencia." *Bulletin of the Comediantes* 36 (1984): 111–24.

———. "The World Picture in Calderón's *Autos Sacramentales*." In *Calderón and the Baroque Tradition*, edited by Kurt Levy, Jesús Ara, and Gethin Hughes, 33–40. Ontario: Wilfrid Laurier University Press, 1985.

Foucault, Michel. *The Order of Things*. New York: Vintage Books, 1971.

Freylas, Alonso de. *Conocimiento, curacion y preservacion de la peste y un tratado de arte de descontagiar las ropas de sedas y un discurso si los melancolicos pueden saber lo que esta por venir con la fuerza de la imaginacion*. Jaen, 1605.

García Carrero, Pedro. *Disputationes medicae super sen primam*. Madrid, 1612.

Garcilaso de la Vega. "Egloga I." In *Poesías castellanas completas,* edited by Elias L. Rivers, 119–34. Madrid: Castalia, 1972.

Garzoni, Tommaso. *The Hospitall of Incurable Fooles*. London, 1600.

Gates, Eunice Joiner. *The Metaphors of Luis de Góngora*. Philadelphia: University of Pennsylvania Press, 1933.

Genfreau-Massaloux, Michèle. "Los locos de amor en el *Quijote*: Psocopatología y creación cervantina." In *Cervantes y su mundo: Actas del I Congreso internacional sobre Cervantes,* edited by Manuel Criado de Val, 687–91. Madrid: EDI-6, 1981.

Gilman, Stephen. *Cervantes y Avellaneda*. Mexico: El Colegio de Mexico, 1951.

———. "The Death of *Lazarillo de Tormes*." *PMLA* 81 (1966): 149–66.

Góngora y Argote, Luis de. *Obras completas*. Edited by Juan Millé y Giménez and Isabel Millé y Giménez. Madrid: Aguilar, 1967.

Gracián, Baltasar. *Agudeza y arte de ingenio*. 2 vols. Edited by Evaristo Correa Calderón. Madrid: Castalia, 1969.

———. *El Criticón*. Edited by Santos Alonso. Madrid: Cátedra, 1984.

Granjel, Luis S. *Cirugía española del Renacimiento*. Salamanca: Universidad de Salamanca, 1968.

———. *El ejercicio de la medicina en la sociedad española del Siglo XVII*. Salamanca: Universidad de Salamanca, 1971.

———. *Humanismo y medicina*. Salamanca: Universidad de Salamanca, 1968.

Green, Otis, H. "El 'Ingenioso' Hidalgo." *Hispanic Review* 25 (1957): 175–93.

———. *Spain and the Western Tradition*. 4 vols. Madison: University of Wisconsin Press, 1963-1966.

Greene, Robert. *The Life and Complete Works in Prose and Verse of Robert Greene*. 15 vols. Edited by Alexander B. Grosart. London, 1881.

Guillén, Claudio. "Toward a Definition of the Picaresque." In *Proceedings of the Third Congress of the International Comparative Literature Association,* 262–66. The Hague: Mouton, 1962.

Gutierrez de Godoy, Juan. *Disputationes Phylosophicae, ac Medicae super libros Aristo-telis de memoria, & reminiscentia, physicis utiles, medicis necessariae duobus libris contentae.* Madrid, 1629.

Gyraldus, Lilius Gregorius. *De deis gentium varia et multiplex historia.* Basel, 1571.

Halka, Chester S. "*Don Quijote* in the Light of Huarte's *Examen de ingenios:* A Reex-amination." *Anales cervantinos* 19 (1981): 3–13.

Harington, Sir John. *A New Discourse on a Stale Subject Called The Metamorphosis of Ajax.* Edited by Elizabeth Story Donno. New York: Columbia University Press, 1962.

Harrison, Stephen. "Magic in the Spanish Golden Age: Cervantes's Second Thoughts." *Renaissance and Reformation* 4 (1980): 47–64.

Hart, Thomas. "The Pilgrim's Role in the First *Solitude.*" *MLN* 92 (1977): 213–26.

Hathaway, Robert L. *Love in the Early Spanish Theatre.* Madrid: Playor, 1975.

Hawkes, Terence. *Metaphor.* London: Methuen, 1972.

Heiple, Daniel L. "The 'Accidens Amoris' in Lyric Poetry." *Neophilologus* 67 (1983): 55–64.

———. "Gutierre's Witty Diagnosis in *El médico de su honra.*" In *Critical Perspectives in Calderón de la Barca,* edited by Frederick A. de Armas, David M. Gitlitz, and José A. Madrigal, 81–90. Lincoln, Neb.: Society of Spanish and Spanish-American Studies, 1981.

———. "Lope de Vega and The Early Conception Of Metaphysical Poetry." *Comparative Literature* 36 (1984): 97–109.

———. "'Lope furioso.'" *Modern Language Review* 83 (1988): 602–11.

———. "Lope's 'Arte Poética.'" In *Renaissance and Golden Age Essays in Honor of D. W. McPheeters,* edited by Bruno M. Damiani, 106–19. Potomac, Md.: Scripta Human-istica, 1986.

———. *Mechanical Imagery in Golden Age Poetry.* Potomac, Md.: Studia Humanitatis, 1983.

———. "Renaissance Medical Psychology in *Don Quijote.*" *Ideologies and Literatures* 2 (1979): 65–72.

Herrero, Javier. "The Great Icons of the *Lazarilo:* The Bull, the Wine, the Sausage and the Turnip." *Ideologies and Literature* 15 (1978): 3–18.

Hidalgo de Aguero, Bartolomé. *Thesoro de la verdadera cirugia y via particular contra la comun.* Barcelona, 1624.

Hippocrates. *Works of Hippocrates.* 4 vols. Translated and edited by W. H. S. Jones and E. T. Withington. Cambridge: Harvard University Press, 1923–1931.

Holzinger, Walter. "Ideology, Imagery and the Literalization of Metaphor in *A secreto agravio, secreta venganza.*" *Bulletin of Hispanic Studies* 54 (1977): 203–14.

Honig, Edwin. *Calderón and the Seizures of Honor.* Cambridge: Harvard University Press, 1972.

Houston, John Porter. *The Rhetoric of Poetry in the Renaissance and Seventeenth Century.* Baton Rouge: Louisiana State University Press, 1983.

Huarte de San Juan, Juan. *Examen de ingenios para las ciencias.* Edited by Esteban Torre. Madrid: Editora Nacional, 1977.

Hutchings, C. M. "The *Examen de ingenios* and the Doctrine of Original Genius." *Hispania* 19 (1936): 273–82.

Hutton, Lewis J. "Salvation and Damnation in Tirso de Molina's Play *Condemned for Unbelief.*" *Christianity and Literature* 30 (1981): 53–62.

Iriarte, M. de. *El doctor Huarte de San Juan y su "Examen de ingenios."* Madrid: Consejo Superior de Investigaciones Científicas, 1948.

Jackson, Stanley W. *Melancholia and Depression: From Hippocratic Times to Modern Times.* New Haven: Yale University Press, 1986.

Jammes, Robert. *Etudes sur l'oeuvre poétique de Don Luis de Góngora y Argote.* Bordeaux: Institut d'Etudes Ibériques et Ibéro-Américaines de l'Université de Bordeaux, 1967.

Johnson, Carroll B. *Inside Guzmán de Alfarache.* Berkeley: University of California Press, 1978.

———. *Madness and Lust: A Psychoanalytical Approach to "Don Quixote."* Berkeley: University of California Press, 1983.

———. "Mateo Alemán y sus fuentes literarias." *Nueva Revista de filología Hispánica* 28 (1979): 360–74.

Jones, Cyril A. "Tirso de Molina's *El melancólico* and Cervantes *El Licenciado Vidriera.*" In *Studia Ibérica: Festschrift für Hans Flasche,* edited by Karl-Hermann Korner and Klaus Ruhl, 295–305. Bern: Francke, 1973.

Jones, J. A. "The Duality and Complexity of *Guzmán de Alfarache.*" In *Knaves and Swindlers: Essays on the Picaresque Novel in Europe,* edited by Christine Whitbourn, 25–46. London: Oxford University Press, 1974.

Jones, R. O. *A Literary History of Spain: The Golden Age Prose and Poetry.* London: Ernest Benn, 1971.

Kaiser, Walter. *Praisers of Folly.* Cambridge: Harvard University Press, 1963.

Kelley, Emilia Navarro de. *La poesía metafísica de Quevedo.* Madrid: Guadarrama, 1973.

Kennedy, Ruth L. "Did Tirso Send to Press a *Primera Parte* of Madrid (1626) which Contained *El condenado por desconfiado?*" *Hispanic Review* 41 (1973): 261–74.

———. "*El condenado por desconfiado:* Various Reasons for Questioning Its Authenticity in Tirso's Theatre." *Kentucky Romance Quarterly* 23 (1976): 129–48.

———. "*El condenado por desconfiado:* Yet Further Reasons for Questioning Its Authenticity in Tirso's Theatre." *Kentucky Romance Quarterly* 23 (1976): 335–56.

Kenyon, Herbert A. "Color Symbolism in Early Spanish Ballads." *Romanic Review* 6 (1915): 327–40.

Kernan, Alvin. *The Cankered Muse: Satire of the English Renaissance.* New Haven: Yale University Press, 1959.

King. Willard F. "*El caballero de Olmedo:* Poetic Justice of Destiny?" In *Homenaje a William L. Fichter: Ensayos sobre el teatro antiguo español y otros ensayos,* edited by A. David Kossoff and José Amor y Vázquez, 367–79. Madrid: Castalia, 1971.

Klibansky, Raymond, Erwin Panofsky, and Fritz Saxl. *Saturn and Melancholy.* New York: Basic Books, 1964.

Koenigsberger, Dorothy. *Renaissance Man and Creative Thinking: A History of Concepts of Harmony 1400–1700.* Atlantic Highlands, N.J.: Humanities Press, 1979.

LaCapra, Dominick. *Rethinking Intellectual History.* Ithaca: Cornell University Press, 1983.

Lazarillo de Tormes. Edited by Francisco Rico. Madrid: Cátedra, 1987.

Lázaro Carreter, Fernando. *Estilo barroco y personalidad creadora.* Madrid: Cátedra, 1974.

Lemnius, Levinus. *The Touchstone of Complexions.* Translated by Thomas Newton. London, 1576.

Leon, Fray Luis de. "Noche serena." In *Renaissance and Baroque Poetry of Spain,* edited by Elias Rivers, 99–101. New York: Charles Scribners, 1966.

Levao, Ronald. *Renaissance Minds and Their Fictions.* Berkeley: University of California Press, 1985.

Lida de Malkiel, María Rosa. *La tradición clásica en España.* Barcelona: Ariel, 1975.

Linocerius, Geofredius. *Mythologiae Musarum libellus.* Paris, 1583.

Lobrera de Avila, Luis. *Remedios de cuerpos humanos y silva de experiencias y otras cosas utilissimas.* Alcalá de Henares, 1542.

López de Villalobos, Francisco. "Anfitrión, Comedia de Plauto." In *Biblioteca de Autores Españoles.* Madrid: Editorial Hernando 36 (1926): 461–93.

———. "Los problemas de Villalobos." In *Biblioteca de Autores Españoles.* Madrid: Editorial Hernando 36 (1926): 405–60.

———. *Sumario de la Medicina,* 1498. Edited by Luis S. Granjel. Salamanca: Real Academia de Medicina de Salamanca, 1977.

López Pinciano, Alonso. *Philosophia antigua poética.* 2 vols. Edited by Alfredo Carballo. Madrid: Consejo Superior de Investigaciones Científicas, 1953.

López Piñero, José María. "La medicina del barroco español." *Revista de la Universidad de Madrid* 2 (1962): 479–515.

———. *Medicina, historia, sociedad (Antología de clásicos médicos).* Barcelona: Ariel, 1973.

Lowes, John L. "The Loveres Maladye of *Hereos.*" *Modern Philology* 11 (1914): 491–546.

Lyman, Stanford M. *The Seven Deadly Sins.* New York: St. Martin's, 1978.

Lyons, Bridget Gellert. *Voices of Melancholy.* New York: W. W. Norton, 1975.

MacCaffrey, Isabel G. *Spencer's Allegory: The Anatomy of Imagination.* Princeton: Princeton University Press, 1976.

McCrary, William C. *The Goldfinch and the Hawk: A Study of Lope de Vega's Tragedy "El caballero de Olmedo."* Chapel Hill: University of North Carolina Press, 1968.

Macey, Samuel L. *Patriarchs of Time: Dualism in Saturn-Cronus, Father Time, the Watchmaker God, and Father Christmas.* Athens: University of Georgia Press, 1987.

Madrigal, Alfonso de. *Tractado por el qualse prueba por la Santa Escriptura como al ome es necessario amar, é el que verdaderamente ama es necessario que se turbe.* Madrid, 1892.

Mancing, Howard. *The Chivalric World of "Don Quijote": Style, Structure, and Narrative Technique.* Columbia: University of Missouri Press, 1982.

Maravall, José Antonio. "Relaciones de dependencia e integración social: criados, graciosos y pícaros." *Ideologies and Literature* 1 (1977): 3–32.

Márquez Villanueva, Francisco. *Personajes y temas del Quijote.* Madrid: Taurus, 1975.

Martínez Arancón, Ana. *La batalla en torno a Góngora.* Barcelona: Antoni Bosch, 1978.

Martínez de Toledo, Alfonso. *Arcipreste de Talavera o Corbacho.* Edited by Michael Gerli. Madrid: Cátedra, 1979.

May, T. E. "*El condenado por desconfiado.* 1. The Enigmas. 2. Anareto." *Bulletin of Hispanic Studies* 35 (1958): 138–56.

———. "The Folly and Wit of Secret Vengeance: Calderón's *A secreto agravio, secreta venganza.*" *Forum for Modern Language Studies* 2 (1966): 114–22.

Melczer, William. "Did Don Quixote Die of Melancholy?" In *Folie et déraison à la Renaissance,* edited by Alois Gerlo, 161–70. Brussels: Université Libre de Bruxelles, 1973.

Mercurial, Geronimo. *Medicina Practica.* Frankfurt, 1611.

Mercado, Luis. *Opera.* 2 vols. Frankfurt, 1619–1620.

Mercado, Pedro. *Dialogos de Philosophia Natural y Moral.* Granda, 1558.

Messick, Alan R. "Tomás Rodaja: A Clinical Case?" *Romance Notes* 11 (1970): 623–28.

Mexía, Pero. *Silva de varia leccion.* Madrid: Sociedad de Bibliófilos Españoles, 1933.

Mohlo, Mauricio. *Cervantes: Raíces Folklóricas.* Madrid: Gredos, 1976.

———. *Les Romans picaresques espagnols.* Paris: La Pléiade, 1968.

Montaña de Monserrate, Bernardino. *Libro de la anatomía del hombre.* Madrid: Instituto Bibliográfico Hispánico, 1973.

Monte, Alberto del. *Itinerario de la novela picaresca española.* Barcelona: Lumen, 1971.

Morell, Hortensia. "La deformación picaresca del mundo ideal en 'Ozmín y Daraja' del *Guzmán de Alfarache.*" *La Torre* 89–90 (1975): 101–25.

Morley, S. Griswold. "Color symbolism in Tirso de Molina." *Romantic Review* 8 (1917): 77–81.

Morón Arroyo, Ciriaco. *Nuevas meditaciones del "Quijote."* Madrid: Gredos, 1976.

Muñiz Fernández, Carmen. "Noticia de médicos españoles (Siglos XV-XIX)." *Cuadernos de Historia de la Medicina Española* 7 (1968): 247–64.

Murillo y Velarde, Thomas. *Aprobacion de ingenios, y curacion de hipochondricos, con observaciones, y remedios muy particulares.* Zaragoza, 1672.

Nashe, Thomas. *The Works of Thomas Nashe.* 5 vols. Edited by Ronald B. McKerrow. Oxford: Oxford University Press, 1958.

Navarro, Gaspar. *Tribunal de supersticion ladina.* Huesca, 1631.

Nelson, Lowry, Jr., ed. *Cervantes: A Collection of Critical Essays.* Englewood Cliffs, N.J.: Prentice-Hall, 1969.

Neugaard, Edward J. "Another Possible Source for Tirso's *El condenado por desconfiado.*" *Hispano* 48 (1973): 19–22.

Nicolson, Marjorie Hope. *The Breaking of the Circle: Studies in the Effect of the "New Science" upon Seventeenth-Century Poetry.* Evanston: Northwestern University Press, 1950.

North, Dudley. *A Forest of Varieties.* London, 1645.

O'Connor, Thomas A. "The Interplay of Prudence and Imprudence in *El médico de su honra.*" *Romanistisches Jahrbuch* 24 (1973): 303–22.

———. "The Knight of Olmedo and Oedipus: Perspectives on a Spanish Tragedy." *Hispanic Review* 48 (1980): 391–413.

Olmedilla y Puis, Joaquín. *Cervantes en ciencias médicas.* Madrid: Administración de la Revista de Medicina y Cirugía Prácticas, 1905.

Osborn, Scott C. "Heroical Love in Dryden's Heroic Drama." *PMLA* 73 (1958): 480–90.

Ostwald, Barbara L. "Fool and Malcontent: The Dramatic Function of the Licensed Commentator in Elizabethan Drama." Ph.D. diss., Indiana University, 1977.

Pabst, Walter. *La creación gongorina en los poemas "Polifemo" y "Soledades."* Madrid: Consejo Superior de Investigaciones Científicas, 1966.

Pacheco, Francisco. *El arte de la pintura.* 2 vols. Edited by F. J. Sánchez Cantón. Madrid: Instituto de Valencia de Don Juan, 1956.

Parker, Alexander A. *Literature and the Delinquent: The Picaresque Novel in Spain and Europe, 1599-1753.* Edinburgh: Edinburgh University Press, 1971.

———. *Polyphemus and Galatea: A Study in the Interpretation of a Baroque Poem.* Austin: University of Texas Press, 1977.

———. "Santos y bandoleros en el teatro español del Siglo de Oro." *Arbor* 13 (1949): 395-416.

Paterson, Alan K. G. "The Comic and Tragic Melancholy of Juan Roca: A Study of Calderón's *El pintor de su deshonra.*" *Forum for Modern Language Studies* 5 (1969): 244-61.

Paul of Aegina. *The Seven Books of Paulus Aeginata.* Translated by Francis Adams. 3 vols. London: Sydenham Society, 1844-1847.

Paulson, Ronald. "The Fool-Knave Relation in Picaresque Satire." *Rice University Studies* 51 (1968): 59-81.

Pérez Bautista, Florencio L. "La medicina y los médicos en el teatro de Calderón de la Barca." *Cuadernos de Historia de la Medicina Española* 7 (1968): 149-245.

———. "La medicina y los médicos en los dramaturgos menores españoles del siglo XVII." *Cuadernos de Historia de la Medicina Española* 8 (1969): 79-110.

Pérez de Herrera, Christobal. *Proverbios morales y consejos christianos muy provechosos para concierto, y espejo de vida, adornados de Lugares, y Textos de los Divinas, y Humanas Letras.* Madrid, 1733.

Pérez de Moya. *Philosophia secreta.* 2 vols. Edited by Eduardo Gómez Baquero. Madrid: Nueva Biblioteca de Autores Españoles, 1928.

Piñera, Estela. "En torno al 'Caballero de la Triste Figura.'" *La Torre* 68 (1970): 135-43.

Platter, Felix, Abdiah Cole, and Nicholas Culpeper. *A Golden Practice of Physick.* London: Peter Cole, 1662.

Quevedo, Francisco. *La vida del Buscón llamado Don Pablos.* Edited by Domingo Ynduráin. Madrid: Cátedra, 1985.

Ramírez, Alejandro. "The Concept of Ignorance in *Don Quijote.*" *Philological Quarterly* 45 (1966): 474-79.

Rand, Edward K. *Ovid and His Influence.* Boston: Marshall Jones, 1925.

Randel, Mary Gaylord. "Metaphor and Fable in Góngora's *Soledad primera.*" *Revista Hispánica Moderna* 40 (1978-79): 97-112.

Read, Malcolm. *Juan Huarte de San Juan.* Boston: Twayne, 1981.

Redondo, Agustín. "El personaje de Don Quijote: Tradiciones folklórico-literarias, contexto histórico y elaboración cervantina." *Nueva revista de filología hispánica* 29 (1980): 36-59.

Reiss, Timothy J. *The Discourse of Modernism.* Ithaca, N.Y: Cornell University Press, 1982.

Revard, Stella P. "'L'Allegro' and 'Il Penseroso': Classical Tradition and Renaissance Mythography." *PMLA* 101 (1986): 338-50.

Rico, Francisco. *Don Quijote.* London: Allen and Unwin, 1986.

———. "Hacia *El caballero de Olmedo,* I." *Nueva Revista de Filología Hispánica* 24 (1975): 329-38.

———. "Hacia *El caballero de Olmedo,* II." *Nueva Revista de Filología Hispánica* 29 (1980): 271-92.

————. "Hacia *El caballero de Olmedo:* amor, muerte, ironía." *Papeles de Son Armadans* 139 (1979): 38–56.

————. *La novela picaresca y el punto de vista.* Barcelona: Seix Barral, 1973.

Riley, E. C. "Cervantes and the Cynics (*El licenciado Vidriera* and *El coloquio de los perros*)." *Bulletin of Hispanic Studies* 53 (1976): 189–99.

————. *Teoría de la novela en Cervantes.* Madrid: Taurus, 1966.

Rivers, Elias L. "El conceptismo del *Polifemo.*" *Atenea* 142 (1961): 102–9.

————. "Nature, Art and Science in Spanish Poetry of the Renaissance." *Bulletin of Hispanic Studies* 44 (1967): 255–66.

Robertson, D. W., Jr. "The Subject of the *De Amore* of Andreas Capellanus." *Modern Philology* 50 (1953): 145–61.

Rogers, Daniel. "Introduction." *El condenado por desconfiado.* By Tirso de Molina, 1–46. Oxford: Pergamon, 1974.

————. "Tienen los celos pasos de ladrones: Silence in Calderón's *El médico de su honra.*" *Hispanic Review* 33 (1965): 273–89.

Ruiz Ramón, Francisco. *Calderón y la tragedia.* Madrid: Alhambra, 1984.

————. "Who's Who in *Don Quijote?* Or an Approach to the Problem of Identity." *MLN* 81 (1961): 113–30.

Russell, P. E. "*Don Quijote* as a Funny Book." *Modern Language Review* 64 (1969): 312–26.

Sabat de Rivers, Georgina. "La moral que Lázaro nos propone." *MLN* 95 (1980): 233–51.

Sage, Jack W. *Lope de Vega: "El caballero de Olmedo."* London: Grant and Cutler, 1974.

Salillas, Rafael. *Un gran inspirador de Cervantes. El doctor Juan Huarte de San Juan.* Madrid: Eduardo Arias, 1905.

Sancho de San Román, Rafael. *La medicina y los médicos en la obra de Tirso de Molina.* Salamanca: Universidad de Salmanca, 1960.

San Pedro, Diego de. *Carcel de amor.* Edited by Keith Whinnom. Madrid: Castalia, 1971.

Santa Cruz, Alfonso de. *Diagnotio et cura affectuum melancholicorum.* In Antonio de Ponce de Santa Cruz, *Opuscula Medica.* Madrid, 1624.

Sarria, Amalia. *La ciencia en la España de los Austrías.* Madrid: Biblioteca Nacional, 1976.

Schafer, Alice E. "Fate versus Responsibility in Lope's *El caballero de Olmedo.*" *Revista Canadiense de Estudios Hispánicos* 3 (1978): 26–39.

Sennert, Daniel. *Practical Physick.* Translated by N. Culpeper and Abdiah Cole. 2 vols. London, 1662–64.

Seznec, Jean. *The Survival of the Pagan Gods.* Translated by Barbara F. Sessions. New York: Harper and Row, 1953.

Shakespeare, William. *The Riverside Shakespeare.* Boston: Houghton Mifflin, 1974.

Shepard, Sanford. *El Pinciano y las teorías literarias del Siglo de Oro.* Madrid: Gredos, 1970.

Shipley, George A. "The Critic as Witness for the Prosecution: Resting the Case Against Lázaro de Tormes." In *Creation and Re-creation: Experiments in Literary Form in Early Modern Spain,* edited by Ramond E. Surtz and Nora Weinerth, 105–24. Newark, Del.: Juan de la Cuesta, 1983.

Sieber Harry. *Language and Society in "La vida de Lazarillo de Tormes."* Baltimore: The Johns Hopkins University Press, 1978.

————. "On Juan Huarte de San Juan and Anselmo's 'locura' in 'El curioso imperti-
nente.'" *Revista Hispánica Moderna* 36 (1970–1971): 1–8.

Smith, Colin. "On the Use of Spanish Theoretical Works in the Debate on Gongorism."
Bulletin of Hispanic Studies 42 (1965): 165–76.

Sobejano, Gonzalo. "Un perfil de la picaresca: el pícaro hablador." In *Studia hispanica in
honorem R. Lapesa*, 3:467–85. Madrid: Gredos, 1975.

Soriano, Geronimo. *Libro de experimentos medicos, faciles, y verdaderos.* Zaragoza,
1676.

Soufas, C. Christopher, Jr. "Lope's Elegy to Góngora and the *Culteranismo* Debate."
Hispanófila 86 (1986): 19–27.

————. "Thinking in *La vida es sueño*." *PMLA* 100 (1985): 287–99.

Soufas, Teresa S. "Beyond Justice and Cruelty: Calderón's King Pedro." *Journal of Hispanic Philology* 6 (1981): 57–65.

————. "Calderón's Joyless Jester: The Humanization of a Stock Character." *Bulletin of
the Comediantes* 34 (1982): 201–8.

————. "Calderón's Melancholy Wife-Murderers." *Hispanic Review* 52 (1984): 181–203.

————. "Religious Melancholy and Tirso's Despairing Monk in *El condenado por desconfiado*." *Romance Quarterly* 34 (1987): 25–35.

————. "The Transvalued Discourse of Heroical Love in Francisco de Rioja's 'A una
rosa amarilla.'" *South Atlantic Review* 52 (1987): 25–35.

Spencer, Theodore. "The Elizabethan Malcontent." In *J. Q. Adams Memorial Studies,*
edited by J. G. McManaway et al., 523–35. Washington: Folger Shakespeare Library,
1948.

Spitzer, Leo. "El barroco español." *Boletín del Instituto de Investigaciones Históricas* 28
(1843–44): 12–30.

Starobinsky, Jean. *History of the Treatment of Melancholy from the Earliest Times to
1900.* Basel: J. R. Geigy, 1962.

Suárez de Figueroa, Cristóbal. *El passagero.* Madrid: Sociedad de Bibliófilos Españoles,
1914.

Sullivan, Henry W. *Tirso de Molina and the Drama of the Counter Reformation.* Amsterdam: Rodopi, 1976.

Talavera, Arcipreste de. *O Corbacho.* Madrid: Cátedra, 1970

ter Horst, Robert. *Calderón: The Secular Plays.* Lexington: University Press of Kentucky, 1982.

Terry, Arthur. "Quevedo and the Metaphysical Conceit." *Bulletin of Hispanic Studies* 35
(1958): 211–22.

Tirso de Molina. *El condenado por desconfiado.* Edited by Ciriaco Morón and Rolena
Adorno. Madrid: Cátedra, 1978.

Trueblood, Alan S. *Experience and Artistic Expression in Lope de Vega.* Cambridge:
Harvard, 1974.

Tyler, Richard W. "La 'flema' en los Siglos de Oro." In *Actas del VIII Congreso de la
Asociación Internacional de Hispanistas (22–27 agosto 1983),* edited by A. David
Kossoff, José Amor y Vázquez, Ruth H. Kossoff, Geoffrey W. Ribbans, 1:653–59.
Madrid: Ediciones Istmo, 1986.

Vaca de Alfaro, Enrique. *Proposicion chirurgica, i censura iudiciosa entre las dos vias
curativas de heridas de cabeça comun i particular, i elecion desta.* Seville, 1618.

Valverde de Hamusco, Juan de. *Historia de la composición del cuerpo humano.* Rome, 1556.

Vega Carpío, Lope de. "Las bizarrías de Belisa." In *Obras escogidas,* edited by Federico Carlos Sainz de Robles, 1:1675–705. Madrid: Aguilar, 1969.

———. *El caballero de Olmedo.* Edited by Joseph Pérez. Madrid: Castalia, 1983.

———. "El castigo sin venganza." In *Lope de Vega: Obras escogidas,* edited by Federico Carlos Sainz de Robles, 1:924–59. Madrid: Aguilar, 1969.

———. "La dama boba." In *Obras escogidas,* edited by Federico Carlos Sainz de Robles, 1:1099–1135. Madrid: Aguilar, 1969.

———. *La Dorotea.* Edited by Edwin S. Morby. Berkeley: University of California Press, 1968.

———. "La niña de plata." In *Obras escogidas,* edited by Federico Carlos Sainz de Robles, 1:647–87. Madrid: Aguilar, 1969.

———. "Los locos de Valencia." In *Obras de Lope de Vega.* 13 vols. 12:409–45. Madrid: Rivadeneyra, 1930.

———. *Obras poéticas.* Edited by José Manuel Blecua. Barcelona: Planeta, 1969.

Velásquez, Andrés. *Libro de la melancholia.* Seville, 1585.

Velázquez de Azevedo, Juan. *El Fenix de Minerva, y arte de memoria.* Madrid, 1626.

Vitoria, Baltasar de. *Teatro de los dioses de la gentilidad.* Madrid, 1676.

Vives, Juan Luis. *Obras completas.* 2 vols. Edited by Lorenzo Riber. Madrid: Aguilar, 1948.

Wade, Gerald. "Love, *Comedia* Style." *Kentucky Romance Quarterly* 29 (1982): 47–60.

Wardropper, Bruce W. "Calderón's Comedy and his Serious Sense of Life." In *Hispanic Studies in Honor of Nicholson B. Adams,* edited by John Esten Keller and Karl-Ludwig Selig, 179–93. Chapel Hill: University of North Carolina Press, 1966.

———. "The Complexity of the Simple in Góngora's *Soledad primera.*" *The Journal of Medieval and Renaissance Studies* 7 (1977): 35–51.

———. "The Criticism of the Spanish *Comedia: El caballero de Olmedo* as Object Lesson." *Philological Quarterly* 51 (1972): 177–96.

———. "El problema de la responsabilidad en la comedia de capa y espada de Calderón." In *Actas del 2 congreso Internacional de Hispanistas,* edited by Jaime Sánchez Romarelo and Norbert Poulussen, 689–94. Nijmegan: Instituto Español de la Universidad de Nimega.

———. "El trastorno de la moral en el *Lazarillo.*" *Nueva Revista de Filología Hispánica* 15 (1961): 441–47.

———. "The Implications of Hypocrisy in the *Lazarillo de Tormes.*" In *Studies in Honor of Everett W. Hesse,* edited by William C. McCrary and José A. Madrigal, 179–86. Lincoln, Neb.: Society of Spanish and Spanish-American Studies, 1981.

———. "La imaginación en el metateatro calderoniano." In *Studia Hispanica in Honorem R. Lapesa,* edited by Eugenio de Bustos et al., 2:613–29. Madrid: Gredos, 1972.

———. "Poetry and Drama in Calderón's *El médico de su honra.*" *Romanic Review* 49 (1958): 3–11.

———. "Temas y problemas del barroco español." In *Historia y crítica de la literatura española (Siglos de Oro: Barroco).* 8 vols. 3:5–48. Barcelona: Editorial Crítica, 1983.

———. "The Unconscious Mind in Calderón's *El pintor de su deshonra.*" *Hispanic Review* 18 (1950): 285–301.

Watson, A. Irvine. "Peter the Cruel or Peter the Just? A Reappraisal of the Role Played by King Peter in Calderón's *El médico de su honra.*" *Romanistisches Jahrbuch* 14 (1963): 322–46.

Weiger, John G. *The Individuated Self: Cervantes and the Emergence of the Individual.* Athens: Ohio University Press, 1979.

Welles, Marcia L. *Arachne's Tapestry: The Transformation of Myth in Seventeenth-Century Spain.* San Antonio: Trinity University Press, 1986.

Wenzel, Siegfried. *The Sin of Sloth: "Acedia" in Medieval Thought and Literature.* Chapel Hill: University of North Carolina Press, 1960.

Weyer, Johann. *Ioannis Wieri de Praestigiis Daemonum, et Incantationibus ac Veneficijs Libri Sex.* Basel, 1568.

Wicks, Ulrich. "The Nature of Picaresque Narrative: A Modal Approach." *PMLA* 89 (1974): 240–49.

Wilson, Edward M. "The Exemplary Nature of *El caballero de Olmedo.*" In *Spanish and English Literature of the 16th and 17th Centuries,* edited by D. W. Cruickshank, 184–200. Cambridge: Cambridge University Press, 1980.

———. "The Four Elements in the Imagery of Calderón." *Modern Language Review* 31 (1936): 34–47.

———. "Hacia una interpretación de *El pintor de su deshonra.*" *Abaco* 3 (1970): 49–85.

———. "La discreción de don Lope de Almeida." *Clavileño* 2 (1951): 1–10.

Wind, Edgar. *Pagan Mysteries in the Renaissance.* London: Faber and Faber, 1968.

Woodward, L. J. "Author-Reader Relationship in the *Lazarillo de Tormes.*" *Forum for Modern Language Studies* 1 (1965): 43–53.

Wright, Thomas, *The Passions of the Minde in Generall.* London, 1621.

Young, R. V. "Versions of Galatea: Renaissance and Baroque Imitation." In *Renaissance Papers 1984,* edited by Dale B. J. Randall and Joseph A. Porter, 57–68. Durham, N.C.: Southeastern Renaissance Conference, 1985.

Zahareas, Anthony. "El género picaresco y las autobiografías de criminales." In *La picaresca: orígenes, textos y estructuras,* edited by Manuel Criado de Val, 79–112. Madrid: Fundación Universitaria Española, 1979.

Ziomek, Henryk. *A History of Spanish Golden Age Drama.* Lexington: University Press of Kentucky, 1984.

———. "La actitud de Cervantes ante la muerte en el *Quijote.*" *Duquesne Hispanic Review* 8 (1969): 13–23.

Index